The Drama of Landscape

Garrett A. Sullivan, Jr.

THE DRAMA OF LANDSCAPE

*Land, Property, and Social Relations
on the Early Modern Stage*

STANFORD UNIVERSITY PRESS
STANFORD, CALIFORNIA

Stanford University Press
Stanford, California
© 1998 by the Board of Trustees of the
Leland Stanford Junior University
Printed in the United States of America

Library of Congress Cataloging-in-Publication Data

Sullivan, Garrett A.
     The drama of landscape : land, property, and social relations on
the early modern stage / Garrett A. Sullivan, Jr.
          p.   cm.
     Includes bibliographical references (p.   ) and index.
     ISBN 0-8047-3303-1 (cloth : alk. paper).
     1. English drama—Early modern, 1500–1700—History and criticism.
2. Landscape in literature.   3. Literature and society—Great Britain—
History—16th century.   4. Literature and society—Great Britain—
History—17th century.   5. Social classes in literature.   6. Land tenure
in literature.   7. Property in literature.   I. Title.

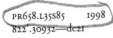
PR658.L35S85   1998
822'.30932—dc21   98-4141
                                                                      CIP

This book is printed on acid-free, recycled paper.

Original printing 1998
Last figure below indicates year of this printing:
07   06   05   04   03   02   01   00   99   98

For Moira

Acknowledgments

For permission to reprint as Chapter One a revised version of "'Arden Lay Murdered in That Plot of Ground': Surveying, Land, and *Arden of Faversham*" (*ELH* 61 [1994]: 231–52), I am grateful to the Johns Hopkins University Press.

In the spirit of a book about landscape, I want to emphasize the happy conjunction of people and places. At Brown, where something faintly resembling this book first took shape, I received encouragement and assistance from many, most notably Karin Coddon, Ashley Cross, Nick Daly, Jen Fleissner, Ed Hardy, Tom Juvan, Tamar Katz, Bill Keach, Ivan Kreilkamp, and Julie Schutzman. Jim Egan, Coppélia Kahn, and Karen Newman were an exemplary dissertation committee: supportive, challenging, engaged, and skeptical when appropriate. Thanks especially to Karen Newman, as fine a director as I could have wished for. At Penn State, where dissertation became book, I have also benefited from a wonderful community of colleagues. I am especially grateful for the support and feedback offered by Patrick Cheney, Laura Knoppers, Francesca Royster, and Linda Woodbridge. Special thanks to Linda Woodbridge, who read the book in its entirety and always offered welcome encouragement and sound advice.

Many others have helped me think about the issues central to this book and have offered advice and support; in particular I am pleased to mention Jim Akerman, Tony Campbell, Denis Cosgrove, Fran

Dolan, Richard Helgerson, Jean Howard, Arthur Kinney, Shannon Miller, Mary Beth Rose, Barb Sebek, Scott Shershow, Bill Waltz, Valerie Wayne, and Eric Wilson. Richard Helgerson and Jean Howard read the manuscript for Stanford University Press, and I gained much from their insightful suggestions. I owe many of the people in the last two paragraphs debts not only scholarly but personal; for friendships only elliptically registered here I remain profoundly thankful.

Thanks to Helen Tartar and John Feneron at Stanford University Press for their work in turning manuscript into book. Laura Rosenthal came up with the book title, much to my delight and relief. I have benefited from institutional support from the College of Liberal Arts' Research and Graduate Studies Office at Penn State and the Newberry Library, and I happily and gratefully acknowledge their assistance here. The support (financial and otherwise) of Don Bialostosky and the English Department at Penn State has been crucial to this project. Thanks also to all the wonderful staff members at the Newberry Library, the British Library, and the Map Library of the British Library—their expertise and generosity greatly accelerated the completion of this book. As a research assistant, Marco Abel assiduously checked sources and quotations, a tedious task he completed in a good-natured and professional manner.

Finally, I want to thank my family: my parents, Cathy and Garry, who have unfailingly offered support and love; and my sisters Tracy, Amy, and Sheila, who have sustained me in countless ways. This book is dedicated to the memory of my sister Moira.

G.A.S.

Contents

The Drama of Landscape

Owning the Land

LANDSCAPE AND ENGLISH
RENAISSANCE DRAMA

The title of this book may read to some as the odd yoking of incompatible categories. After all, *landscape* seems to have precious little to do with *drama*. Moreover, the period under discussion precedes the heyday of English landscape painting and country-house poetry. It is this book's aim, however, to complicate our understanding of what is and can be meant by the seemingly simple term "landscape." The purpose of this introduction is twofold: to offer an alternative, drawn from the discipline of human geography, to conceptions of landscape associated with poetry and the graphic arts; and to argue for the crucial nature of that alternative not only to the study of early modern drama but to the way in which we configure the social relations that emerge around and on the land.

"Landscape" is a familiar term, but its very familiarity has blinded us to its relevance to the early modern theater. The term most immediately suggests either a view of a particular location or the representation in words or pictorial images of that location. These two meanings are unpacked by Denis Cosgrove, a geographer whose work on landscape is important to my project:

Between the early fifteenth century and the late nineteenth century, at first in Italy and Flanders and then throughout western Europe the idea of landscape came to denote the artistic and literary representation of the visible world, the scenery (literally that which is *seen*) which is viewed by a

spectator. It implied a particular sensibility, a way of experiencing and ex-
pressing feelings towards the external world, natural and man-made, an
articulation of a human relationship with it. That sensibility was closely
connected to a growing dependency on the faculty of sight as the medium
through which truth was to be attained: 'seeing is believing.' . . . Landscape's second usage is in contemporary geography and related environmental studies. Here it denotes the integration of natural and human phenomena which can be empirically verified and analysed by the methods of
scientific enquiry over a delimited portion of the earth's surface.[1]

One might be tempted to create an opposition between these two
conceptions of landscape predicated upon a distinction between
the man-made—artistic representation—and the natural—a "delimited portion of the earth's surface." However, Cosgrove makes
clear that both of these landscapes register the "integration of natural and human phenomena"—an integration so complete, I would
add, that disentangling the natural and human is impossible.[2]
Moreover, Cosgrove goes on to suggest that these two versions of
landscape, one aesthetic and the other scientific, are significantly
similar. As he puts it, "landscape [in both its meanings] denotes the
external world mediated through subjective human experience in a
way that neither region nor area immediately suggest. Landscape is
not merely the world we see, it is a construction, a composition of
that world. Landscape is a way of seeing the world."[3]

Both a construction and a way of seeing the world: this paired
definition insists that landscape is not merely an aesthetic product
or the object of scientific inquiry. Instead, a landscape is a materi-
alization of the external world, a way by which topography is
brought into discourse and into knowledge. As such, landscape is
profoundly ideological,[4] for it simultaneously reflects and instantiates attitudes not only toward the land but to a whole range of social phenomena that are indivisible from the land. The ideological
nature of landscape has been fruitfully discussed not only by geographers like Cosgrove but by literary critics such as Raymond Wil-

liams, James Turner, and Don Wayne, whose work on poetry and landscape has admirably revealed the complex ways in which the aesthetic, social, and topographical interpenetrate.[5] However, what these and other critics have failed to consider is that an ideological understanding of landscape (as simultaneously a construction and a way of seeing the world, the means by which social relations are negotiated across topography) allows us to abstract the category from a narrow set of aesthetic products or practices. A partial exception is to be found in the recent work of Chris Fitter, work that has suggested as I do here the historical contingency and construction of different landscapes. Fitter draws the important distinction between "landscape" and "landskip": the former describes, in terms similar to Cosgrove's, "the dialectical construction of environmental 'reality' through the interplay of the physical with the psychical universe," whereas the latter refers to "the narrower, technical concern, in painting or poetry, for naturalistic, pictorial effects and the composed 'view.'"[6] Fitter's definition of "landskip," a term used to describe seventeenth-century poetry, accommodates what I call *the landscape arts*, which are exemplified by texts such as country-house poems or landscape paintings. Importantly, Fitter's schema separates landskip (or "the landscape arts") from landscape. He rightly asserts that landskip "is but one, historically contingent form of conceptualizing and perceiving natural space": that is, it is one form of landscape. Nevertheless, Fitter's book focuses on "the rise and fall of landskip," ensuring that he reproduces the aesthetic and literary-historical emphases of earlier critical work on landscape.[7] It is my contention that landscape can be deployed as an ideological category that is isolable from the landscape arts. Specifically, I intend to focus on the multiple ways in which a range of late-sixteenth- and early-seventeenth-century dramatic texts participate in the construction of a number of early modern landscapes.

I should first point out that while I will refer to material landscapes throughout this book, my emphasis is less on them than on the ways in which they are construed—the ways in which they enter into discourse. Thus, while I will not offer readings of, say, the geography of a particular estate—a geography that has obviously been shaped in accordance with both material needs and ideological pressures and imperatives—I will explore how such a geography is represented and understood, and how it intersects with a variety of social relationships. While my approach involves the privileging of representations and experiences of the land over "the land itself," these obviously cannot be separated when studying "actual" landscapes. As Alan R. H. Baker points out,

'Actual' landscapes are constructions, 'ideal' landscapes are conceptualizations. At the same time, 'actual' landscapes are moulded by ideologies and ideologies are themselves fashioned by 'actual' landscapes: the relationship is reciprocal, the product is a dialectical landscape which is a resolution of nature and culture, of practice and philosophy, of reason and imagination, of 'real' and 'symbolic.'[8]

Nevertheless, for the purposes of this analysis, the landscapes I refer to will almost always be less material than discursive ones.

Cosgrove has linked two meanings of landscape—topographical region and artistic representation—through their shared status as both constructions and ways of seeing the world. However, once we understand landscape in all its forms as constructed and thus ideological, as a social relationship with and experience of the land, then we need no longer imagine landscape as something that is materialized in a discrete set of texts. "Landscape" refers not merely to the landscape arts, but to a relationship to the land, or, more precisely, to one among many possible conceptions of social relations mediated by land. Such a relationship both manifests itself in representations and exceeds them. That is, landscape is both a rendering that reflects or naturalizes social relations—a painting or play—and a subjective purchase on land and relations. Such a conception of landscape makes possible different, even contestatory, landscapes—as there are multiple relationships to the land, so must there be multiple landscapes. This means that there are such things as distinct subjective landscapes, though they may be evidence less of individuality than of the subject's position within a social network. These landscapes are structured both by texts and by custom and practice, by the subject's concrete modes of engagement with both land and the social environment inseparable from it.

This notion of multiple landscapes is not identical with multiple perspectives on the land, for the perspective itself constitutes one historical form that landscape can take. This is made clear by Barbara Bender in her definition and discussion of landscape:

Landscapes are created by people—through their experience and engagement with the world around them. They may be close-grained, worked-upon, lived-in places, or they may be distant and half-fantasised. In contemporary western societies they involve only the surface of the land; in other parts of the world, or in pre-modern Europe, what lies above the surface, or below, may be as or more important. In the contemporary western world we 'perceive' landscapes, we are the point from which the 'seeing' occurs. It is thus an ego-centred landscape, a perspectival landscape, a landscape of views and vistas. In other times and other places the visual may not be the most significant aspect, and the conception of the land may not be ego-centred. . . . [T]he experience of landscape is too important and too interesting to be confined to a particular time, place and class. True, the word was originally coined in the emergent capitalist world of western Europe by aesthetes, antiquarians and landed gentry—all men. It is also true that this coinage is a fine example of how those with power can use language and image to conceptualise and naturalise a particular, and in this case, deeply unequal, way of relating to the land and to other people. But it is inescapably true that even at the historical moment when the word 'landscape' was coined and used to its most powerful effect, there were, at the same time and the same place, other ways of understanding and relating to the land—other landscapes.[9]

Bender makes a crucial point that I will return to later, that one kind of landscape, the "ego-centred" and "perspectival" landscape, is routinely taken to be the only kind. As we shall see, the perspectival landscape is that of both the landscape arts and the landowner. By insisting on multiple landscapes (and, again, not simply on multiple perspectives), we foreground "other ways of understanding and relating to the land."

As diverse and multiple as landscapes might be, in my discussion of the estate I emphasize three overlapping but isolable categories of landscape crucial to the early modern period, what I have termed the landscapes of absolute property, stewardship, and custom. In order to define these categories as clearly as possible, I will first turn to a few examples of an early modern trope, that of land converted into clothing, that both champions a particular landscape and reveals the influence of others. Through these examples, we can begin to recognize both the conflicting cultural meanings of land in the early modern period and the landscapes through which those meanings are constructed. I will begin with John Williams's critique of the worldliness and sartorial extravagance of a rich landowner:[10]

To see a man (who is but a *Steward* of what hee possesseth, and to render a fearefull account of the same) to haue a *Farme* clapt vpon his feete, a *Coppy holde* dangling vp and downe his legges, a *Manor* wrapt about his body, a *Lordship* hanging vpon his shoulders, nay (peraduenture) the *Tythes* (*Christs patrymonie*) turn'd to a Cap, and the *bread* of the poore to a plume of feathers: and all this waste to no *ende* then this, that people might come out and see, *this man cloathed in soft rayments.*[11]

This example reveals what is at issue in an early modern representation of the uses and abuses of land. To a twentieth-century reader, Williams's narrative of the conversion of land into clothing may seem at first glance like an account of the simple, if admittedly lopsided, sale of one commodity in order to purchase another, land for us being like clothing in that it is to be bought, sold, or traded.[12] To an early modern moralist like Williams, however, this exchange constitutes a scandal, one that can only be made sense of by recognizing that land is crucial to the moral economy of the period. Unsurprisingly, this moral economy is a decidedly manorial one, and by turning his land into cloth the lord of the manor is shrugging off a set of estate-based relationships in favor of a new suit. The hospitality the lord once offered to the poor in the form of food is relinquished for a plume of feathers; the set of obligations and expectations inscribed in manorial copy rolls are given over in favor of an adornment perhaps akin to Malvolio's yellow garters; and even tithes once presented for the maintenance of the church are "turn'd to a Cap." Thus, much more is suggested here than the conversion of one commodity into another; what is actually referred to is the passing of a social order through the sale of lands, a sale that tears at the very fabric of that order even as it makes possible the lavish adornment of the seller.

Williams warns the would-be fashion plate that while he may technically be within his rights to sell his land, he owes an obligation not only to the tenants below but to the Lord above him. The landowner "is but a Steward of what hee possesseth," and he will one day have to make an account of his holdings. Williams conflates a steward's presentation to his lord of the manorial records he keeps, a phenomenon we see represented in *A Jovial Crew*, with the Last Judgment, thereby situating the business of the estate in terms of the rendering up of spiritual account books. This is not an idle conflation, for, as I make clear in Chapter One, the temporal and spiritual orders are seen in this period as both analogous and interconnected. Such interconnections underwrite Williams's conception of stewardship, which combines careful maintenance of the estate with moral stewardship of its inhabitants. We can see what is at stake, then, in the lord's turn to a life of foppery and leisure: not merely a few parcels of land, but a complex set of interconnecting relationships to which both land and landowner are central.

The land-into-clothing trope is one dear to early modern drama, just as many of the plays I discuss in this book are centrally concerned with a paternalistic, land-based moral economy. We see versions of this trope in various texts, one of which I take up in Chapter Two, but especially in the works of Ben Jonson. In *Every Man Out of His Humour*, for instance, the following suspect advice is offered:

First, to be an accomplished gentleman, that is, a gentleman of the time, you must give o'er housekeeping in the country, and live altogether in the city amongst gallants; where, at your first appearance, 'twere good you turned four or five hundred acres of your best land into two or three trunks of apparel (you may do it without going to a conjuror) and be sure, you mix yourself still with such as flourish in the spring of the fashion, and are least popular.[13]

Four or five hundred acres to two or three trunks—the disparity in scale does satirical work, suggesting that much is given up for little. Responsibilities are given up as well: as I stress in Chapter Five, "housekeeping" refers not merely to the maintenance of a household but to hospitality and the social obligations attendant upon being lord of the manor. These responsibilities, associated with a traditional, seemingly timeless social order, are abandoned in order to become "a gentleman of the time"; for Jonson and many others in this period, being fashionable means being socially irresponsible.

In *Epicoene*, Truewit says the following of a prospective wife for the woman-loathing Morose:

Then if you love your wife, or rather dote on her, sir, oh how she'll torture you . . . [S]he must have that rich gown for such a great day, a new one for the next, a richer for the third; be serv'd in silver, have the chamber fill'd with a succession of grooms, footmen, ushers, and other messengers, besides embroiderers, jewelers, tirewomen, sempsters, feathermen, perfumers; while she feels not how the land drops away, nor the acres melt, nor foresees the change when the mercer has your woods for her velvets.[14]

The land drops away and the acres melt; what replaces the social order that evaporates with them is a household comprised solely of servants for Morose's imagined wife. While even post-feudal manorial relations are ideologically (and ideally) predicated upon social reciprocity, as is made clear in Jonson's "To Penshurst," the world of the fashionable housewife replaces reciprocity with vanity. That is, we witness here not a hierarchical social order to which all of its members, from peasant to freeholder to lord of the manor, contribute, but a succession of attendants and tradespeople who wait upon the lady of the house. Moreover, the escalation of the wife's desires—each day demands a more extravagant dress—means that Morose will run through all of his lands to provide her with gowns.

Jonson's reference to a conjurer in the first quotation, evocative of his larger interest in alchemy, suggests that the conversion of land into cloth resembles a kind of magic trick, as does the melting away of acres. But what kind of transformation has taken place? While in terms of cultural capital or even market value the conversion of land into clothing could conceivably be advantageous to the landseller, Jonson's satire is predicated upon the assumption that another stick should be used to measure the wisdom of this transaction. We have already seen that in moral terms the exchange is a suspect one, but I want to talk of two other possible reasons for its flawed nature. First and most obvious is that Jonson's landsellers are exchanging a renewable resource, a source of steady and regular revenue, for that which makes one no more than a fashionable "gentleman of the time." Even given that clothing was both often costly and recycled over several years, its long-term value (at least usually) fell far short of that offered by land.

The second reason demands more detailed explanation, but gets closer to accounting for why Jonson invokes the conjurer. Insofar as it suggests to him a kind of transubstantiation, such a conversion is for Jonson the reverse alchemical transformation into dross of what, in social terms, is gold. Put somewhat differently, we witness in these passages traffic between regimes of value that Jonson believes to be fundamentally distinct. To see this more clearly, consider what Igor Kopytoff says about "commoditization" as a process:

> From a cultural perspective, the production of commodities is also a cultural and cognitive process: commodities must be not only produced materially as things, but also culturally marked as being a certain kind of thing. Out of the total range of things available in a society, only some of them are considered appropriate for marking as commodities. Moreover, the same thing may be treated as a commodity at one time and not at another. And finally, the same thing may at the same time, be seen as a commodity by one person and as something else by another.[15]

The conversion of land into clothing through the sale of the former and purchase of the latter marks both acres and velvets as commodities. However, for Jonson and many other early modern thinkers the ascription of commodity status to land violates their notion of what both a commodity and land should be. Certainly Jonson is aware that land was constantly bought and sold, but land, like a wedding ring (or the wife who wears it), was expected to efface its commodity status by taking on a social meaning that would override the fact of its onetime entry into the market. As we have seen, land formed the basis for a social world; to identify it as first and foremost a commodity was to expose the fragility of that world, or, at least, to dislocate land from the moral economy that was supposed to be inseparable from it. However, Jonson was writing at a time when the land market was expanding dramatically. Discussing the period 1560–1699, Lawrence Stone refers to "the tremendous upheaval in the mobility of land in this country, which is without parallel in either the later Middle Ages or the late seventeenth and eighteenth centuries." According to Stone, land sales rose steadily from 1560 and peaked around 1610.[16] Such changes put pressure on traditional ways of construing land by foregrounding its commodity status, the status that the writings of Jonson and other moralists both register and resist.

With the world of the estate in mind, let us look at one last quotation from Jonson. In this, also from *Epicoene*, LaFoole reflects on his own sartorial splendor:

I had as fair a gold jerkin on that day as any was worn in the Island Voyage or at Caliz, none disprais'd, and I came over in it hither, show'd myself to my friends in court and after went down to my tenants in the country and survey'd my lands, let new leases, took their money, spent it in the eye o' the land here, upon ladies—and now I can take up [i.e., borrow] at my pleasure.[17]

Whereas in the first quotation from *Epicoene* we have acres melting into velvets, here we have a precise articulation of how the land is exploited in pursuit of a cognate commodity to "a gold jerkin." LaFoole does not sell his lands, though surely his borrowing points in that direction, but he does take steps to increase his revenues from them. In order to maintain an opulent appearance at court, he surveys his lands and then renegotiates leases with his tenants based on the higher land values generated by the survey. With the money gained by this, LaFoole returns to London, importantly described as "the eye o' the land," and promptly spends all he has gained. No matter, though, because his show of wealth establishes him as a good credit risk, and therefore he can "take up at [his] pleasure." This example introduces us to topics crucial to this book: the tension between notions of land as exploitable resource and social site; the complex intersections between country estate, town, and nation (the "land" that London is the eye of); and the use of written texts such as the survey for the construction of what I will now describe as a landscape of absolute property.

WHAT WE WITNESS in the above anecdotes is an early modern
cultural struggle over the meaning of landed property. This struggle can be understood in terms of the conflict between three conceptions of landscape, each of which represents a particular kind of
construction of the land, a way in which the land is brought into
knowledge and meaning. Williams and Jonson decry the decline of
hospitality, survey-engendered abuses of the tenantry through rack-
renting or "progressive estate management," sartorial excess, conspicuous consumption, the migration of landlords to London, and
spiritual decay: all of these phenomena are linked to and bespeak a
landscape of absolute property which both manifests itself in specific
texts and their uses—think of LaFoole's survey—and for them constitutes a fundamentally exploitative and acquisitive vision of land
and tenantry that was perceived to threaten the entire social order
and that pointed toward the era of private property. My reference
in the last sentence to vision is deliberate: the landscape of absolute
property is often manifested in and engendered by the "ego-
centred" and "perspectival" landscape discussed above. It is no accident that the estate map, which generates a perspectival landscape, is routinely seen as a tool of exploitation. Satirists and moralists like Jonson and Williams favor a *landscape of stewardship*, one
that presupposes and champions a land-based moral order at the
center of which stands the beneficent landlord, moral steward of
his estate. Less frequently or fully represented is the *landscape of
custom*: a landscape structured by custom—those activities performed by lord and tenantry, but especially the latter, that "haue
been used, time out of memorie of man"[18]—and everyday practice.
Customs both give tenants certain rights—for instance, to collect
firewood on rented lands, or to cross another's fields to gain access
to the river—and place them under specific obligations to the
landlord. However, because my aim is to excavate the forgotten
landscape(s) of the tenantry, custom is here defined as those rights
and activities of the tenants that are often perceived to be threat-

ened by the avarice of the landlord, usually via the employment of a surveyor.[19] Obviously, the landscape of custom is often compatible with that of stewardship, but it differs in that its emphasis is not on the landlord: imagine what "To Penshurst" would be like if the landscape it produced were centered on the village or marketplace and not the manor house.

Of course these three kinds of landscape are not always easy to distinguish from one another, and they do not exist in a pure form unmarked by the influence of other conceptualizations of and relationships to the land. While I have for the purpose of analysis differentiated between the landscapes of absolute property, stewardship, and custom, the latter two in particular can overlap and interanimate one another in important ways. In addition, one could imagine a landscape of absolute property, such as a survey, being used in a fashion reconcilable with the imperatives of custom; the potential compatibility of these landscapes should not be denied. As we shall see, however, the survey is routinely represented as corrosive of custom—as Andrew McRae puts it, surveyors "promote a rational definition of social and economic relationships, in preference to the network of duties and responsibilities which constitutes the conservative ideal"[20]—and this theoretical compatibility was, at the level of representation, seldom recognized.

It is my contention that through the examination of these historically specific landscapes we encounter the complex relations between landed property and a range of social practices from which it is inseparable. It should be noted, however, that the landscapes described here for the most part reflect the beliefs, values, and sometimes even the language of moralists and traditionalists; what we will not encounter in this book are many sympathetic accounts or advocates of absolute property. This is not to say that such sympathetic advocacy was impossible in this period; as McRae has so ably shown, by the mid-seventeenth century there had fully developed an influential discourse of agrarian improvement that endorsed as necessary and right "the primacy of individual rights over ties of community, and link[ed] enclosed fields to ideals of order and freedom."[21] Largely because that primacy has come to seem as natural to us as property itself, I have chosen to focus on texts in which the landscape of absolute property is revealed to be only one possibility among several.

In referring to the property that is natural to us, I am of course describing a particular conception of property whose "naturalness" represents the historical victory of ideas not always widely held. The transition from precapitalist to capitalist conceptions of property is one that requires the move from seeing property as a *relation to* (others through) objects to seeing it *as* an object. C. B. Macpherson explains this development in terms of land: "As rights in land became more absolute, and parcels of land became more freely marketable commodities, it became natural to think of the land itself as the property. . . . It appeared to be the things themselves, the actual parcels of land and portions of commercial capital, not just rights in them, that were exchanged in the market."[22] This alteration in the nature of rights in land requires not only economic change, but the broad acceptance of a conceptualization of land not as a site of customary relations but as a fungible "plot." Such acceptance has as a necessary if not sufficient cause the triumph of a landscape of absolute property. The story that this book tells is that of the agon preceding that triumph.

A LANDSCAPE IS built out of inclusions and exclusions; it is a structuring of knowledge and a valorizing of some things at the expense of others. For instance, the landscape of absolute property understands a forest as uncultivated and thus as *vacant* or *reclaimable* land—this is obviously the language of "progressive estate management"[23]—while the landscape of custom sees the forest as the site of traditional economic activities such as wood gathering. Of course both literary criticism and the literary tradition operate in an analogous way; like landscape, they are simultaneously a construction and a way of seeing the world. Thus far, this tradition has seen the category of landscape as inseparable from texts produced at the behest of the landowner, texts that reinforce his authority and register his hegemony: paintings, poems, gardens, etc. Arguably that hegemony is inevitable in a culture to which landowning gentry or aristocrats were so conceptually and materially central; certainly I will not be looking at dramatic texts that suggest anything too radically different. What we will encounter, however, is a fuller interrogation of the nature and imperatives of that hegemony, and the more complete rendering of "perspectives" other than those of the landowner or the artist whose efforts he underwrites. That is, we will encounter different and competing landscapes, ones that register multiple relations to and apprehensions of the land.

This difference is possible, in part, because we are dealing with texts that largely predate the emergence in England of both the category of landscape (as it is traditionally construed) and those artifacts identified as landscapes: while the "seminal estate poem" is "To Penshurst," only with "the triumph of Augustan georgic [did] estate poems [come] into their own";[24] prospect paintings appear in the late seventeenth century; landscape gardening flourishes in the eighteenth century, and so on.[25] The important point, though, is that the institutionalization of landscape marks the triumph of landscapes of absolute property. We see this in prospect painting,[26] or in the difference between Jonson's "To Penshurst" and Marvell's "Upon Appleton House."[27] The connections between landscape painting and landscapes of absolute property are elegantly summarized by Kenneth Robert Olwig as follows:

Landscape was framed and reified as a cultural object, to be bought and sold as cultural capital on the burgeoning new art market, much as land itself was being divided up according to the geometric coordinates of the map, to be sold and traded on the property market. This whole process, in turn, went hand-in-hand with a transformation by which reciprocal, inherited, customary cultural relations, rooted in the organic cosmology of feudalism, were replaced by money relations in which the particular was commodified through a universal system of quantifiable monetary value that was independent of that which was exchanged. There is thus a certain poetic appropriateness to the fact that the first representations of landscape scenery in painting tended to be views seen from the window of the urban patron whose portrait was being painted, and that the same persons who imported Dutch surveyors and engineers to England to restructure and rationalise their properties, imported landscape paintings and hired landscape architects.[28]

Land "divided up according to the geometric coordinates of the map, to be sold and traded on the property market": this process is conducive to the construction of, and depends upon, landscapes of absolute property, which are clearly linked here to estate cartography, painting, landscape architecture, and, running through all of these, the perspective of the landlord.[29] This perspective is just that, a mode of detachment from rather than immersion in the social relations of the estate. Such detachment lends itself to the construction of land as plot to be bought or sold rather than place to be inhabited and worked on.[30] In contrast to this perspective are "reciprocal, inherited, customary cultural relations"—that is, customary landscapes. If what the landscape arts provide us with is inseparable from the emergence of private property, we encounter again and again in the drama of the late sixteenth and early seventeenth centuries the landscape of absolute property not as a given but as a contestant in an ideological agon, as in competition with the landscapes of custom and stewardship. By talking of landscapes before the institutionalization of landscape, we catch a crucial glimpse of the conceptual struggles attendant upon the uneasy emergence of private property.

MY PURPOSE IN this book is not merely to complicate or criticize a literary tradition. It is also to attempt to step outside of that tradition not only by offering alternative landscapes but by situating literary texts in a broad social and discursive context. In this regard, I have been influenced by new historicism, which has worked to position texts in relation to larger cultural phenomena. For the study of the early modern period this is a particularly significant innovation, given the anachronistic nature of a notion of literariness that works to abstract the production and consumption of texts deemed "literary" from broader social processes. Critics like Stephen Greenblatt have relocated "literature" in terms of "the circulation of social energy,"[31] thereby making possible the tracing of relations between texts once viewed as categorically distinct from and thus incommensurate with one another. My project deals not merely with the landscapes of drama, but also with those conceptually related landscapes registered in and generated by a range of early modern texts and practices. It is my contention that by adducing these we are able to offer important alternatives to the landscapes of absolute property which, instantiated in the *landscape arts*, have traditionally registered as defining *landscape* itself.[32] Consider, for instance, a topic briefly addressed in Chapter One, the difference between a Rogationtide ceremony, which involved integrating the young into a sense of the community through what was known as "the beating of the bounds," and tenants perambulating estate lands with a surveyor. Both practices involve the traversing of the land, but the first activity is in the service of the inculcation in all parish residents of a sense of belonging, of community ownership and participation; the second usually works instead to define a landscape of absolute property, to make clear, with the aid of long-time tenants and in the service of increasing revenues, the exact dimensions of what the landlord owns. On the one hand, the Rogationtide ritual integrates members of the community into a customary landscape; on the other, the survey works to generate a map that offers the lord a view of his estate akin to that of the prospect painting—it instantiates and produces a landscape of absolute property.[33] By placing these two disparate practices next to one another, we see what is implied in accepting the landscape of absolute property as all landscape: the effacement or distortion of the customary, the erasure of certain relations to the land in the name of a limiting, limited (and, in terms of its largely uncontested dominance, anachronistic) conception of absolute ownership. This is, of course, what private property portends. It is also what many of the plays that I discuss in this book resist.

Over the preceding pages I have turned and returned to the issue of property, obviously a crucial one for any discussion of landscape. However, this book also concerns itself with landscapes that cannot be immediately understood in terms of landed property: in particular the landscapes of London and the nation. What will become clear, though, is that the estate intersects in significant ways with city and nation. For instance, we will see that the emergence of a landscape of absolute property was spurred on by the flight of landlords to London, whereas changes in the management of the estate, particularly enclosure, both fueled the growth of the city and put pressure on the sociospatial tropes that gave shape to its landscape. We will also see the estate construed as a model for the nation, and the mismanagement of the nation compared to the abuse of the estate. In short, the landscapes of the estate existed not in conceptual isolation but often emerged out of material and conceptual cross-fertilizations with those of city and nation.

Despite these cross-fertilizations, nation and city might still seem to pose problems for my notion of landscape. The category makes most obvious sense when used to describe the estate, which obviously has long associations with the traditional definition of landscape. Arguably, to talk of nation and city is to run the risk of reducing landscape to an empty metaphor; after all, the nation is an imagined community, a locus of identification whose instantiation owed a great deal to Tudor efforts to consolidate state authority, whereas the city as a conceptual unit can be less easily configured in terms of property and seignorial authority than an estate can.[34] However, if we adhere to the notion of landscape as an ideological category—that is, if we let go of its association with the landscape arts—then its utility here becomes clear. Landscape is a construction and a way of seeing, the means by which social relations are negotiated across land, a way that topography is brought into discourse and into knowledge: this can be said not only about the estate, but of both the urban landscape of the city and the imagined landscape of the nation (which, as we shall see in Chapters Three and Four, bears a complex relationship to the topography of Britain). This "imagined landscape" has two forms specific to it: the *landscape of imagined community*, which refers to the way in which the map of the nation makes possible the acts of identification necessary for the construction of an imagined community; and the *landscape of sovereignty*, which manifests itself in one of these two ways: it reflects and shapes the ambitions and imperatives of those who control or would control the kingdom; and, more broadly but distinctly, it represents the conceptual annexation of distinct cultural spaces in the name of monarch or (a culturally homogenized) nation. In Chapter Six we will see that such a landscape of sovereignty poses a threat to Heywood's London, represented in terms of a customary landscape understood as both emerging out of traditional economic practice and giving shape to the city.

IN THE PLACE OF the landscape arts, this book locates sixteenth- and seventeenth-century dramatic texts that are concerned with the construction and implications of a range of landscapes. Of course, this concern is not peculiar to drama; Jonson's depiction of LaFoole's avarice bespeaks a broader cultural awareness of the troubling implications of social and commercial innovations. However, what makes the professional theater particularly intriguing here is that in crucial ways its development required those innovations. Theatrical companies relied upon both absentee landlords and displaced rural workers for their audiences; the theaters became sites for the kinds of conspicuous consumption Jonson both decried and, for a time, depended upon for his livelihood; plays were the product of a mixed system, evidence both of aristocratic patronage and, more emphatically, a burgeoning entrepreneurial culture that turned them into commodities. In addition, players were seen as posing a similar kind of threat to the stability of the social order as were elaborately bedizened gallants eagerly selling their lands. When John Williams alludes to the fop motivated by the hope "that people might come out and see, this man cloathed in soft rayments," he could be easily referring to a gallant perched upon a stool at the stage's edge, or for that matter to a player. Thus, in concrete and multiple ways the theater was fueled by as well as implicated in the social transformations that it represented and attempted symbolically to manage.

While the theater was a largely entrepreneurial institution, the plays discussed here suggest that it was not capitalism's champion. In the face of survey-enabled attempts to rationalize land management—that is, to generate out of estate and nation a landscape of absolute property—*Arden of Faversham* and *Woodstock* gesture toward customary landscapes; *1 Edward IV* symbolically resists the growth of a protocapitalist economy that troubles the city's sociospatial self-identification. The seeming contradiction between the theater's entrepreneurialism and its apparent critique of capitalism should not surprise us, however. For these plays to be read as resistant to capitalism, we must assume that the late sixteenth and early seventeenth centuries knew exactly what capitalism was. That is, these plays only thumb their noses at capitalism if we read them through the lens of a fully developed and culturally available articulation of capitalism, one absent from Tudor-Stuart England. A more fruitful way of construing them is in terms of resistance to specific practices and the landscapes those practices imply. This is not to suggest that those practices do not gesture toward capitalism or represent some of its preconditions, but it is instead to focus on ideological contradictions and skirmishes that partly defined the long period of uneven transition from feudalism to capitalism.[35]

If a play discussed below resists specific practices and the landscapes they imply, then it should also be noted that it represents them. This obvious point suggests another reason why I have chosen to focus on plays—their multivocality. A play in its very form lends itself to the enunciation of a myriad of "viewpoints," the representation of multiple landscapes. However, I do not want merely to replace the landscape arts with plays, texts which may not fit the traditional definition of landscape but do sit squarely in a (constructed) literary tradition.[36] I also want to consider the way in which certain non-literary texts construct landscapes: in particular, estate, county, and national maps and surveys, coronation and Rogationtide accounts, surveying manuals, road tables, and atlases. This list clearly does not exhaust the texts that could be construed in terms of the category of landscape; one could also look at, say, accounts of royal progresses or Lord Mayor's shows, or plans for land reclamation. (Similarly, one might examine a range of practices or sociospatial networks constitutive of local or national landscapes: postal networks, river traffic, peddler's routes, and so on.) What unites the texts I focus on, though, is the way in which they were central to material practices that delimit space and represent the complex interpenetrations of the topographical and the social. My interests lean toward the cartographic. I situate maps in terms of the practices governing their production and consumption, practices intertwined with the social transformations that characterize this period. Thus, the map is taken up less as an aesthetic artifact—one that has been intriguingly connected to landscape painting by Svetlana Alpers[37]—than as a text implicated in broader social processes that inform the construction of disparate landscapes.

I began by talking about the commodification of land, and of course estate maps functioned to facilitate the exploitation and sale of lands. Landscape as it has traditionally been discussed also colludes with commodification insofar as it participates in the fetishization of the estate, rendering it in terms of what I have called the landscape of absolute property. In this regard, the landscape arts are in line with the landscape of the estate survey, but this book will show that the survey offers only one possible conception of landscape, and not an uncontested one. In contrast to this landscape, we will encounter customary ones that emphasize not the fetishized singularity of the estate, a singularity shaped by the perspective of the landowner, but the estate's status as a sociospatial nexus. This nexus is marked not only by relations between landlord and tenantry, but emerges out of both material exchanges between estate and city and conceptual ones between estate and nation. Tracing these exchanges is one of the ways in which this book works to complicate our sense of the landscape(s) of early modern England.

This book is divided into three sections, the first focusing on the estate, the second on roads, and the third on the city. This design describes (not without a measure of irony) the path of a landlord like Arden, moving from estate to city via the roads; of course it also traces the journey of many a displaced rural worker turned itinerant wage laborer. As tidy as this structure seems, the divisions do not hold absolutely—the estate is discussed in Section Two, as the city is in Section One. Moreover, the nation is taken up throughout. In short, while this partitioning works to demarcate subjects of analysis, the analysis itself insists on the practical inseparability of those subjects.

Section One, "Of Landlords and Kings: The Landscapes of Estate and Nation," concerns itself with the effects of developments in cartography and surveying on conceptions of land, estate, and nation. The first chapter, "'Arden Lay Murdered in That Plot of

Ground': Surveying, Land, and *Arden of Faversham*," elaborates upon the above discussion of the interconnectedness of land and social practices centered upon it. It then examines *Arden of Faversham*'s response to the historical erosion of one form that that interconnectedness could take, an erosion made possible in part by developments in surveying technology that altered estate relations between lord and tenant. Produced during what one historian has called "the golden age of estate surveying," *Arden of Faversham* (1591) imagines the social price paid for the values that underwrite the development of surveying. The play resists the beliefs undergirding the survey's construction of a landscape of absolute property through its valorization of an ethic of stewardship and its simultaneous critique of the "covetousness" understood to motivate estate managers such as Arden.

The second chapter, "Strange Metamorphoses: Landscape and the Nation in *Woodstock*," focuses on the anonymous *Woodstock* (1592), a play that represents Richard II's abuses of authority in a way that both dovetails with and diverges from Shakespeare's later dramatic account of the deposed king. In *Woodstock*, Richard authorizes the dissemination of "blank charters . . . through all the shires of England." Through these charters and related documents, Richard will both extract wealth from and accumulate information on all landholders. In other words, the charters function as surveys of the country, informing the monarch "what rents / What lands, or what revenues [the people] spend by th' year." The play represents a struggle over the nature of the rural landscape—is its meaning to continue to be constituted through local social practice, or will it emerge out of its place in Richard's map and survey? *Woodstock* offers an anxious vision of nationhood predicated upon the monarchical exploitation of information gathered in villages and marketplaces and collected in surveys and maps.

Chapter Three, "Reading Shakespeare's Maps," sketches a social history of the early modern map, paying particular attention to its

perceived status as a scientific text that generates a landscape of absolute property while seemingly authoritatively defining the land.
An elite document that seemed to allow gentlemen directly to "behold"—both look at and hold near—that which was only represented, the map nonetheless engendered an epistemological confusion that is explored in map-reading scenes in William Shakespeare's *1 Henry IV* (1597) and *King Lear* (1605). Shakespeare's *Richard II* (1595), however, stands as both the most sustained and most
elliptical of dramatic explorations of the meaning of maps. I focus
on John of Gaunt's famous map-inspired description of England in
relation to the play's insistent questioning of the nature and (largely
geographic) limits of Richard's authority. By doing so, I consider
the way in which *Richard II* raises questions about the conventions
of reading and conceptions of spatiality and sociality apparently
embedded in maps themselves—conventions and conceptions central to the imaginative construction of the landscapes of the nation.

In Section Two, "Where All Roads Lead: Land, Travel, and
Identity," I focus on the role of roads in defining or problematizing
definitions of estate and nation. As the Romans understood, roads
are a precondition for the formation of an integrated nation; by the
sixteenth century, the road system was shambolic, comprised
mostly of muddy, ill-maintained tracks and highways that were a
clear falling off from the much-heralded glories of the Roman
roads. Both chapters in this section concern themselves with the
idea (or ideal) of the road in relation to its material reality, a relationship with powerful implications for conceptions of private
property and national integrity. Chapter Four, "Civilizing Wales:
Cymbeline, Roads, and the Landscapes of Early Modern Britain,"
begins with the simple problem of how long it will take Imogen to
get to Milford Haven. This problem leads to a discussion of road
measurement that impinges upon Anglo-Welsh relations. Seen by
the English as both alien and familiar, both separate and integrated,
the Welsh landscape resists assimilation into an English landscape

of sovereignty (and the statute mile) while also functioning as the backdrop for English history. This dynamic is apparent in Shakespeare's *Cymbeline* (1609), a play whose conception of pre-Roman Britain bespeaks the symbolic annexation of Wales through its articulation of a *British* history understood finally as an *English* one. *Cymbeline* also embraces ancient Britain's Roman future, thereby simultaneously gesturing toward both Roman and Jacobean dreams of a unified island, the former pursued through the construction of a national network of roads.

Chapter Five, "Knowing One's Place: The Highway, the Estate, and *A Jovial Crew*," focuses on the significance of the highway to the landscape of absolute property. The highway is generally understood as the empty space of travel, as a space between places, and yet it is also "home" to an ever expanding vagabond population. The estate, on the other hand, functioned culturally as the embodiment of a threatened social order and as an emblem of local identity. However, as I argue in my *Arden* chapter, the estate survey rendered the land abstract, making it less a place than a plot to be bought or sold. I explore the relationship between the highway and these contradictory conceptions of the estate—place or plot— through a discussion of Richard Brome's *A Jovial Crew* (1641), a comedy about vagabonds in which Springlove is torn between, on the one hand, the emplacedness of the estate that he manages and putatively surveys, and, on the other, the supposed placelessness of the road. For Brome, the highway is part of a customary landscape to which an emergent conception of private property is hostile. As an alternative to this conception, Brome champions both estate-based hospitality, which suggests a landscape of stewardship, and his jovial crew of vagabonds, who for Brome act in the service of custom by following the highway.

Section Three, "London Under Fire: Landscape, Space, and the Representation of Revolt," focuses on assaults on London in plays by Thomas Heywood and William Shakespeare, assaults that symbolically negotiate a late-sixteenth-century crisis in the meaning and nature of the landscape of the city. The precise nature of this crisis is made clear through the discussion of landscape in terms of a broader critical category, that of space. Chapter Six, "The Beleaguered City: Guild Culture and Urban Space in Heywood's *1 Edward IV* and Shakespeare's *2 Henry VI*," shows that Heywood's London takes shape as a customary landscape unified by guild culture. The play represents the threat to guilds and London posed by the city's astonishing and unsettling growth and its economic expansion. More specifically, it considers the impact on London of both a nascent capitalist suburban industry and a sometimes rapacious Crown. At stake is the landscape of London, alternately figured as site of customary practice and as exploitable resource. Shakespeare offers a different vision of the city, following the logic of the coronation account in figuring it less as the instantiation of social practice—as, that is, a customary landscape—than as the vacant backdrop for the aristocratic struggles of the Wars of the Roses, as landscape of sovereignty. In short, this chapter considers the way in which the dramatic representation of London's spaces is implicated in a broader negotiation of the meanings and imperatives of urban landscapes.

IT IS WORTH reiterating that *The Drama of Landscape* does not serve as an exhaustive compendium of all possible versions of the relationship between land and social relations; for instance, a different project could take as its primary focus the crucially important ways in which landscapes are gendered. Nor does this book take up in any detail the kinds of texts more traditionally associated with landscape, both for what I hope are by now obvious theoretical reasons (it attempts to loosen the critical stranglehold that the landscape arts have on the category of landscape) and for practical ones (drama *and* the landscape arts would require another or a vastly different book). What I do hope that the book offers is not merely new

readings of old plays, but more importantly a disciplinary intervention that will force us to rethink the relationship between an ideological category and the aesthetic artifacts with which it has been in-
variably associated. Such an act of rethinking should remind us yet
again of what is at stake in the construction of both literary traditions and aesthetic categories: not merely the selection of some texts
over others, but the privileging of a certain way of seeing the world.
In the case of landscape as it has traditionally been read, this way of
seeing neatly coincides with the landowner's view from the manor
house. That the landowner's view has been taken as the only one attests less to either the power of his vision or the splendor of his prospect than it does to the fact that, by now, the only other available
views are obstructed ones. More precisely, insofar as the word evokes
the perspective, they are not "views" at all.

Of Landlords and Kings

THE LANDSCAPES OF ESTATE AND NATION

CHAPTER ONE

"Arden Lay Murdered in That Plot of Ground"

SURVEYING, LAND, AND 'ARDEN OF FAVERSHAM'

Without the habit of conceptualising space, a traveller going to war or work could not link his separate impressions to the nature of his route as a whole . . . [A] man could not visualise the country to which he belonged; a landowner, unable to "see" his properties as a whole was not concerned to concentrate his scattered holdings by sale or exchanges.[1]

According to its epilogue, *Arden of Faversham* tells us "the truth of Arden's death."[2] That "truth" refers not only to the homicidal machinations that lead up to the murder of Arden, but also to a certain relationship between the killing and the land: "Arden lay murdered in that plot of ground / Which he by force and violence held from Reede; / And in the grass his body's print was seen / Two years and more after the deed was done" (10–13). The murderous actions taken against Arden mirror the "force and violence" with which he withheld the "plot of ground," and the bloody print seen in the grass attests to the indignation of both Reede, who earlier cursed his landlord, and the land itself. The epilogue reminds us that in the late sixteenth century land is not solely thought of in terms of its utility or its fungibility, its status as a commodity; here the land speaks an ethics of stewardship that has its origins in feudalism. What I shall argue, though, is that in Elizabethan England, thanks to changes in a variety of social and material practices, and to technological innovations such as those that revolutionize estate surveying, the meaning of land begins to undergo a profound transformation. *Arden of Faversham* takes sides in an Elizabethan struggle over the cultural function of land, a struggle in which older conceptions of property as social office are troubled by emergent ideologies and technologies that imply a radically different view of what it means to be a landowner. That is, *Arden of Faversham* symbolically enacts a cultural conflict between the imperatives of landscapes of stewardship, custom, and absolute property.

LET US BEGIN with that "plot of ground." Returning from Shorlow, Arden is met by the ocean-bound Dick Reede, who confronts him as follows:

> My coming to you was about the plot of ground
> Which wrongfully you detain from me.
> Although the rent of it be very small,
> Yet will it help my wife and children,
> Which here I leave in Faversham, God knows,
> Needy and bare. (13.12–17)

In reply, Arden, who states he "dearly bought" the land, angrily asserts that if Reede continues to "rail on [him]," he will "banish pity" from his actions (19–27). Then follows Reede's curse, also a request beseeched of God:

> That plot of ground which thou detains from me . . .
> Be ruinous and fatal unto thee!
> Either there be butchered by thy dearest friends,
> Or else be brought for men to wonder at,
> Or thou or thine miscarry in that place,
> Or there run mad and end thy cursed days. (32–38)

This curse is one that Reede shall "leave with [his] distressful wife; / [His] children shall be taught such prayers as these" (51–52). Interestingly, though, Arden is not murdered on the contested land; he is only later dragged to the plot of ground necessary for the maintenance of Reede's family.

What we see here is land positioned variously in relationship to intersecting feudal, religious, and familial discourses. In banishing pity, Arden rhetorically casts off the mantle of the beneficent lord, the model for whom might be found in this "popular eulogy" for the third earl of Huntingdon:

> His tenants that daily repaired to his house
> Was fed with his bacon, his beef, & his souse.
> Their rents were not raised, their fines were but small,
> And many poore tenants paid nothing at all.
> No groves he enclosed, nor felled no wood,
> No pastures he paled to do himself good.
> To commons and country he lived a good friend,
> And gave to the needy what God did him send.[3]

Even in this paean to the generous lord, one who fulfills the moral responsibilities of his office by providing, fatherlike, for his tenants, we see in references to enclosure and to the felling of woods an alternative, more instrumental conception of the land—a conception in which the social relations at the center of the above verse are marginalized. Of course it is social and familial relations that Reede insistently foregrounds, first by appealing to the image of his "needy and bare" wife and children, and then by promising that they will regularly curse Arden's name. Mention of the bitter "prayers" Reede says his children will utter echoes ironically religious discourse epitomized by a tenant's prayer regarding his landlord in *The Book of Private Prayer*, a text issued by Edward VI in 1553:

We heartily pray thee to send thy holy spirit into the hearts of them that possess the grounds, pastures, and dwelling-places of the earth, that they, remembering themselves to be thy [i.e. God's] tenants, may not rack and

stretch out the rents of their houses and lands . . . after the manner of covetous worldlings . . . but so behave themselves in letting out their tenements, lands and pastures, that after this life they may be received into ev-
erlasting dwelling places.[4]

The prayer transposes feudal relations onto the heavenly sphere, arguing that landlords should be kind to tenants in the hopes that
they will be treated well in the afterlife by God, the Lord upon
whom they are dependent. For landlords to act as "covetous worldlings," to deny the reciprocal social relations that constitute the
feudal ideal central to a landscape of stewardship, to "banish pity"
as Arden does, is for them to run the risk of losing their "ever-
lasting dwelling places." Greed causes the mismanagement of their
heavenly estates.

Reede ends his curse with his children's prayers; he begins it by
wishing that Arden be "butchered by [his] dearest friends," a wish
that largely comes true, and one whose enactment is spatially inscribed. Arden is murdered not only by dear friends, but in his own
home. The curse of the tenant insinuates itself into the domestic
and social spaces—the house and friendships—of the pitiless landlord.

What I have been trying to suggest is that *Arden of Faversham*
and the various ideologies sketchily adduced here see land as fully
implicated in a range of social practices and relations; it is understood in terms of the enactment of lordly beneficence (a landscape
of stewardship) and the traditional benefits and rights of the tenant
(a landscape of custom). And yet, the shadow we saw cast over the
above eulogy, that of instrumental conceptions of the land, also
stretches over both the culture and the play, and while that shadow
may be dramatically dispelled by Arden's death, the culture cannot
so easily shrug off its effects. With that in mind and before returning to the play, I want to talk about changes in Elizabethan land
management practices and in estate surveying, both of which have

the potential to destabilize the social relations we saw delineated above and which underwrite a landscape of absolute property.

KEITH WRIGHTSON tells us of the "fundamental contradiction between the realities of an individualistic agrarian capitalism and the ethics of traditional social obligations which so often surfaced in the course of the sixteenth and seventeenth centuries."[5] In such a situation, he argues, what is crucial for the maintenance of social order is

the whole world of regular personal contact, at work, after church services, in the streets . . .What was vital in this daily social intercourse was the regularity of direct face-to-face contact both between comparative equals and between superiors and inferiors. Indeed in the latter case, individual demeanour in direct personal interaction was of singular importance, for it could simultaneously reinforce consciousness of the bond of personal identification and the reality of social differentiation upon which the whole structure of paternalism and deference rested.[6]

In manorial relations, this paternalism necessitated on the part of the tenantry a loyalty analogous to that of children to their father, a loyalty that could even take the form of armed service in the name of the lord. Increasingly, however, such relationships of fealty had begun slowly to erode. The reasons for this are multiple; one involves the formation during the Tudor era of the nation-state, an ideological construct which required a consolidation of authority in which, as texts such as *The Homily on Obedience* make clear, feudal or manorial loyalties are carefully circumscribed by, and shaped within the parameters of, loyalty to Crown and country. Another reason, however, is the shift in the late sixteenth and early seventeenth centuries toward a more unabashedly economic relationship between lord and tenant. Speaking of the 1590's, Lawrence Stone says that

This decade saw the last of the age-old habit of regarding land not only as a source of money, but also as a means of obtaining military aid and outward signs of loyalty and esteem. The rapid rise in agricultural prices during this decade must have opened landlords' eyes to the necessity and justice of tampering with ancient customs in order to cope with the effects of inflation.[7]

Similarly, Martin White argues that the final years of Elizabeth's reign witnessed the beginning of the end of the idea of a "moral economy" and the emergence in embryonic form of a fundamentally economic conception of the self.[8] Of course, as both Stone and White are aware, the kind of paradigm shift alluded to here neither takes place at a precise historical moment nor constitutes the emergence of a univocal or unvariegated social form. The feudal ideal of the beneficent, fatherly landlord continued to play a part in the public imagination and to influence social relations long beyond the Elizabethan and Jacobean periods. At the same time, Stone tells us that "The influence of the nobles over client gentry and tenantry was being weakened by their increasing absenteeism due to attendance at Court . . ."[9] While he sees this phenomenon as reaching its peak in the early seventeenth century, Elizabethan proclamations attest to Tudor anxiety regarding this migration.

In 1587, Elizabeth writes of "sundry persons of good wealth and calling" who have left their homes in coastal shires for "inland countries, and . . . the city of London," a flight that compromises both coastal defense, a crucial consideration in pre-Armada England, and the "accustomed hospitality in those places."[10] Nine years later, Elizabeth has been informed of "sundry persons of ability to keep hospitality in their countries" who are "leaving the relief of their poor neighbors as well for food as for good rule" to live in London. Elizabeth attributes the desire of these "persons of ability" to abandon the kinds of responsibilities we saw delineated above to their "covetous minds."[11] Similarly, shortly after his coronation, James urges the landed gentry and aristocrats who came to court for the festivities to return to their country seats to relieve the poor and maintain order:

We have entred into consideration of the state of the severall parts of the body of our Realme, And therein do finde, that the absence of the Noblemen and Gentlemen which are used to reside there in severall quarters, is accompanied with great inconvenience, aswell in the want of reliefe which the poorer sort did receive by their ordinary Hospitalitie, as also chiefly in the defect of Government, whereby besides other inconveniences, through lacke of order, the infection of the Plague spreadeth and scattereth itselfe into divers places of the Realme, and is like further to increase, if by the presence and care of such as are in authority and credit amongst our people, they be not contained in some good course, for the preventing of that contagion.[12]

James begins by talking of the state of the "body of our Realme" and ends by alluding to the plague which threatens that body thanks to the absence of those who "are in authority and credit amongst our people." Of course one cannot underestimate the literal threat of contagion in this period, and the need in such a situation for the material aid offered by "Noblemen and Gentlemen," but what is striking in James's statement is the slide from hospitality to disease, the implicit equation between absentee landlordism and, not only disorder, but the plague. Contagion functions as a real threat and as an unsettling metaphor for the erosion of relations of "hospitalitie" and "good rule."

What we see then is that the feudal conception of social relations that has been under strain since at least the beginning of rampant enclosure is by the Elizabethan era finally near collapse. The ideology of paternalistic interdependence could hardly flourish in its feudal form for long with the "covetous" father of the manor moving to the big city and relinquishing all his familial responsibilities. Neither could it survive the more quotidian phenomenon alluded to above, the gradual but general move to a solely rent-based conception of landlord-tenant relations. What is important about this last development for our purposes is that such a move necessitates a reconceptualization of the land, an emergent view of land not as social space but as commodity, as salable, manipulable lot. We see the beginning of that reconceptualization in the practices of estate surveying.

IN DISCUSSING Christopher Saxton's 1579 atlas, each sheet of which bears the queen's arms, Richard Helgerson argues that the "maps proclaim royal sovereignty over the kingdom as a whole and over each of its provinces."[13] However, the centrality of land in such maps eventually necessitates that the queen's arms be consigned to the edges of the map; as a result, "explicit symbols of royal control are necessarily made to look marginal, merely decorative, and thus ultimately dispensable."[14] The effect of all of this, says Helgerson, is to "[strengthen] the sense of both local and national identity at the expense of an identity based on dynastic loyalty."[15] For Helgerson, cartographic (or, in his term, chorographic) productions signify primarily through their relationship to king and country; his interpretive model is informed by new historicist paradigms that see the text as created out of the author's polyvalent negotiation of sovereign power.[16] Moreover, his account of maps as discursive artifacts, while richly suggestive, insufficiently distinguishes those artifacts from "literary" ones,[17] and does not fully address either the material circumstances of their production or the range of contexts within which they might be read. I would argue that estate maps—Helgerson focuses on county and national ones—can be understood in terms different from the ones adduced in *Forms of Nationhood*; most significantly, they can be read in light of developments in early modern surveying.

"The period 1558–1598," Peter Eden tells us, "was one of great change in surveying practice. At its commencement estate maps were a rarity; by the end of it they were a commonplace."[18] The results of surveying practices before this period took the form of written records; in the fourteenth and fifteenth centuries we are told of written accounts of landholdings known as terriers which "describ[ed] . . . individually owned plots and strips one after the other."[19] P. D. A. Harvey states that while there is a surveying tradition, the "drawing of maps and plans . . . can hardly be said to have had any tradition at all by 1500."[20] However, "By the time of Cecil's death techniques of measuring and drawing were fully developed, though cartographic embellishment long continued to recall . . . earlier panoramas" and other forms of visual representation not associated with surveying.[21] What we see, then, during this period—a period dubbed by one historian of surveying as the "golden age of estate cartography"[22]—is the fusing of written and visual traditions, a fusion that makes possible a new way of construing the land.[23]

One of the most important factors in making this fusion possible is the development of advanced surveying instruments. J. A. Bennett shows how the early modern rediscovery of mathematical texts such as Euclid's *Elements* transformed and professionalized surveying. Surveyors first drew upon and adapted instruments such as the astrolabe and quadrant, instruments used previously by astronomers and navigators. As Bennett puts it,

Renaissance mathematicians . . . saw in surveying an opportunity to demonstrate again the practical usefulness of geometry, and the importance of mathematical science. Success would require a propaganda effort directed at the surveyor—who, as likely as not, preferred to be left in peace with his familiar techniques—and at his patron. They would need to be convinced of the value of a new type of surveying . . . and of a new image of the surveyor as a geometer, whose badge of office would not be a notebook and pole, but a theodolite [an azimuth instrument adapted from astronomy].[24]

The "propaganda effort" Bennett refers to seems eventually to have worked. Training in mathematics in this period was largely limited to the upper classes; the average surveyor was ignorant of the mathematical principles and practices required to utilize advanced surveying techniques.[25] The effects of this were, first, to inspire the production of a number of texts designed to instruct the surveyor in the necessary mathematics; notable among these are Leonard Digges's *Pantometria* (1571), William Cunningham's *Cosmographical Glasse* (1559), and, a text to which we shall return, John Norden's *The Surueyor's Dialogue* (1607). Second, however, we see the denigration of instruments which are both cruder in form and which, more importantly, do not require mathematical knowledge. Most mocked of all late-sixteenth-century surveying instruments was the plane table. This device, A. W. Richeson tells us, "provided the practitioner who was not adept at calculations with an instrument that would perform more or less mechanically the many arithmetical calculations in land measuring."[26] The plane table, says Thomas Digges, son of Leonard and publisher of the *Pantometria* after his father's death, is "an Instrument onely for the ignorante and unlearned, that have no knowledge of Noumbers." Arthur Hopton writes in his *Topographicall Glasse* (1611) that the plane table "hath begot itselfe a wonderfull affection of the vulgar, whereby they vainly thinke noe work doth relish well unlesse it bee served upon this plaine Table."[27] Most interestingly, Aaron Rathborne in *The Surveyor* (1616) expresses an anxiety that the instrument is so straightforward that

the multitude of simple and ignorant persons (vsing, or rather abusing, that good plaine Instrument, called the *Plaine Table*) who hauing but once obserued a Surueyor, by looking ouer his shoulder, how and in what manner he directs his sights, and drawes his lines thereon; they presently apprehend the businesse, prouide them of some cast *Plaine Table*, and within small time after, you shall heare them tell you wonders, and what rare feats they can performe.[28]

What all of this tells us is that the introduction of mathematics works to professionalize surveying by privileging practices that require specialized knowledge and by denigrating those that are accessible to "the vulgar," "the multitude of simple and ignorant persons." In wearing the badge of the theodolite, the surveyor attests to his status as master of a set of practices inaccessible to most. More importantly, these practices, rooted as they are in mathematics, lend to surveying the credibility of a science. Thus, surveys begin to make scientific truth claims; they take on the status of fact.

Of Elizabethan estate plans, Maurice Beresford says the following:

Some were commissioned by landlords anxious to develop their estates and some by landlords who were nervous of their tenants' claims; some were the result of litigation and some were designed to avoid it: but, whatever the motive, the plan had to descend to the smallest parcels of land, the smallest differences of tenure and the most accurate record of occupancy.[29]

The potentially problematic nature of this last requirement was registered in the outraged voice of a fictional farmer who appears in John Norden's surveying textbook, *The Surueyor's Dialogue*. Of surveyors, the farmer says:

You pry into mens tytles and estates ... whereby you [bring?] men and matter in question often times, that would (as long time they haue) [?] without any question. And oftentimes you are the cause that men lose their land: and sometimes they are abridged of such liberties as they have long used in Mannors; and customes are altred, broken, and sometimes peruerted or taken away by your meanes.[30]

Norden's surveyor responds by asserting that all the lands belong to the lord, and that consequently the lord has the right to pry in order to discover the exact dimensions of what is rightly his. The fictional farmer is, eventually, placated, and even desires to become a surveyor; one imagines that flesh-and-blood farmers might not be so easily appeased. Norden's text tells us what J. B. Harley asserts in another context: "The surveyor ever more frequently walks at the side of the landlord ..."[31] Harley's focus is on the spread of "capitalist forms of agriculture," but his insight might be more broadly

applied. Norden's farmer describes, to import Foucauldian termi-
nology, a "technology of power" that alters customs and abridges
liberties as it also makes of the land an object of knowledge.[32] For
Norden, though, it is not only the land—and by "the land" I mean
to include here all issues pertaining to measurement, leases, boundaries, etc.—but also the tenantry that are an object of pow-
er/knowledge; it is part of the surveyor's job, for instance, to discover if the tenant is a bastard, or if he is guilty of treason.[33] The
end result of all this is to create

a plot rightly drawne by true information, describ[ing] so the liuely image
of a Mannor, and euery branch and member of the same, as the Lord sitting in his chayre, may see what he hath, where and how it lyeth, and in
whose use and occupation euery particular is upon the suddaine view.[34]

In an image that tells us we've moved beyond the world of terriers
alone, Norden uses the language of the prospect or panoramic view-
—from his chair the lord can take it all in, as if he were Milton's Sa-
tan perched atop the tree of life. The map, or "plot," seems a substitute for the land itself, but what the lord sees is a representation of
social and spatial relations that bleaches them of their particularity
and their humanness. At the same time, this representation presents
itself as *fact*, as *reality*. As Harley asserts, in the sixteenth century "the
acceptability of the cartographic message began to be coloured by a
perception of its detailed accuracy in representing what was believed
to be scientific or geographical truth."[35] Consequently, this reduction of land and tenantry to their graphic and written representations takes on the status of truth. Moreover, as we see in the above
passage, surveys valorize a particular relationship between lord and
estate; Norden's lord is less source of "hospitalitie" than he is (literally) overseer. In addition, estate cartography both textualizes that
relationship and creates a peculiar new subject position for the landowner: to be lord of the manor is to have a relationship with one's
tenants that is both mediated and defined by a relationship with

specific kinds of texts. Stone describes the effect of surveying innovations on the status of landed gentlemen as follows:

New surveying and mapping techniques and the growth of more systematic accounting methods gave great lords the same intimate sense of control of their estates as did the more direct knowledge of his every field possessed by the smaller gentleman. . . . When the process was complete, when prices had levelled off and the landlord had become a rentier pure and simple, it could safely be said that 'a gentleman's account is a trifle to a merchant's—one hour or two a week will do it.'[36]

Paradoxically, the survey and plot allow a simultaneous registering and effacing of both the social and the spatial. While the lord is given more specific information on his lands and tenantry than ever before, both are deconcretized, rendered abstract, turned into objects of knowledge and power—into, that is, features of a landscape of absolute property. Through the survey, "Landownership is figured as reducible to facts and figures: a conception which inevitably undermines the matrix of duties and responsibilities which had previously been seen to define the manorial community."[37] At the same time, the plot and survey give the lord a precise sense of and control over his holdings while also allowing him to be absent from his lands; with the plot spread before him, the prospect mentioned above is available to the lord from *any* chair.[38] The crucial point, though, is that through the survey the social meaning of land is reconfigured. Sarah Bendall makes this clear as follows:

As the concept of landed property as a collection of rights gave way to that of ownership of a definable piece of land, it was no longer sufficient to rely upon oral tradition and local knowledge, and the simple 'landmeater' who had accompanied the steward was replaced by a professional surveyor who could prepare a well-executed and ornamented estate plan.[39]

Surveyor and survey ease the transition from land defined in terms of "a collection of rights"—a landscape of custom—to "ownership of a definable piece of land"—a landscape of absolute property.[40]

In arguing the above I don't want to suggest that estate maps single-handedly usher in the era of absolute property, of capitalist conceptions of land. Nor do I intend to gesture toward an idealized feudal past, a gesture Raymond Williams has so convincingly warned us against making.[41] Covetousness, abuse of the tenantry, even surveying—none of these emerge in Elizabethan England. Concern about engrossing or enclosing or greedy landlords precedes this period by centuries. The important point is that the interplay among surveying innovations, economic phenomena—the fluid land market, increasing inflation, the gradual and relative impoverishment of the aristocracy—and certain social forms leads toward an increasingly instrumental conception of both the tenantry and the land they occupy.[42] It is important to emphasize that Norden does not see his text as working in this way. What is striking about *The Surueyor's Dialogue* is that it pointedly attempts to shore up feudal relations that had already significantly eroded by 1607. Norden sees surveying as preserving the "union . . . between the Lord and tenants . . . by the Lords true knowledge of the particulars that euery tenant holdeth, & a fauorable course in fines and rents."[43] Whether or not we lend Norden's argument any credence (and it is easy enough to see it as a desperate attempt to resuscitate a dying feudal ideology), we must remember that the ideological and epistemological implications of technological innovations are never immediately realized. Estate maps threaten social relations based on the feudal ideal of social interconnectedness, but they do not topple the old order in a single stroke. One might place next to innovations in surveying an older set of practices used to define and delimit land. Rogationtide ceremonies, which began in England around 750 and continued beyond the Elizabethan period, centered upon what is known as the "beating of the bounds":

The clockwise circuit of the bounds involved a walk of anything from three to ten miles, depending on the size and shape of a parish . . . Quite apart from the distance to be covered [over a three-day period], there were halts to inspect boundary points and to resolve any disputes. It was usual to recite a passage from scripture at the major turning points . . . The procession would have had to make its way along the edge of ploughed and sown land, along the marshy edge of rivers and through woodland scrub. Only when it came to common grassland and the fallow field could the procession quicken its pace.[44]

This procession was made not only by clerics and town elders but by young members of the village or parish; it "was both a statement of the past rights of a village and the means by which these rights should be preserved. . . . The social purpose . . . was the education of the young in this important set of facts."[45] Moreover, while the procession had largely lost its religious component in this period, it was seen as being too socially useful to be suspended.[46]

Norden also advocates taking both old and young along the boundaries of an estate; the former provide information, while the latter learn the limits of the land.[47] However, while his efforts work at the estate level to reinforce the absolute sovereignty of the lord— tenants go along with the surveyor so as to tell or to learn what belongs not to them, but to the landowner—the "beating of the bounds" introduces a range of people to what is in a sense *their* land; it reinforces a sense of communal identity tied to the parish or village. Of course, each of these practices has a different purpose and operates on a different scale, but what is striking about the Rogationtide ceremony is both that it reads the land along a social axis, and that the land is measured if not in feet then in footsteps; it is understood in terms of the negotiation on foot of marsh and scrub, plowed land and fallow field. This ceremony exists side by side with the new surveying practices and technologies discussed above, and attests to the coexistence of and conflict between landscapes of custom and of absolute property.[48] Nevertheless, such technologies do have an impact, if not an immediate one, on the way in which land is understood. Capitalist conceptions of space, as David Harvey points out, insist on fragmenting land "into freely alienable parcels of private property, to be bought and traded at will upon the market."[49] We catch glimpses of such conceptions in the making in the shift to rentier-tenant relationships and, I would argue, in the transformations in estate-surveying practices. Plots and surveys play a small but important part in leading us away from ideologies of feudal reciprocity and toward capitalist conceptions of space which, at a systemic level, carve space into fungible units and, in doing so, efface the social.[50]

THE HISTORICAL Thomas Arden (or Ardern), Martin White tells us in his introduction to the New Mermaids edition of the play, was one of "those 'new men' who had benefitted from the distribution of land that followed the dissolution of the monasteries, and who looked on that land as the passport to wealth and social status, to gain which they were prepared to break the traditional bonds between landlord and tenant."[51] White goes on to say that "the [play's] social comment constitutes the 'public' world of the play (with the central motif of *land*), and the exploration of the personalities and relationships of Arden, Alice, and Mosby constitutes the 'private'. . ."[52] While White immediately adds a disclaimer warning against any such simple division, he nevertheless adheres to those categories throughout his introduction. Catherine Belsey offers a more complicated, but finally problematic, formulation, again based on an opposition between public and private. On the one hand, she focuses on a struggle over the meaning of marriage in which the state works "to create a private realm and to take control of it in the interests of the public good."[53] In this instance, as in her later account of the installation of the liberal humanist family,[54] the private, domestic realm is an unstable, emergent construct. On the other hand, Belsey seems to follow without problematizing Holinshed's account of the murder as one which, in Belsey's words, "transgresses the normal boundaries between public and private . . ."[55] Moreover, this

distinction implicitly informs her assertion that there are "two versions of Arden—as loving husband and as rapacious landlord—
[which] coexist equally uneasily in the play."[56] I would argue that
the roles of husband and landlord cannot be separated in the way
Belsey suggests. Arden's status as estate manager collapses these roles
and the categories of public and private concomitant with them, a
fact that helps explain the apparent contradiction between the "two
versions" of Arden.

Lena Cowen Orlin has recently offered a reading of the relationship between public and private, both in the play and in the life of
Thomas Ardern, that is sensitive to the inseparability of Belsey's
"two versions." Orlin deploys the language of public and private,
often in the service of an examination of the commonplace analogy
between the governments of the household and the state. However,
even as she does so, she insists that in this period "the public was
private" and "the private was . . . public in consequence."[57] The
interpenetration of the two terms gets at the untenability of their
putative distinctiveness, an untenability that thus undoes other
distinctions commonly and anachronistically mapped onto this one
(such as business and home, male and female spheres of activity, or,
read along the single axis of male action, landlord and husband).
Admittedly, that Orlin feels compelled to talk in terms of public
and private reveals the extreme difficulty of thinking beyond or
outside these overdetermined categories and the binarism they support. Nevertheless, Orlin's account is sensitive to the fact that the
roles of husband and landlord cannot be separated in the way that
Belsey suggests. While White's and Belsey's readings of *Arden* have
largely relied on a public/private opposition more appropriate to
the late eighteenth and nineteenth centuries than to early modern
England,[58] Orlin assumes and analyzes the inseparability of these
two categories, an inseparability that erodes their supposed distinctiveness.[59]

In early modern England, the activities and duties of the head of household could not be neatly divided into public and private spheres. In *House and Household in Elizabethan England*, Alice T. Friedman offers an historical example, albeit on a larger scale, that helps to define the kind of estate management I will discuss. Friedman shows that Wollaton Hall's Sir Francis Willoughby (1546–96) "dispensed hospitality to the poor and to every sort of visitor. . . . Wollaton was . . . both a residence and a place of business; bailiffs, agents, and neighboring landowners came and went in a never-ending parade of visitors."[60] Friedman's evidence suggests that a separation cannot easily be made between "inside" and "outside" or, in Belsey's and White's terms, between public and private; the manor is both domestic site and place of business. The "great house was not isolated from its surroundings but very much a part of them."[61] The lord's vigilance descends to the smallest social level in exercising control over the household—one of Willoughby's orders to his butler, for example, was to see that "no filching of bread or beer be suffer'd."[62] In short, Willoughby's duties and activities could not be divided into public and private spheres, but encompassed a range of activities from estate to household management, from providing hospitality to the poor to monitoring the larder.

As with Wollaton Hall, estate management in *Arden* refers not only to the control and use of land, but to the governance of an array of material and social relations; the play resists a reductive rent-based relationship between landlord and tenants. Also, Arden, like Willoughby, is at the center of a social world, a world whose inhabitants—not only his wife, Alice, but his servants, Michael and Susan, his former tenants, Greene and Reede, and his sometime guest, Mosby—turn on him. Moreover, issues of marital fidelity are inextricably linked with the fate of lands given to Arden. In the first fifteen lines of the play we see mentioned letters from the king granting Arden ownership of abbey lands and love letters that pass between Mosby and Alice. This juxtaposition is hardly accidental, and it is echoed later in the first scene. Mosby, who characteristically focuses on Arden's lands, tells Arden that Greene has offered them to him. Arden replies, "As for the lands, Mosby, they are mine / By letters patents from his majesty. / But I must have a mandate [i.e., a deed of ownership] for my wife; / They say you seek to rob me of her love" (1.300–303). The point is not merely that Arden sees Alice as a piece of property who might be stolen by Mosby, but that Arden's relationship to the land is intertwined with his relationship with his wife. Mosby constitutes a threat to the passing down of Arden's property to his heirs, and Alice's love for Mosby cannot be separated from the potential mismanagement of her husband's affairs. (It is both obvious and consequential that in the play property and children are assumed to be "his," a formulation that both speaks to the patriarchal imperatives of early modern society and, as I shall discuss below, masks the active role women played in family and estate; Alice is seen as jeopardizing what "belongs" to her husband.) Consider Sir Walter Raleigh, who, in a letter of advice to his son, argues that one proof of a wife's love for her husband is "if thou perceive she have care of thy estate and exercise herself therein."[63] Alice's lack of love for Arden takes the material form of undermining the stability of his estate. She promises Greene land and money, and pledges the hand of her servant, Mosby's sister Susan, to both Michael and Clarke. She also tells Mosby, "My saving husband hoards up bags of gold / To make our children rich, and now is he / Gone to unload *the goods that shall be thine*, / And he and Franklin will to London straight" (1.220–23, emphasis mine). Again we see Alice's transgressive sexual relationship with Mosby as a threat not only to Arden, but to his estate, to his offspring, and to patriarchy; the (presumably male) children who would inherit his wealth and carry on his name are cheated by Alice's affair.

That Alice promises to pass goods from her "saving husband" to her lover reveals the extent to which both she and the play understand the estate in terms of men. The estate is threatened, not contributed to, by Alice, and her engagement with estate business, as in her meeting with Greene, only advances the threat. Such a representation obviously fails to do justice to the multiple roles women played in the management and maintenance of an estate, roles which further trouble the public / private binary discussed above. An examination of *The Lisle Letters* reveals not only that the home is a site of business, but that Lady Lisle is very much involved in the kinds of matters construed by the nineteenth century as part of the male, "public" domain: she handles bills; she works to gain influence at court through gifts to the queen; and, most intriguingly, she receives information regarding the payment of rents and the behavior of tenants.[64] Similarly, in a survey of manuals for householders, Susan Amussen shows that "Wives were joined with their husbands in the management and supervision of the household. The household manuals expected women to make an important economic contribution to the household: they emphasized the wife's role in provisioning the household, and the importance of her thrift."[65] As we have seen, though, for Alice (and *Arden of Faversham*) estate and wealth are not the product of the joint activity of husband and wife, but are "goods" to be transferred from one man to another.

Important for our purposes is not only that Alice's contempt for her husband is reflected in the profligate and sinister mismanagement of his estate, but also that it is Arden's *absence* that allows the formation of a series of nefarious alliances dedicated both to his demise and to the pillaging of his possessions. For example, when Greene first meets Alice, he says, "I am sorry that your husband is from home / Whenas my purposed journey was to him" (1.451–52). However, by meeting Alice and not Arden, Greene secures her promise of access to the lands he desires. In return, Greene pledges to "pay [Arden] home [i.e., kill him], whatever hap to me" (515). Later on, this pledge is referred to by Mosby as follows: "For Greene doth ear the land and weed [Arden] up / To make my harvest nothing but pure corn" (8.24–25). Mosby's utterance is not emptily metaphoric, for Arden's absence and the efforts of men like Greene make it possible for him briefly to take over Arden's estate.

In the soliloquy from which the above quotation is drawn, Mosby talks further of what it would take to maintain control of Arden's land and possessions. In doing so, he uses the language of domestic and estate management. After Greene kills Arden, he must be "heave[d] . . . up" and "smother[ed] . . . to have his wax" (8.26–27); Mosby compares Greene to bees who must be driven from their hives so that he might collect their wax and honey. Michael and Clarke are two "curs" to whom he has thrown a single bone (Susan) so that each might "pluck out [the] other's throat" (35). Finally, even Alice must be gotten rid of so that she does not "extirpen [Mosby] to plant another" (41).[66] The end result of all this would be that Mosby would become "sole ruler of [his] own" (36). Mosby engages in a fantasy of ownership in which he is "sole ruler," a fantasy that at the same time reveals its very instability; the rapid rhetorical proliferation of obstacles to Mosby's ownership attests to the fragility of his projected authority. Most importantly, we see the destruction of these obstacles described in terms of practices associated with the management of land and estate—the keeping of bees, the killing of animals, the plucking out of weeds. The irony, of course, is that those whom he plans to destroy are the ones upon whose efforts the "sole rule of his own" must be *built*. The estate, as we have seen, is understood in the play not in terms of individual ownership of land, but as the management of a set of customary social relations. Mosby's daydream is a testament both to his covetousness and to a vision of land stripped of a particular social meaning. It is also, as I have suggested, a threat to Arden's estate made possible by Arden's absence.

What compounds the problem created by Arden's absence is his baffling willingness to allow, or invite, those who desire to do him harm into his home and household. (As we shall see, such willingness is paralleled by his traveling to London in the first place. Despite being acutely conscious of the threat Mosby poses to both his marriage and his estate, Arden accepts Franklin's illogical advice that he sojourn in the city.) One example is Susan, Mosby's sister, who both is involved in Arden's murder and, as the object of their desire, is the reason for Clarke's and Michael's involvement. After reading Michael's love letter to Susan, Arden insists that "once at home / [he will] rouse her from remaining in [his] house" (3.29–30). This he never does, and immediately after speaking so, Arden says, "Now, Master Franklin, let us go walk in [St.] Paul's. / Come, but a turn or two and then away" (31–32). This scene contains elements crucial to Arden's failure as manager of his household and estate. Susan is a threat to his stability that he ignores, and, instead of heading home, he stays in London, a decision emblematized by the stroll through St. Paul's. Moreover, St. Paul's in Elizabethan England was a notorious site of conspicuous consumption, a place where "courtiers and gallants . . . [came] to see and salute one another, to hear and discuss the latest news of domestic politics, home affairs, notorious current litigation or just plain gossip about the actions and passions of such people as were attracting general attention."[67] The above "turn or two" evokes the image of those profligate landlords drawn to the life of leisure offered by London.

While Susan threatens Arden's estate, a greater threat is posed by Mosby, whom Arden characterizes as

> A botcher, and no better at the first,
> Who, by base brokage getting some small stock,
> Crept into service of a nobleman,
> And by his servile flattery and fawning
> Is now become the steward of his house,
> And bravely jets it in his silken gown. (1.25–30)

This description notwithstanding, Arden, to prevent appearing jealous of Alice, urges Mosby to come often to his house: "Nay, rather frequent [the house] more. / The world shall see that I distrust her not" (1.349–50). Only eight lines later, Arden informs us that he will "lie at London all this term / To let them [i.e., those "enemies" who suggest Mosby and Alice are having an affair] see how light I weigh their words" (358–59). Arden does "lie at London," despite his realization from the beginning of the play that, as he once puts it, "base Mosby doth usurp my room / And *makes his triumph of my being thence*" (4.29–30, emphasis mine). This is just one of the ways in which the play represents Arden as, in Orlin's words, "having ceded his domestic territory"; it "indict[s] him for household [and, I would add, estate] mismanagement."[68]

One of the play's great ironies is that Arden is finally "paid home" *in* his home. As it happens, the play seems to suggest that Arden can only be murdered at home. Attempts at St. Paul's, in "his house at Aldersgate" (3.172), near Rainham Down, and on the way to Lord Cheiny's all fail both near-comically and, in one case, pseudo-providentially: a mysterious fog protects Arden and dissipates shortly after he is delivered from Black Will and Shakebag. When he is finally killed, it is not only by agents hired by Alice and Mosby, but also by friends, family, and members of the household. More specifically, he is murdered shortly after having been successfully manipulated by Alice into urging Mosby to stay, even inviting him to play "a game at tables" (14.222). After the killing, Alice tells Mosby to "sit you in my husband's seat" (287). Mosby's ascension to the position of head of household fulfills, albeit briefly, the hopes expressed in his harvest metaphor. At the same time, however, the social world of which Arden was the center dissolves upon his demise. Frank Whigham, drawing on Frances Dolan's brilliant discussion of period legal conceptions of the murder of husband or master as "petty treason," describes the effects of this dissolution masterfully:

The successful petty treason reorients not only the marriage (the wife replaces Arden with Mosby), but the relation of servants to masters (Michael and Susan become peers of their [former] masters). Indeed, it is even more complex: the sister also no longer has to wait on her brother, who originally owned the gendered right of sexual disposal of her. Kinship, rank, and gender determinations are suddenly all in flux.[69]

In short, what is so striking about the end of the play is that it presents us with a stark image of a dehierarchized and solipsistic world. Not only do Michael and Susan refuse to wait upon their mistress and new master, but Michael talks of poisoning Alice (14.288–96); Shakebag and Black Will are last seen each on his own, having, in the words of the latter, "come unto no sanctuary" (17.4); the final scene shows us the conspirators, all members or guests of Arden's household, bitterly divided, and, in the Mayor's words, "accus[ing] each other" (18.26). Intriguingly, the killers are discovered because Franklin realizes "[Arden] was murdered in this house / And carried to the fields [i.e., Reede's plot], for from that place / Backwards and forwards may you see / The print of many feet within the snow" (14.393–96). The "print of many feet" echoes and foreshadows the "body's print" seen in the grass for two years after Arden's death.

David Attwell argues that *Arden of Faversham* offers a "depiction of unrestrained appetitiveness . . . which looks forward to the . . . emergent bourgeoisie."[70] This appetitiveness "suggests in many ways (sometimes ironically) the necessity for a code of fair play enshrined in the law."[71] I would argue that the play also looks backward longingly to ideologies (nearly) lost, in particular to the ideal of paternalism hinted at in the curse scene with which we began, an ideal with its own "code of fair play" articulated in a landscape of stewardship. In addition, the play presents us with a cautionary tale of an estate mismanaged. Let us remember the world of daily personal contact that Wrightson suggests is necessary for the maintenance of paternalistic, hierarchized social relations. Arden exempts himself from that contact; he spends most of the play away from home, much of the time, like Elizabeth's and James's covetous landlords, in London. What the play shows us is the disastrous effects of Arden's absentee landlordism. Moreover, the details of the murder link Arden's role as landowner to his role as husband. The play posits a continuum between Arden's neglect of both his responsibilities as governor of a household and his responsibilities as governor of the larger estate—the curse made by Reede, the curse of the tenant, is executed by members of Arden's household. The play insists upon the interconnectedness of land with social and personal relations, an interconnectedness increasingly denied by a rent-based economy and by cartographic conceptions of the land which help make possible absences like Arden's. Of course to link such conceptions to the play is not to posit a reductive relationship between surveying and cartographic innovation on the one hand and theatrical representation on the other—to say, for instance, that Arden consulted estate maps or surveys, or that the author of the play had surveys in mind as s/he wrote. Instead it is to note that both estate survey and play are active participants in an ongoing struggle over the nature and meaning of land and ownership, a struggle between landscapes of absolute property, of custom, and of stewardship.

In this regard, let us consider the quotation with which I began this chapter. Estate maps enable a landowner "to 'see' his properties as a whole," and "to concentrate his scattered holdings by sale or exchanges." What both *Arden* and the above discussion of estate surveying tell us is that such sight is not as ideologically neutral as Hale would seem to suggest, that it requires the development of a particular kind of blindness well suited to a landscape of absolute property. As we noted above, the play ends with an image of the land bearing the marks of the "force and violence" with which Arden withheld the plot from Reede. This final image offers us a near-metaphysics of land, a mystified conception of the land as a force offended by Arden's covetousness and social irresponsibility.

As fantastic as this conception may seem, it is of a piece with the landscapes of stewardship and custom, foregrounding as it does both a traditional ethic of landownership and the plight of those betrayed by a covetous landowner. Significantly, the land's indignation takes the form of a silhouette of a body. As is the case with the beating of the bounds, the land, whether through the "body's print" or the "print of many feet within the snow," is situated within a dense social matrix. It speaks the language of Norden's farmer, protesting the alteration of custom that allows Arden to "banish pity," and it suggests that there is more to itself and to the social relations in which it is imbricated than that which can be "seen" by "the Lord sitting in his chayre."

CHAPTER TWO

Strange Metamorphoses

LANDSCAPE AND THE NATION IN
'WOODSTOCK'

We have seen that the land itself registers the wrongness of Arden's actions—the bloody print of Arden's body, which reflects the judgment passed on an absent and covetous landowner, attests to the fact that in Tudor-Stuart England land was central to the traditional moral economy of the nation. At the same time, I have also suggested that increasingly the imperatives of that moral economy conflicted with those that drove the land market and influenced new generations of landowners. *Arden of Faversham* registers the tensions between these conflicting imperatives, as does another late sixteenth-century play that I want to discuss here, the anonymous *Woodstock*. However, while *Arden* focuses on the estate and symbolically manages the implications of survey- and map-generated shifts in land management, *Woodstock* considers what would happen were the governance of the entire nation to be simultaneously modeled after that of the estate and divorced from the land-based moral economy I discuss above. King Richard is disparagingly referred to as "no king, but landlord,"[1] a characterization that bespeaks his renunciation of his duties and his reduction to the level of an exploitative landowner.[2] Moreover, while landowners like Arden benefit from surveys and maps produced by the surveyors they hire, *Woodstock* represents the royally sanctioned construction of such a survey, a process that not only provides the king with the information necessary to farm out the kingdom and rack his subjects, but also threatens to destroy the regional communities whose assets and attributes are recorded in the survey. The play situates Richard's abuses of power in terms of the moral economy we encountered in the last chapter, while at the same time amplifying upon the skepticism of John Norden's farmer regarding the social function of the survey. *Woodstock* understands the construction of a national survey in two ways: as a violence done to the communities represented within it, and as a process culminating in the construction of a landscape that exists at the expense of those communities. By focusing on the play's representation of both the construction of the survey and the exploitation of it and the map it makes possible, I will consider the complex and vexed relationship between the landscape of the nation, modeled upon that of absolute property, and the regions which exist as much more than the parts out of which a national whole is built.[3]

Before turning to my analysis of *Woodstock*, I want briefly to supply important plot details for this underread play and to touch upon its relation to the more famous play to which it is usually compared and which I discuss at length in Chapter Three, Shakespeare's *Richard II*. *Woodstock* depicts the early reign of Richard and focuses on his abuses of authority, most notably represented by the courtly extravagance made possible through the unjust taxation of the commons. In contrast to Richard and his young, frivolous favorites, who are active partners in and beneficiaries of the King's abuses, are his dead father's loyal advisers, exemplified by Thomas of Woodstock, duke of Gloucester. Richard sloughs off their influence, removing Woodstock from his position as Lord Protector once he comes of age, and embarks with his greedy favorites on the scheme of the blank charters, described below. Richard's exploitation is resisted by Woodstock, who Richard subsequently has abducted, even participating in the kidnapping himself. By play's end Richard feels repentant, partly because of the death of the charitable and sympathetic Queen Anne, but he is not in time to save

Woodstock, whose murder he has authorized. The play, from which a final fraction is missing, ends in the middle of a rebellion against the unjust king, one in which Richard and his corrupt followers and favorites have seemingly been defeated.

While *Woodstock* foregrounds certain nefarious acts of the greedy monarch, in *Richard II* these transgressions fade into the background; Richard's farming out of the kingdom, which is central to *Woodstock*, appears in Shakespeare as only one complaint among John of Gaunt's many. Shakespeare's downplaying of Richard's misdeeds obviously serves his emphasis on the psychology of the king, whereas *Woodstock* focuses on a constellation of social relations affected by a monarch's misrule. Nevertheless, there are continuities between the two texts that suggest either shared interests or, as I believe, direct influence. Most critics accept A. P. Rossiter's argument that *Woodstock* preceded and influenced *Richard II*.[4] For example, Edgar Schell traces the history of Richard's "farming out of the kingdom" as follows: "[A] rumor reported by Holinshed that Richard had farmed out the realm to his flatterers is taken in *Woodstock* to be a fact and is elaborately dramatized. That translation of historical rumor into dramatic fact is then assumed in *Richard II*, and the farming of the realm is included in the catalogue of Richard's political sins."[5] That Shakespeare never explains what is referred to by the farming out of the kingdom supports Schell's contention—the play assumes knowledge of its predecessor and of the social phenomena registered within it. I would also suggest that while no map appears directly in *Richard II*, the play echoes and builds upon *Woodstock*'s investigation of the nature and social function of maps, an investigation that, as I shall soon show, has important implications for the creation of certain conceptions of nationhood.

I WILL BEGIN with *Woodstock*'s version of a trope discussed in the Introduction—that of land converted into clothing. "Plain

Thomas" of Woodstock is known in the world of the play for his
plain speech, plain dealing, and plain clothes: "his mind suits with
his habit / Homely and plain" (1.1.106–7). However, in honor of
the king's wedding Woodstock agrees "For once [to] sumpter a
gaudy wardrobe . . ." (211). Upon being teased by the king for his
opulent attire, however, the earnest and humorless Woodstock rails
against both the clothing he only reluctantly donned and the fashions of the court:

> A hundred oaks upon these shoulders hang
> To make me brave upon your wedding-day,
> And more than that:—To make my horse more tire[d
>   under Woodstock's opulence],
> Ten acres of good land are stitched up here. (1.3.95–98)

Woodstock then refers to his usual humble attire in the form of his
"tother [i.e., other] hose," asserting that

> There's honest plain dealing in my tother hose.
> Should this fashion last I must raise new rents,
> Undo my poor tenants, turn away my servants,
> And guard myself with lace; nay, sell more land
> And lordships too, by th' rood. Hear me, King Richard:
> If thus I jet in pride, I still shall lose;
> But I'll build castles in my tother hose. (103–9)

Woodstock articulates the common viewpoint that the sartorial ex-
cesses of gentlemen, especially those in and around the court, are
underwritten by the exploitation of the lands and tenants under
their control. That is, the land is mismanaged to finance the gentleman's conspicuous consumption: a hundred oaks and ten acres
are converted into a gaudy wardrobe. Woodstock goes farther than
this, however—he suggests that as a result of the landlord's extravagant expenditure, tenants are abused and the servants loyal to
him are turned away, leaving him with only his clothing to protect
him. Woodstock speaks of affairs at the level of the estate, but that

he is also referring to the nation is revealed over the course of the play—the dismissed servants are Woodstock and other loyal advisers of the king, while the exploited tenants are Richard's subjects. Woodstock makes this latter point clear two lines later when he says, "Tother hose! did some here wear that fashion / They would not tax and pill the Commons so!" (111–12). Exploitation of the estate and of the nation are aligned, paving the way for our understanding of Richard as "no king, but landlord."

Richard is referred to as landlord because he "farms out" his kingdom—that is, he leaves the management of the nation to his four extravagantly attired favorites, Bushy, Bagot, Greene, and Scroope, in return for a monthly fee of seven thousand pounds (4.1.180–84). In return for this fee, Richard is to give them control of

all [his] crown lands, lordships: manors, rents: taxes, subsidies, fifteens, imposts; foreign customs, staples for wool, tin, lead and cloth: all forfeitures of goods or lands confiscate; and all other duties that *do*, shall, or may appertain to the king or crown's revenues. (185–90)

As Edgar Schell puts it, Richard's foppish favorites are to become "tributary kings, each with absolute power over a part of England . . ."[6] However, this "farming out" would be impossible without the earlier dissemination of blank charters "through all the shires of England" to "All landed men, freeholders, farmers, graziers, / Or any else that have ability" (3.1.16–20). The charters are blank pieces of paper that are to be signed by the king's subjects and later filled in by the Crown; thereafter, subjects can be taxed for an amount filled in by Richard in accordance with his desires and his subjects' assets. Crucially, the charters are supplemented by information about those who sign. Tresilian, whom Richard has made Lord Chief Justice, asks that his henchman Nimble "Inquire what rents / What lands, or what revenues they spend by th' year, / And let me straight receive intelligence" (127–29). The collection of such information "Shall [allow] King Richard [to] seize into his hands /

The forfeiture of all their goods and lands" (135–36). However, as we have seen, once Richard farms out the kingdom, it is his favorites who will acquire the wealth of the king's subjects. "Never had English subjects such a landlord" (4.1.210), Richard smugly proclaims, and it is not clear whether he refers here only to his four favorites, who call themselves his "tenants" (208), or to all of those over whom he rules.

The important thing about the gathering of evidence to supplement the charters, though, is that it makes possible unjust taxation through the construction of a survey. Compare Tresilian's instructions to Nimble with John Norden's description of a professional surveyor's duties: "measuring the quantity, obseruing the quality, recounting the value, and acquainting the Lords with the estates of all mens liuings . . ."[7] As we shall see, the procedures by which Nimble collects this information echo those followed by surveyors at this time. Before turning to the scenes in which Nimble coerces property owners in Dunstable to sign the charters, however, I want to talk about the Crown as landlord in Elizabethan England. By doing so, I will both show what the government thought it could gain from a national survey and discuss one of the ways in which the Crown's actions as landowner generated controversy in the period, thereby identifying a crucial reason for *Woodstock*'s anxiety about the survey and a set of practices aligned with the process of its construction.

HISTORIANS HAVE OFTEN characterized the Tudor Crown's management of its lands from the reign of Henry VIII on as the steady if not systematic sale of its properties. While this view suggests the enormous expansion, if not the invention, of the land market in Tudor England,[8] it fails to do justice to the continued significance of the Crown as landowner in this period. Richard Hoyle describes the Crown as landlord as follows:

Throughout the early modern period (and despite their progressive dimi-nution) the Crown's estates were the biggest and most widely scattered of all English estates. . . . They were much more than a source of rental in-come, but formed an important part of the Crown's armoury of patronage and rewards. . . . There was, of course, a tension between the estates as a source of revenue and their role as a source of patronage. But because they served that patronage purpose, the management of the estates was not a private matter between the Crown and its tenants but a highly public one which concerned the society of provincial England as a whole.[9]

The fiscally strained Elizabethan government often rewarded gen-tlemen in its favor with favorable leases, fee-farms, or portions of land. Moreover, these rewards were sometimes translated immedi-ately into cash: "Elizabeth's reversionary leases, fee-farm grants and exchanges were often made not to the courtiers she wished to re-ward but to nominees who would act for them in selling the prop-erty. Many resales took place so quickly that the buyer must have been found before the Crown grant was made . . ."[10] Thus, the pos-sibility of the rapid conversion of either acres or the right to the revenues from them into opulent clothing was a readily achievable one in the late sixteenth century.

The kind of exchange I describe here attests to what Hoyle identifies as the "highly public" nature of the Crown's actions as landlord, for it poses a threat to the moral economy I discuss above. The benefits to be gained by the Crown's patrons could conflict with the interests of smaller tenants and of village commu-nities, much as the actions of Richard's "tributary kings" serve their avarice at the expense of those over whom they "reign." The ex-change of property for cash (and thus clothing) obviously suggests the protocapitalist exploitation of land rather than the maintenance of the paternalistic, land-based social order I discuss in Chapter One. However, such exchanges also mark a recent innovation in English history:

For the very idea that land was a commodity, subject to sale, was a relatively new one. Land had been sufficiently stable in pre-Tudor England that its ownership had seemed a part of the natural order. The estates of the lords, for example, had been bound by ancient entails to descent by rule of primogeniture to eldest sons. . . . Then, during the reigns of the early Tudors, these lords were given the right to break their entails and alienate their property, and many chose to emulate their king by selling land to put money in their purses. The novelty of the idea of the sale of the land is apparent in the procedure by which it was accomplished, an awkward adaptation of feudal laws . . . The buyer and seller negotiated the transfer by engaging in a legal suit that resulted in the purchaser's being fined in the amount of the purchase price. . . . The more abstract concept of capital value had yet to be employed.[11]

While ideologies construing land as private property had not yet emerged, we can see that the land market was headed in that direction. Moreover, as was made clear in the previous chapter, this was a direction that was understood to pose a threat to ideologies of stewardship and custom that still exercised considerable authority throughout the early modern period.

The Crown was hampered in its efforts both to exchange lands and to accrue revenues from them by the fact that the value and extent of much Crown property was unknown. This was because of the lack of what countless advisers to the Crown continually advocated the production of: an exact survey of Crown lands. That no such survey was produced in the period meant first of all that the values ascribed to Crown properties were out of date.[12] Thus, were a courtier to acquire a piece of land from the Crown at its valued rates, he would then be able to determine through a survey its current value, raise the price considerably, and make a huge profit that could have fallen to the Crown itself—a scheme quite close to the one that, with aid of the information derived from the survey, is to be implemented by Richard's favorites. The same opportunities for profit would obtain in the case of rental properties: were the land fee-farmed to a courtier, he could reestimate the value of the property under his control and raise the rents of his tenants. Given this, it is no wonder that "surveyors appeared as essentially landlords' men, inquisitive, prying and vexatious men . . . intent all the time on squeezing the tenantry."[13]

The significance of the survey extended beyond the promise of an accurate valuation of existing Crown lands, however; it also offered the possibility of locating what were known as concealed lands. These were "those properties where the owner or tenant had allegedly 'concealed' the Crown's title and so 'defrauded' the Crown of revenue in the shape of purchase price, entry fines, rent, or otherwise."[14] A significant opportunity for profit lay in the acquisition of a royal license to search for concealed lands, for the discovery of these lands depended upon the actions of private parties whose searches were sanctioned by the Crown. As David Thomas puts it, "Concealment hunting was the Crown's private enterprise solution to the problem of its ignorance about its lands."[15] Moreover, these hunters were appointed not because of special abilities, but thanks to their success at attaining the favor of an influential patron.[16] Concealment hunters were often greeted with suspicion and animosity by landholders, as they posed the same kind of threat to customary rights and practices as did surveyors. Also, since the licenses usually offered profits only to those who discovered concealed lands, hunters found it in their best interest to locate, if not invent, such lands wherever possible.[17]

Both locating and inventing concealed lands often proved easier than one might expect, not merely because of the paucity of accurate old or new surveys, but because the category of concealed lands was quite inclusive. Joan Thirsk describes five kinds of concealed lands: forest lands that had been cleared and improved upon by squatting peasants; lands held under defective titles; productive land that had at one time been covered by rivers or the sea; extraparochial lands, usually in forests or fens or along the borders of parishes; and cultivable land within waste areas, such as those of the moors.[18] Land reclaimed from the sea or in waste could be claimed by the Crown, and when made worthy of cultivation become a potentially valuable holding.[19] That such lands were in many cases already being cultivated by squatters raises an important issue: it is not barren lands but "invisible" communities that are discovered and disrupted by concealment hunters. Richard Hoyle addresses this topic in the context of a discussion of disafforestation and drainage, two of the projects embarked upon by the Crown in order to reclaim land often located by concealment hunters:

It must . . . be recognised that to speak of drainage and clearance as 'progressive economic activities' is to share the early modern prejudice against the pastoral economies of forests and fens. We are not talking here of waste ground in the sense of vacant land, rather, land which might on first sight appear to be used unintensively, but which in fact supported a whole range of pastoral and semi-industrial activities to which migrants were drawn. A petition against the disafforestation of Leicester Forest spoke of 'a great confluence of poor people [that] hath been made to this place by reason of the benefit which the chace hath afforded them, who being still to inhabit there will be destitute of means to live if it be disafforested, the ancient towns not being able to relieve them'. Every forest or fen had its role in the local and regional economy.[20]

What we see, then, is the threat posed by concealment hunters, who, like Tresilian's henchmen and those "landlords' men" the surveyors, trouble the customary economic and social practices of entire regions. Of course surveyors also worked in the service of "progressive economic activities" and at the expense of communities in forests and fens—Thirsk tells us of the disdain of surveyors toward the "disorderly, idle rabble" that had settled in the forests, while Christopher Hill notes the "notoriously hostile" actions of surveyors toward cottagers, actions which provided "one of the reasons for the unpopularity of the profession."[21]

It is hardly surprising that concealment hunters were extremely

unpopular and that their activities generated a great deal of controversy under both Elizabeth and James. The first patent for concealment hunting was issued between 1559 and 1561, and already by
the 1570's reports of abuses of authority by those holding such patents prompted the first of a series of (largely ineffectual) governmental reforms. Complaints continued to pour in. A list of grievances was drawn up in 1592, but little changed.[22] Under James the
actions of the concealment hunters grew even more egregious. But
what form did these abuses take? The activities of a Jacobean concealment hunter, while perhaps worse than those of any acting under Elizabeth, provide us with an answer to that question. The actions with which Sir Giles Mompesson was charged

are a catalogue of the problems caused by [the Crown's] method of dis-
covering concealed lands. It was alleged that he had undervalued properties, claimed that land was concealed when rent was being paid to the
Crown, attacked people who had spent vast sums draining land or em-
banking it against the sea and had pretended to discover concealed land by
the simple process of copying out the records of the Elizabethan concealment hunters.[23]

Focusing on Elizabethan concealment hunters, Herbert Hope Lockwood adds another practice to the catalogue. Before proper investigation for concealed lands had even begun, some hunters would exploit landholders' uncertainty about the stability of their titles to
land by

convey[ing] a new title to those willing to pay and enrol the conveyance in
Chancery . . . By 1589 a number were enrolled on the day after the
[Letters] Patent [i.e., the Crown license allowing hunters to search for
concealments in a given area were] issued showing that many tenants had
been investigated and coerced into compounding before the Letters Patent
were issued.[24]

It is clear that the concealment hunter, like the surveyor, has a corrosive effect on customary practice, prying as he does into titles and

estates. In fact, it is not always easy to separate the functions of surveyor and concealment hunter, as each is a "landlord's man" who
locates and registers the Crown's properties. Moreover, the responsibilities of the surveyor could include the location of concealed
lands. The surveyor's office, Thomas Clay writes, is "to view and
suruey all and singular the Honors, Mannors, Lordships, Lands &
Tenements of his Lord, and to search out all the profits, Royalties,
priuiledges, and customes thereunto belonging . . ." In addition,
the surveyor is "[t]o take notice of such encroachments, conceale-
ments, purprestures, and such like, as hee shall meet withall in his
view and perambulation, and to certifie the Lord or his Commis-
sioners thereof, that the same may bee reformed . . . to the Lord his
profit."[25] Not surprisingly the survey was understood as performing
a function that would eradicate the need for concealment hunters,
who would be rendered redundant; with accurate and extensive
surveys, "[t]heoretically concealment would become impossible and
the Crown surveyors could decide how rents and fines could be
'improved'."[26] Until that time landholders in England would have
found the choice between surveyor and concealment hunter a particularly unpalatable one, given both the status of each and the possible deleterious effects of the "reformation" of land management
on existing social relations.

Both surveyor and concealment hunter act much like Tresilian's
men in "measuring the quantity, obseruing the quality, recounting
the value, and acquainting the Lords with the estates of all mens liuings . . ." One difference between the two lies in the fact that the
hunters made their living at the direct expense of the tenants whose
concealments they located—delinquent tenants were to negotiate
with the hunters for back payments, a portion of which the hunter
received. If tenants didn't pay, the land was confiscated, and the
Crown's agents were able to claim a portion of the land.[27] Like the
favorites to whom Richard farms out his kingdom, the concealment hunters benefited from the privileges awarded by the Crown

at the expense of landholders. Moreover, the granting of licenses for these hunters was a matter of royal prerogative, and was thus not subject to parliamentary control.[28] Significantly, Richard not only underwrites the actions of those who carry out his survey but also dismisses Woodstock and his other old advisers, and the emergency parliamentary session they called. In short, *Woodstock*'s survey is not far removed from the Crown's project to ascertain the nature and value of lands both visible and concealed, a project understood to be carried out at the Crown's prerogative and to the detriment of those who lived and worked on the land—a project, that is, performed in the service of a landscape of absolute property and at the expense of landscapes of custom.

I want to draw two major conclusions from what I have just discussed. The first should be obvious from the above and from a similar discussion in the first chapter—the intervention of these agents of the state into the affairs of landowners and landholders involves at least the possibility of the radical disruption of local customs and practices. Second, both the survey and the search for concealed lands render visible to the Crown that which previously was not—not only parcels of land such as those that had been underwater, uncultivated, or in the no-man's-land between parishes, but also those displaced or migratory populations that worked or lived upon the land, no longer able to be sustained by the economies of "ancient towns." The process of constructing a survey brings that which is concealed into knowledge and, significantly, into ownership: until rendered visible these properties did not belong to the Crown; the discovery of once-concealed land was actually the laying claim to it, and often at the expense of the heretofore "invisible" inhabitants of the land. Of course this bringing of the land into knowledge is actually the privileging of one form of knowledge over another, of the survey over the attitudes, practices, and beliefs of those surveyed. "Progressive economic activities" and the knowledge they engender exist at the expense of those who work on lands concealed not to them but to the Crown. Both the survey and the search for concealed lands transformed land into (Crown) property, an act that threatened to violate social practices to which the land was central.

I HAVE FOCUSED on the Crown's search for concealed lands in order to suggest a historical phenomenon crucial to *Woodstock*'s anxious representation of Tresilian's efforts to collect information about "the estates of all mens liuings." However, the play's concern about the construction of a survey of the nation extends beyond topical references to the actions of the Crown's concealment hunters. The creation and deployment of the survey need to be understood in terms of the play's representation of the struggle between two models of estate and, by extension, nation management, models that imply radically different conceptions of the dissemination and consumption of knowledge.

The survey was generally constructed not only from knowledge produced through the instrument-driven measurement of parcels of land, but also through the aid of those who lived on the land. This was clearly the case for what one map historian labels as "[t]he first modern topographical survey of England and Wales," that of the Elizabethan surveyor and cartographer Christopher Saxton.[29] This survey was a massive effort performed roughly between 1574 and 1579, one that involved the surveying of all of England and Wales, albeit with Saxton often taking shortcuts through the aid of existing surveys and other forms of cartographic information.[30] Saxton's project, both the initial survey and also the later publication of an atlas of county maps (1579) and a wall map (1583), was one that "had the backing of the central government."[31] This is made clear by the letter given Saxton in 1576 to present to Welsh Justices of the Peace asking that "the said Justic[e]s shalbe aiding and assisting unto him to see him conducted unto any towre, castle, highe place or hill to view that countrey . . ." Saxton was to

be accompanied w[i]th ii or iij honest men such as do best know the cun-
trey, for the better accomplishement of that service, and that at his
dep[ar]ture from any towne or place that he hath taken the view of the
said towne do set forth a horseman that can speke both welsh and englishe
to safe conduct him to the next market towne . . .[32]

That Saxton might need "safe conduct . . . to the next market
towne" should be clear from the above discussion of attitudes toward surveyors, but the immediate point is that the knowledge of
"honest men" was to be exploited in order to help accumulate information about the lands Saxton surveys; in particular, these men
were to give details about land, villages, or hamlets not visible from
the hills which Saxton periodically scaled to get the lay of the land.
While this process may seem benign enough, it is worth remembering the nature of the activities of the concealment hunters, those
other representatives of the Crown who pried into the life and
lands of rural communities, activities that as we have seen are
closely aligned to those performed by the surveyor. Moreover,
Saxton's efforts faintly echo those undertaken by Tresilian's men
for more obviously sinister purposes.

It is of course important to notice that the construction of Saxton's survey provides a less immediately credible model for the activities of Tresilian's men than does that of an estate survey, which,
as I showed in Chapter One, could involve not only the community-
assisted measurement of property, but also the ascertaining of information about tenants—whether or not, for instance, they are
treasonous or bastards. However, Richard exploits the information
provided by a national survey in order to farm out his kingdom; that
is, he uses the information produced by such a survey to treat the
nation as if it were an estate under his (mis)management, once again
proving himself less king than bad landlord. Before we take up this
topic more fully, however, we must first consider the means and
procedures by which *Woodstock*'s national survey is conducted. To
do that, I want to talk first of the market town and some of the social

practices to which it is central, and then turn to *Woodstock*'s representation of Dunstable, a market town in which not the surveyor but the town's inhabitants could use the promise of safe conduct.

Alan Everitt suggests that despite the rise of private trading in the late sixteenth century, "the market town was still, and was destined to remain, the normal place of sale and purchase for the great majority of country people." The market town, of which there were approximately 760 in Tudor and Stuart England, was a center not only of commerce and local culture, but also of the dissemination of information, of the construction and consumption of knowledge.[33] As Everitt puts it, "The market town . . . was the focus of the rural life around it. Its squares and taverns provided the meeting place for yeomen and husbandmen, not only to buy and sell, but to hear the news, listen to sermons, criticize the government, or organize insurrection." During the reign of Henry VIII, the king's actions "were frankly discussed in Fakenham market place in 1534, where 'honest men . . . marvelled much what the king meant by polling and pilling the realm . . . and thought he intended to make a great hand by money, and then to avoid the realm and let the people shift as they could.'"[34] Henry VIII's actions as described here of course echo those taken by Richard in farming out and taxing his kingdom. What's most important, though, is the resistance offered to the king's edicts by the commons, resistance that, as we shall see, Nimble seems to detect everywhere in Dunstable's market square.

Such resistance, however, is arguably a by-product of the workings of rural culture. It is important to remember that in the late sixteenth century England is still largely illiterate; David Cressy's study of court depositions in Norwich suggests that while illiteracy was "rare among shopkeepers, men of commerce and the ruling elite," between a third and a half of the skilled craftsmen on record could not sign their names, while around three-quarters of all laborers were illiterate.[35] Moreover, literacy was much more common in cities than in rural areas. One of the implications of this is that "oral communication was still the chief means by which technical skills were transmitted, political information circulated, and personal relationships conducted. . . . [O]nly a tiny fraction of social knowledge was transmitted via the written word."[36] While this was so, oral communication often existed in a symbiotic relationship with written communication; that is, written texts were often central to acts of oral communication. What Roger Chartier says of early modern France is also true of England in this period:

Thanks to the various social situations in which reading aloud occurred, there existed . . . a culture dependent on writing, even among people incapable of producing or reading a written text. Full comprehension of that culture presupposes the view that access to the written word was a process much more broadly defined than simply silent reading of an individual in isolation, literacy in the classic sense.[37]

Or, as Tessa Watt in her superb study of English cheap print puts it,

oral and literate modes of communication were closely intertwined. Printed works were disseminated by word of mouth, transforming the culture of the 'illiterate', and oral modes of communication shaped the structure of printed works. The interesting process was not only the spread of literacy and readership, but the complex interweaving of the printed word with existing cultural practices.[38]

This complex interweaving could take other forms, such as the reading aloud of a proclamation, ballad or broadside by one person to others unable to read, a process that would often lead to a discussion of the material transmitted by the reader. This was one way in which news was disseminated; what P. M. Handover calls "newsbooks," texts produced not regularly but to report on a major event, were quite common at the end of the sixteenth century.[39] Moreover, while such texts were usually produced in London, they were distributed throughout the country by networks of itinerant peddlers such as ballad singers and chapmen.[40] Peter Burke quotes from R.

Cotgrave's *A Dictionary of the French and English Tongues* (1611), in which a chapman is described in terms that, despite the absence of any reference to purse cutting, remind us of Shakespeare's Autolycus: "'a paltry pedlar, who in a long pack or maund (which he carries for the most part open and, hanging from his neck, before him) hath almanacs, books of news, or other trifling wares to sell'. . . . These chapmen would provision themselves with materials from booksellers in towns and then make their way from village to village."[41] Certain social sites in rural and market towns became centers for the consumption of these texts. As Watt puts it, "Texts and their effects radiated outward to local communities from certain focal points: the marketplace, the parish church, the godly household, the inn or alehouse"; in addition, the collective consumption of texts produced what Watt calls a "shared culture."[42] It is such a culture that is both exploited and threatened by Nimble's quest for information.

Nimble and various officers of the law take advantage of the market's status as both a local gathering place and a site for the dissemination of news in order to forward the scheme of the blank charters. As Saxton was aided by "honest men," Nimble requires the assistance of the Bailey (or bailiff) of Dunstable, who informs him of the wealth and identities of various of Dunstable's inhabitants (e.g., 3.3.20–23, 58–59). At the same time, much like surveyors looking for evidence of treason, they all search carefully for signs of resistance, a search in which the Bailey is directly involved (145). Fleming talks of "strange songs and libels cast about the market-place against my lord Tresilian" and the other favorites (27–29); Nimble repeatedly alludes to the treasonous talk of "privy whisperers" (e.g., 3.3.144).[43] There is undoubtedly resistance to the unjust scheme for taxing the commons via the blank charters, but the play sympathizes with that resistance and makes it clear that the response of Nimble is excessive: one man is arrested for having "whistled treason" (228), for humming the tune of a ballad believed to be treasonous. What is most important, though, is to realize that the kinds of actions construed as treasonous—the singing of songs, the humming of ballads, the collecting into groups of "privy whisperers"—are all crucial to the dissemination of information, subversive or otherwise, in rural, largely illiterate communities: crucial, that is, to the workings of the culture. Ballads and songs were frequently topical and often functioned as sources of news—in *Woodstock* the writer of a ballad commenting on the blank charters is arrested (154–215)—and this news would be mulled over or evaluated in various social groups. We witness one such group in action: a farmer, grazier, and butcher discussing affairs of state. Intriguingly, the Butcher's landlord, a "good knight," has told him "that King Richard's new Councillors ... had crept into honester men's places than themselves were" (63–68). It is this information that the Butcher passes along, and it is this information, which Nimble refers to as "what your landlord told ye" (139), that leads to the three men's being arrested as privy whisperers. In quashing resistance to Tresilian's actions, Nimble takes advantage of the social structures necessary for the circulation and dissemination of information; he exploits the circuits of communication. He also threatens to dismantle them, for all privy whisperers, all those acting as did the three men, are arrested. The three men are vulnerable, not only because of what they say, but also because their gathering in the marketplace, that "focal point" out from which "texts and their effects radiated," exposes them to the scrutiny and machinations of Nimble. In short, the project of collecting information and signatures for Richard's survey is understood as both undermining and exploiting rural social structures governing the circulation of information. At the same time, this project leads to the production of a text, the survey, that is consumed not in the marketplace, but behind royal walls. An elitist text is generated at the expense of popular forms of textual consumption.

In another play these scenes of textual consumption might seem as sinister or worthy of disruption as they do to Tresilian. As readers of Shakespeare, we are familiar with accounts of collective discussion or the dissemination of information that stress the malleability, if not maliciousness, of a rude mob that is treated dismissively for either its susceptibility to rhetoric or its illiteracy: think of the effect on the citizens of Rome of Antony's valedictory remarks about Julius Caesar (3.2.73–259); or, in *Coriolanus*, of the citizens' protests to the Senate scornfully described as "shreds" (i.e., proverbs) with which they "vented their complainings" (1.1.203–4); or the famous hostility toward writing evinced by Jack Cade and his rebellious followers in *2 Henry VI*. This last text provides us with a passage that reflects interestingly on the scenes I have discussed above. Cade states, "Is not this a lamentable thing, that of the skin of an innocent lamb should be made parchment? that parchment, being scribbled o'er, should undo a man? Some say the bee stings, but I say 'tis the bee's wax; *for I did but seal once to a thing, and I was never mine own man since*" (4.2.71–76, my emphasis).[44] While the exact nature of Cade's complaint is obscure, the writing he has sealed, writing which he claims has kept him in thrall to an undefined other, reminds us of Tresilian's blank charters. However, Cade's critique of the oppressive power of writing fails to hold the reader's sympathy when, around twenty lines later, he sentences a clerk to death. What is interesting about *Woodstock* is that its collective discussion and its complaints are understood not as threatening but as threatened. While a figure such as the whistler of treason is to some extent comic, the overall effect is not laughter at his expense, or relief at his apprehension. *Woodstock*'s sympathies lie with the signer of the blank charters, the one who "did but seal once to a thing, and . . . was never [his] own man since." Moreover, while these Shakespearean texts denigrate and misrepresent the means by which information is transmitted among "the illiterate mob," *Woodstock* sees those means as integral to the workings of a culture.

Any discussion of the dissemination of information threatens to figure that process as more passive than it is, as the mere passing on of "shreds," the simple reading of a proclamation to an audience in the marketplace. However, I am not suggesting that the circulation of information is no more than the transmission of preexisting textual "facts" through a social structure designed merely to facilitate that transmission. I want to insist that the dissemination of information is a productive process, that knowledge is not transmitted but produced.[45] To understand the culture of the marketplace in this way is to resist a reading of rural culture that assumes knowledge to be generated elsewhere, by someone else, and then distributed to people who benefit from but are presumably incapable of producing such knowledge.[46] This is not simply a theoretical point, for *Woodstock* reinforces it—among those arrested in the Dunstable marketplace is the composer of a ballad that depicts and critiques the actions of Tresilian. Moreover, even if that same ballad had arrived from London in the pack of a petty chapman, the singing of it in a public setting would involve the recontextualizing of it, the positioning of it in a culture that potentially puts it to use in ways very different from those imagined or intended by those who first penned it or set its type.[47] This is not merely a reappropriation or the act of an early modern *détournier*. It is the production of knowledge—knowledge, after all, is produced everywhere, although even in the early modern period (and especially under the empirical regime that in the late sixteenth century was only beginning to emerge) little can bear up under the formal category's epistemological weight. Moreover, the dissemination of printed texts in a rural culture implies a kind of knowledge radically different from the knowledge manifested in the survey and map and in the social relations that their consumption presupposes.

The survey and map connote both exclusive, aristocratic relations with texts and, as we have seen in Chapter One, the consolidation of a scientific knowledge of the land. Consider again Norden's lord of the surveyed manor who "sitting in his chayre, may see what he hath, where and how it lyeth, and in whose use and occupation euery particular is upon the suddaine view"[48]—we see his analogue in Thomas Elyot's account of the aristocratic map reader:

For what pleasure is it, in one houre, to beholde those realmes, cities, sees, ryuers, and mountaynes, that uneth in an olde mannes life can nat be iournaide and pursued: what incredible delite is taken in beholding the diuersities of people, beastis, foules, fisshes, trees, frutes, and herbes: to knowe the sondry maners and conditions of people, and the varietie of their natures, and that in a warme studie or perler, without perill of the see, or daunger of longe and paynfull iournayes: I can nat tell what more pleasure shulde happen to a gentil witte, than to beholde in his owne house euery thynge that with in all the worlde is contained.[49]

I will deal in greater detail with this passage in the next chapter; for now suffice it to say that the reading of the map takes place in "a warme studie or parler," in the reader's "owne house." Consumption of the map is a matter far removed from the shared culture of the marketplace. This is confirmed by the inventory of the study or closet of William More of Loseley, which, while it includes a range of texts, from ballads and proverb books to Castiglione and Petrarch,[50] is most important for our purposes because of the presence of maps and surveying manuals. F. J. Levy adds to this inventory a description of what More's closet would have looked like during his lifetime:

When that learned gentleman sat down in his closet, one day in 1556, he could gaze at walls hung with maps of the world and of England, France, and Scotland; he could date his letters from a framed perpetual calendar, and check his references from a framed, one-sheet chronicle. On his shelves stood balances and weights, together with a globe; pens, seals, a pair of compasses rested on his desk.[51]

Here knowledge takes the form of various sources of information that the gentleman can consult—not only a calendar and chronicle, but also maps and a globe. Much as with once-concealed lands made manifest by a surveyor, the land is registered here in the form of its cartographic representation, not as lived site but as an object of, or that comes into, knowledge. The gentleman is surrounded by texts that provide him with information and attest to his privileged position in the world; the closet inscribes both a relation to the world and a social position, both of which exist in stark contrast to the image of the collective consumption of texts in the market-place.[52]

Of course it is not only the *consumption* of texts that takes place in the marketplace and, more generally, in rural communities. Tre-silian's search for privy whisperers is motivated not only by the de-sire to squelch resistance to the blank charters, but also by fear of a response to Crown actions that predated Nimble's trip into the countryside. In a description that echoes the aforementioned ac-count of marketplace resistance to the actions of Henry VIII, we are told by Lancaster, one of Richard's wise advisers and a compatriot of Woodstock, that "The Commons murmur gainst the *dissolute* king / Treason is whispered at each common table / As customary as their thanks to heaven" (1.1.157–59). Such whispering later takes more concrete form. Even before Nimble is sent out to collect in-formation "through all the shires of England," these shires make their presence felt at court through the agency of Woodstock. "Plain Thomas" presents the king with "petitions ... Sent from each sev-eral shire of all the kingdom" (2.2.4–6). Woodstock then slides from these petitions to the people whose opinions they record; he says to Richard shortly thereafter that "From every province are the people come / With open mouths exclaiming on the wrongs / Thou and these upstarts have imposed on them" (43–45). It is not clear whether Woodstock refers here to the physical presence of people from every province, or if he is talking about the petitions which he takes to represent the voices of those people. In either case, he clearly conflates written grievances with the voices of those abused by Rich-ard. The petitions are understood by Woodstock as clear transmit-ters of the outraged voices; they are associated with "open mouths exclaiming on wrongs," and as such the petitions stand in stark contrast to the data accumulated by Nimble, which informs Richard and his favorites only "what rents / [and] What lands [they have], or what revenues they spend by th' year."

Thus far I have contrasted two worlds of textual consumption and production—that of the marketplace and that of the gentleman's closet. It would of course be a mistake to map onto this seeming opposition, which is hardly an absolute one in this period, a distinction between the illiterate country and literate city, the benighted provinces and the enlightened court. Or, to put it slightly differently, it would be a mistake to oppose the occupant of the closet, whether the map reader or the landlord scrutinizing his survey, to the butcher, grazier, and farmer who produce and consume knowledge in the marketplace. Such an opposition would not only be conceptually simplistic—remember Chartier and Watt on the mixed nature of textual consumption in this period—it would also fail to account for the butcher's landlord, the "good knight" who rightly criticizes the king's favorites. Unlike the lord managing his estate from his chair, the butcher's landlord is understood as being a vital part of the life of the community, part of a shared culture.[53] He is a major source of information about the blank charters, and he states that "we should never have a merry world" until Richard's "new Councillors" are put down (3.3.66–70). The "merry world" or "merry England" topos is one recognizable from popular literature, and the term is usually deployed to describe an idealized time gone by. John Selden, for instance, laments that "There was never a merry world since the Fairies left Dancing . . ."; Lawrence Ramsey talks of "howe it was merrie, when Robin Hoods playe / Was in everie Towne."[54] These particular complaints suggest that the world is less merry because of the eradication under Protestantism of popular cultural forms, of folktales and plays celebrating England's legendary heroes. That the "good knight" deploys rhetoric akin to this is intriguing. It suggests that he is aligned with popular cultural forms, with the maintenance of traditions and structures of behavior threatened by Richard's advisers and, by extension, by the survey itself. That is, *Woodstock*'s good landlord is spokesperson for a range of popular cultural practices widely understood in this period as having been undermined by the official state religion, a religion whose authority is of course inseparable from that of the Crown. Moreover, that the spokesperson for these practices is a landlord should remind us that the play reads only some landlords in negative terms—Richard would be most precisely described as "not king but *bad* landlord." The bad landlord opposes the good one; the authority of the monarch, an authority here enacted by the creation and nefarious use of the survey, opposes popular cultural forms, just as it exploits and assaults existing structures of communication.

Importantly, the "good knight" is aligned in the logic of the play with Thomas of Woodstock, the play's major critic of the actions taken by Richard and his men and a favorite of the people. While the nation is loosely understood as a badly managed estate, the play also approvingly gestures toward examples of traditional feudal estate management performed at the local level. Woodstock is a paternalistic landlord; he is recognizably one of those who, in R. H. Tawney's words, sees "Property [as] not a mere aggregate of economic privileges, but a responsible office."[55] Woodstock and certain others resist the destabilizing effects of Richard's actions by returning to their estates and shoring up local, manorial structures of authority—"Let each man hie him to his several home," Woodstock says, ". . . And, in the mildest part of lenity, / Seek to restrain [the people] from rebellion" (3.2.91–94). At the same time, we have already seen Woodstock as a defender of the rights of the very people he here seeks to restrain. Woodstock performs the proper function of the local landlord, exercising authority at the regional level for the good of both tenants and commonwealth—that is, he acts like the beneficent landlord whose actions are instantiated in a landscape of stewardship. More precisely, while Richard repudiates his responsibilities as king, Woodstock performs properly the role understood as being analogous to that of the king. Susan Amussen has explored the implications of the commonplace analogy between head of household and head of state, an analogy that she also sees operating in other social arenas:

The bonds of deference and responsibility which were supposed to hold the family together also operated throughout society. In the village, hundred and county (as well as the nation) those of higher status were to govern and care for their inferiors, and in return receive obedience and respect from the governed.[56]

In practice, these are analogies and not equivalencies, but the preservation of order at the local level can obviously work to shore up paternalistic relations at the national one.[57] Thus, the manorial landowner is a crucial figure for the maintenance of authority and order throughout England.[58] While Richard exploits rural communities in the name of the Crown, Woodstock's actions to defend both monarch and people work to integrate the local and the national; he acts in service of analogous models for management of both estate and country, models that Richard deliberately repudiates when he banishes Woodstock and his other advisers from the court. Moreover, Richard's actions threaten to profoundly unsettle the local social order; Nimble tells us that those imprisoned by him "begin already to offer their lands for liberty" (4.3.80–81), thereby being coerced to undermine the paternalistic social relations to which the landlord was central.

It is worth remembering that while Richard is exploiting rural communities, the means by which he does so also provide information that allows him to create a representation of the nation. That is, from Richard's act of violence done to England and Wales comes a textual representation of the same in the form of the national survey—an inventory of the nation out of an assault upon it. I would also argue that a cartographic image of the nation emerges out of this process, for *Woodstock* boasts a scene in which Richard divides his kingdom among his favorites through the use of a map. While the play does not directly suggest that the map is a result of the survey, it invites such a conclusion by presenting the map only after both blank charters and the information associated with them are collected—symbolically, the map is a product of the survey, a product that is used to farm out the kingdom. Thus, much as the maps produced out of Saxton's survey of the nation were used to tax various counties, Richard the landlord-king uses his survey and map to "rack [his subjects] soundly" (4.1.170–71). Map and survey produce a landscape of absolute property.

In a scene that strongly echoes and probably influenced the episode of the division of the kingdom in *King Lear*, Richard states, "Reach me the map, [that] we may allot their [i.e., Bushy, Bagot, Greene, and Scroope's] portions, and part the realm amongst them equally" (220–21). In enacting this division, Richard catalogues counties as if reading them off a wall map such as Saxton's: for example, "Bagot, thy lot / betwixt the Thames and sea thus lies: Kent, Surrey, / Sussex, Hampshire, Berkshire, Wiltshire, Dorsetshire, / Somersetshire, Devonshire, Cornwall, those parts are thine / As amply, Bagot, as the crown is mine" (226–30). Moreover, just as Lear offers Cordelia a portion "more opulent than [her] sisters,"[59] Richard, despite claiming the equal partitioning of the realm, grants Greene a portion that he identifies as "the greatest" (presumably in quality and not in size [246]). What is most important, though, is Richard's systematic dismantling of his nation, his reduction of it into its counties to be lorded over by his favorites. If survey and map make possible the cartographic construction of the nation, the use of the same also allows the management of the constituent parts of the nation in a way that is understood as detrimental to it both at the local level and as a whole. While the play applauds the way in which Woodstock can pass between court and estate, can act in the best interests of both the monarchical state and the local community, it simultaneously fears that this particular representation of the nation will be the means to abuse it.

This can be seen clearly two scenes later. Shortly after Richard has granted a lease for the rule of Kent to Bagot, a shrieve of Kent who has been arrested by Tresilian pleads his county's "ancient liberties / Recorded and enrolled in the king's Crown-office, / Wherein the men of Kent are clear discharged / Of fines, fifteens, or any other taxes" (4.3.19–22). Kentish rights are trampled upon through Richard's use of the survey, blank charters, and map, a use that violates "ancient liberties" much as the actions of the surveyor, in Norden's terms, alter and pervert customs. The shrieve asserts the particularity of Kent; its customs are different from those of other counties. This is in contrast to Richard's list of county names, which understands Kent only as one county among many casually granted by lease to his favorites. Just as the voices registered in the petitions Woodstock presents to the king offer a corrective to a view of individuals as the sum total of their assets, the shrieve insists on the particularity of his county, of its incommensurability with the counties that surround it—an incommensurability that Richard's reading of the map allows him to ignore. The map enables the effacement, if not eradication, of a landscape of custom.

What should be clear by now is that *Woodstock* is very concerned with negotiating the conflicting imperatives of the nation as a whole and of the regions that both help constitute it and are distinguishable from it. This process of negotiation takes place in part through the construction and use of the survey and map, documents that exist in this play as records and means of exploitation. If we understand the map to represent, as Richard Helgerson has suggested, a crucial (if not unproblematic) document for the construction of both local allegiance and nationhood,[60] then we also have to understand *Woodstock* as representing in symbolic terms resistance to that process of construction. This is made clear through the play's fundamental premise, that the management of the nation is closely analogous to that of the estate. Such a premise insists that we think of England in terms of the paternalistic moral economy delineated in Chapter One, an economy that, here as there, can be threatened by the construction and use of surveys and maps. In short, *Woodstock* asks what the costs of this construction of nationhood are—it wonders at whose expense the nation is formed.

BUT THAT DOES NOT go far enough to describe the complexity of this play's construction of the relationship between the management of the land and of the nation. If map and survey are the vehicles of a coercive sense of nationhood understood in terms of a mismanaged estate, then the play also offers a benign, if embattled, social vision in which the local and national are symbolically integrated through both the person and actions of Plain Thomas and the register of clothing.

In response to Woodstock's wearing of his one opulent outfit, Richard jestingly asks, "How comes this golden metamorphosis / From homespun housewifry?" (1.3.75–76). Woodstock's "tother hose," his supposedly homespun attire, are associated with housewifery—domestic economy, the management of household affairs (OED 1)[61]—and, later in this scene, "homespun judgements" (191).[62] The slide from apparel to domestic economy to judgment is telling, indicating that Woodstock's clothes register in multiple and complex ways. For now I want us to consider the term "homespun": the term, all of the relevant meanings of which, according to the OED, were coined in the late sixteenth or early seventeenth century, refers firstly to that which is of domestic manufacture (OED A1, 1591).[63] However, "homespun" in its adjectival form can also refer to something that is "simple, unsophisticated, unvarnished; plain, homely" (OED A2, 1600).[64] In addition, "homespun" is the material itself, the "cloth made of yarn spun at home" (OED B1, 1607). In *Woodstock*, all of these meanings intersect in the characterization of Plain Thomas's "homespun housewifry" or "homespun judgements." These mocking descriptions reveal unwittingly what the play takes to be the truth about Woodstock, a truth worth unpacking in some detail.

Lurking behind this characterization is the domestic production of cloth, alluded to in Woodstock's "homespun housewifry." In the second half of the sixteenth century English cloth production was central to the nation's economy, and cloth and cloth products were the major exports of the period. Moreover, the production of cloth was a household affair; in rural areas, farm laborers would "divid[e their] time between the loom and the plough" as "[v]illage after village developed into industrial as well as agricultural units . . ."[65] That the cloth market was driven by exporting did nothing to dismantle the association of Englishness with homespun industry and plain cloth. A common complaint in the period registered both the fate of that cloth once it left England's shores and England's increasing dependence upon foreign goods. Writing in 1549, Sir Thomas Smith in *A Discourse of the Common Weal of This Realm of England* bemoans first the proliferation of foreign goods that alters the commercial and physical landscape of London: "I have seen within these twenty years, when there were not of these haberdashers that sell French or Milan caps, glasses, daggers, swords, girdles, and such things not a dozen in all London. And now, from the Tower to Westminster along, every street is full of them." He then goes on to suggest that some of these goods are English in origin: "What grossness be we of . . . that will suffer our own commodities to go and set strangers on work, and then to buy them again at their hands; as of our wool, they make and dye kersies, frisadoes, broad cloths, and caps beyond the seas, and bring them hither to be sold again."[66] Smith laments the consumption of luxurious foreign goods over English ones, but he also resents the fact that some of these goods were at one point English products. The importation and sale of these foreign goods most clearly articulates what he sees as a loss of English self-sufficiency—the products consumed are caught up in a global market that puts

strangers to work, and that at least adulterates, if not totally obliter-
ates, the Englishness of those products. The homespun becomes fri-
sado, and the transformation is offensive to England and, at the level
of the commodity, corrosive of Englishness.[67]

Of course, Richard and his court are associated with foreign fashions imported into England, the kinds of fashions that required
landowners to convert acres into silks. Cheyney describes Richard
sitting "in council" with his favorites as follows:

> They sit . . . to devise strange fashions,
> And suit themselves in wild and antic habits
> Such as this kingdom never yet beheld:
> French hose, Italian cloaks, and Spanish hats,
> Polonian shoes with peaks a hand full long,
> Tied to their knees with chains of pearl and gold.
> Their plumed tops fly waving in the air
> A cubit high above their wanton heads.   (2.3.88–95)

The extravagance of this attire (and of Cheyney's description) is
borne out by the later appearance before Woodstock of a foppish
messenger who models his sartorial choices after those made by the
court. Echoing Richard's earlier response to his opulent attire,
Woodstock cries, "O strange metamorphosis! Is't possible that this
fellow that's all made of fashions should be an Englishman?"
(3.2.154–56).[68] Strange metamorphoses: Woodstock to wedding
guest, English wool to foreign kersies, Englishman to one "all made
of fashions."

I want us to take the idea of metamorphosis seriously here, as we
might when we remember Elizabethan sumptuary legislation which
understood clothing as a crucial indicator of identity.[69] However,
whereas that legislation usually concerned itself with rank- or gen-
der-based transgressions of a (putatively) sartorially fixed social order, here it is national identity that is at stake, that is unfixed by the
assumption of French hose and Italian cloaks—the messenger is all

made of foreign fashions.[70] We see an echo of this in William Harrison's *Description of England* when Harrison states that "Neither was it ever merrier with England than when an Englishman was known abroad [i.e., in public] by his own cloth and contented himself at home with his fine kersey hosen and a mean slop . . ."; when this was the case, the commonwealth was not "oppressed by unreasonable exactions made upon rich farmers and of poor tenants, wherewith to maintain [such apparel]."[71] Like the distribution of blank charters, the assumption of elaborate imported clothing is antithetical to the practices associated with a merry England; it is corrosive of English identity, a strange metamorphosis the implications of which extend far beyond a simple change of clothing. On the other hand, Woodstock, homespun in his clothing, judgment, and housekeeping, is figured as the exemplary Englishman, unadulterated by the pernicious influence of foreign garb.

Representations of what Karen Newman has called "sartorial extravagance" are of a piece with period accounts of the decay of hospitality; the "unreasonable exactions made upon rich farmers and of poor tenants," exactions made necessary by the need for new items of apparel, necessitated a decline in hospitality in the name of self-interest. While Arden's stroll through St. Paul's suggested both his repudiation of his responsibilities and the allure of that center of conspicuous consumption, Woodstock's "homespun housewifry" refers to the proper management of his affairs at the level of household and estate; as I have suggested above, he is the play's exemplary estate manager. Moreover, period ideologies outlining the ideal attributes of the nobleman see as inseparable the management of the household and the practice of hospitality, which is made clear by the fact that the terms "housekeeping" and "hospitality" both connote acts of lordly generosity.[72] In addition, "The essence of noble identity was supposed to hinge on housekeeping, that being the most conspicuous sign of a nobleman's worth. If hospitality was declining, then so was the state of England's gentry."[73] I will talk at length about early modern hospitality and its decline in Chapter Five; for now we need only note that Woodstock is the model of hospitality in the play, and that his hospitality gets him killed. When Richard and his cohorts, disguised as "some country gentlemen [who desire] / To show their dear affection" to Woodstock (4.2.85–86), arrive unannounced at Plashey Castle, Woodstock not only lets them enter but "embrace[s] their loves most kindly" (90) and prepares a banquet for them. The masque that these guests perform is putatively in Woodstock's honor, but it is actually the means by which Richard kidnaps Woodstock, prelude both to Plain Thomas's secret deportation to Calais and his murder.[74] We encounter the clearest evidence of Richard's depravity through his brutal abuse of Woodstock's hospitality, an abuse that attests to the threat posed by Richard to the moral order of which hospitality was a crucial part.

At the same time, however, Woodstock's hospitality finds its ironic counterpart in Richard's extravagant plans to "build again the hall at Westminster / To feast and revel in" (2.3.98–99). While this hall is planned as a source of hospitality for more than just Richard's immediate favorites, the queen immediately points out the hypocrisy of Richard's actions: "O certain ruin of this famous kingdom! / Fond Richard! thou buildst a hall to feast in / And starv'st thy wretched subjects to erect it" (101–3). Richard's "hospitality" marks the ruin of the kingdom, the extension of the exploitation of his subjects enacted by the scheme of the blank charters. While hospitality in its true form is integral to English noble identity, Richard's reign represents a perversion of its practices, the subordination of hospitality to the willful pursuit of the Crown's prerogatives and pleasures.

We have seen that Richard is aligned with those who convert land into opulent attire, and in a sense that is what he does. While Richard is not represented as either selling land or increasing its revenues through "progressive economic activities," his farming out of the kingdom reads the land not as social site but as landscape of absolute property, as a resource to be exploited by his favorites in return for an annual fee—like the survey-aided landlords we discussed in the last chapter, Richard becomes "a rentier pure and simple."[75] Moreover, this annual fee is metamorphosed into his French hose and Italian cloaks. The hospitality he offers is a dark parody of that advanced by Woodstock, but it is important to note a version of true hospitality, in the form of aid to the poor, is offered by Queen Anne, who converts her wealth into charity. As Anne herself says,

> Distressed poverty o'erspreads the kingdom:
> In Essex, Surrey, Kent and Middlesex
> Are seventeen thousand poor and indigent
> Which I have numbered; and to help their wants
> My jewels and my plate are turned to coin
> And shared amongst them.   (2.3.18–23)

In striking contrast to the distribution of the blank charters, Anne distributes aid; while Richard's map-enabled catalogue of counties is in the service of his parceling land out to his favorites, here the counties are specified in terms of their suffering inhabitants. Moreover, Anne defines the kingdom in terms of its people and the hardships they face, while for Richard those people are understood solely as sources of revenue. In the face of Richard's cruelty, however, Anne finally dies, and while her death helps prompt Richard to regret his actions and attempt to annul his order to execute Woodstock, the damage has been done. Hospitality is a casualty both of Richard's avarice and of the cartographic construction of the nation that enables and feeds that avarice.

I HAVE DISCUSSED in relation to *Woodstock* a wide range of topics: the actions of concealment hunters, the surveying of the kingdom, the cartographic construction of nationhood, the production and dissemination of knowledge in the marketplace, sartorial excess, and hospitality.[76] What I hope is clear is that what brings these disparate subjects together is the implication of each in *Woodstock*'s construction of the landscapes of region and nation. Each topic is a crucial site for the construction of (sometimes intersecting, sometimes conflicting) conceptions of land and its social uses. What I have tried to elucidate through a discussion of these practices is the complex relationship between the local and the national, a relationship that can lead one to the conclusion drawn by *Woodstock*—that the formation of a landscape of the nation (as absolute property) may constitute an act of violence done to the regions (landscapes of custom) that are supposedly a part of it. Interestingly, *Woodstock* not only depicts this violence but resists it, and not only through the actions of "privy whisperers"—the play, which is incomplete, ends during a seemingly successful rebellion against Richard and his favorites, a rebellion that Plain Thomas would not have sanctioned but one that, rather shockingly, the play does.[77] Interestingly, victory is marked by and partly made possible through the dissemination and consumption of texts. Whereas Tresilian sent out proclamations to discredit the likes of Lancaster and York, it is proclamations distributed by the rebels that lead to Tresilian's demise. Nimble betrays his onetime master in order to claim the reward and pardon promised in such a proclamation. After informing Tresilian of his plan, Nimble says, "You heard not the proclamation? . . . O sir, all the country's full of them" (5.5.42–45). The inventor of the scheme of the blank charters, a scheme that made possible the nefarious survey of the nation, is brought down because of his failure to attend to a kind of text around which a shared rural culture emerges—the very culture he earlier exploits and dismantles. While the *country*, meaning either countryside or country as a whole, may be full of these proclamations, Tresilian and Richard's *nation* finally wants no part of them or, for that matter, of the local cultures that consume them.

CHAPTER THREE

Reading Shakespeare's Maps

Arden of Faversham and *Woodstock* both promulgate an ethic of stewardship that stands in stark contrast to the landscapes of absolute property implied by maps as we have thus far seen them used. I have focused on the estate map and the map of the nation, and while the imperatives of a landscape of absolute property fit more obviously with the former than the latter, *Woodstock* understands the nation as a mismanaged estate, and the king as an exploitative landlord—that is, it understands the national map as a version of an estate map. Now that we turn to Shakespeare, however, we encounter a landscape distinct from but related to that of absolute property. The three texts I discuss here, *1 Henry IV, King Lear,* and *Richard II,* critique what I call a landscape of sovereignty—a political landscape that reflects and shapes the ambitions and imperatives of those who control or would control the nation. In such a landscape, the nation becomes the venue for the enactment of certain characters' sovereign acts and ambitions.

The landscape of sovereignty represents only one form that imaginary identification of or with the nation can take. As it happens, the map is one of the texts that enables the creation of what Benedict Anderson has called an "imagined community."[1] Brian S. Osborne discusses the landscape of the nation in relation to "the transition of societies from *Gemeinschaft* (community) to *Gesellschaft* (society)":

Gemeinschaft is essentially local and immediate. As such, the lived-in land-scape becomes a fundamental concept central to a people's sense of community, heritage and nationhood. It is the setting for the day-to-day economic, social and ideological activities that serve to unite a distinctive people. All these culturally significant actions serve to imbue that place with evocative associations and transform it into a symbolically charged repository of past practices and events. Some sites are elevated to the level of shrines or sacred places. Such a landscape supports the culture as its 'hearth' of origin, its home for the present, and its refuge for the future. The idea of this common residence in a particular place is often the matrix binding the nation together.

Gesellschaft requires that people identify with an abstraction—the territory of an artificially constituted unit, the state. Long-standing localisms are replaced by new centralizing structures of government, communications and bureaucracy that facilitate the functional interaction of the state. Attempting to cultivate the sense of 'oneness' that was so strong in the pre-state *Gemeinschaft*, states consciously nurture shared symbolic constructs that reinforce the sense of membership to the group and the development of a sense of distinctiveness. . . . Through these symbolic contributions, states are able to establish identities and thus create collective memories or 'imagined communities.'[2]

Identification with an abstraction—this is enabled by maps, and the possibilities for such identification are obviously not summed up in the landscape of sovereignty. *Richard II* makes clear that in early modern England there are different conceptions of nationhood with which characters identify, and which offer alternatives to (or alternative versions of) a landscape of sovereignty. Moreover, the map helps engender the creation of different landscapes—both of sovereignty and of imagined community—and that it does so tells us something important: that it is open to multiple and conflicting interpretations. We will see this through not only a discussion of *1 Henry IV*, *King Lear*, and especially *Richard II*, but also an examination of early modern map reading.

IN A FAMOUS MOMENT in *1 Henry IV*, we witness the projected division of the kingdom amongst the three rebels, Mortimer, Glendower, and Hotspur. This scene offers us a model for reading maps, a model that suggests the peculiar efficacy of the carto-graphic texts whose production in England underwent a profound transformation during Shakespeare's lifetime. "Come, here is the map," Glendower says; "shall we divide our right / According to our threefold order ta'en?"[3] Mortimer replies, "The Archdeacon hath divided it / Into three limits very equally" (3.1.68–69), but Hotspur has doubts about the equality of that division:

> Methinks my moiety, north from Burton here,
> In quantity equals not one of yours:
> See how this river comes me cranking in,
> And cuts me from the best of all my land
> A huge half-moon, a monstrous cantle out.
> I'll have the current in this place damm'd up,
> And here the smug and silver Trent shall run
> In a new channel fair and evenly;
> It shall not wind with such a deep indent,
> To rob me of so rich a bottom here. (92–101)

Here Shakespeare pushes the logic of carving up the kingdom to an odd extreme, as Hotspur imagines redirecting the river, thereby gaining access to "the best of all [his] land." What is most impor-tant about this scene, however, is that Hotspur imagines not alter-ing the *map* so as to increase the value or nature of his property, but rather he plans to alter the *land itself*.[4] Instead of arguing that his portion as represented on the map be enlarged or modified, Hotspur angrily asserts that he will reconstruct that which is con-tained within the boundaries of that portion; he eschews discussion of changing the cartographic terms of the agreement in favor of the more costly, elaborate, and time-consuming process of redirecting the river, of altering the land itself. Hotspur imagines that it is not the allocation of land made possible by the map that robs him of a portion of dry land, but it is the river that "wind[s] with such a deep indent, / To rob me of so rich a bottom here." For Hotspur, the land is both intending and manipulable; it is its cartographic partitioning into thirds that is inviolable. Of course the irony is that if Hotspur does redirect the river, then the cartographic representation of the land must be modified. And yet, at this moment it is the boundaries marked out on the map that are obdurate; apparently land yields more readily than do the abstract portions of space created through the Archdeacon's division "Into three limits very equally."[5]

I begin with this scene because it reminds us that maps are not transparent, that their meanings are not self-evident and that they can be multiply construed. More pointedly, I will show that map readings such as this one tell us much about the way in which early modern culture fitfully came to terms with a new (or, more precisely, an importantly modified) textual form that posed unsettling interpretive or epistemological questions. Moreover, it should be noticed that Hotspur's reading, were it to be transformed into action, would have important material effects; it is not merely a desocialized land that Hotspur threatens to submerge, for, as I have emphasized throughout this book, land is inevitably imbricated in a range of cultural activities and practices. Also, Hotspur resembles here those unsavory figures we encountered in the last chapter, the concealment hunters. This resemblance is telling, for it links Hotspur's impetuosity and hubris to that of those agents of the Crown who, like surveyors, unsettled traditional social relations in the name of profit—that is, whose actions asserted the prerogatives of a landscape of absolute property over one of custom. The crucial point is that the map makes that process possible; at both the representational and the material level it helps erase households, tenants, and working inhabitants of the land.

In order to pursue further some of the issues skeletally adduced here, I want to sketch a social history of the map in the Elizabethan and Jacobean periods. I will then explore the ways in which Shake-spearean drama intervenes in that history, interrogating the domi-nant modes of cartographic consumption—an interrogation that raises questions about the conventions of reading and conceptions of spatiality and sociality apparently embedded in maps themselves. Af-ter turning briefly to *King Lear*, I will focus on the buried cartograph-ic rhetoric of *Richard II*, a rhetoric that raises significant questions about the map's construction of English nationhood and the land.

Richard Helgerson's important essay on early modern cartogra-phy has sparked interest in the way in which maps help shape the identity of the map reader by making possible his or her imagina-tive identification with county or nation.[6] What Helgerson does not focus on, however, are period representations of map reading. These representations confirm Helgerson's sense of the potency of the map, but they also open up a new avenue of inquiry. While Helgerson rightly considers the ways in which maps imaginatively locate the reader in relation to, say, the political unit of the county, an examination of representations of map reading suggests that the map also performs the surprising function of realizing the spaces of textual consumption. A representative description of a man and his map is to be found in Sir Thomas Elyot's *The Boke Named the Governour*, in which the narrator describes the joys of map reading:

For what pleasure is it, in one houre, to beholde those realmes, cities, sees, ryuers, and mountaynes, that uneth in an olde mannes life can nat be iournaide and pursued: what incredible delite is taken in beholding the diuersities of people, beastis, foules, fisshes, trees, frutes, and herbes: to knowe the sondry maners and conditions of people, and the varietie of their natures, and that in a warme studie or perler, without perill of the see, or daunger of longe and paynfull iournayes: I can nat tell what more pleasure shulde happen to a gentil witte, than to beholde in his owne house euery thynge that with in all the worlde is contained.[7]

Elyot describes the potential that to many Elizabethans maps seemed to represent: the possibility of viewing in one's own house "euery thynge that with in all the worlde is contained." What is striking about this passage is the relationship, commonly delineated in this period, between the whole, vast world represented by the map and the cozy spaces of the study within which the map is read. Elyot's map reader "beholds"—a verb used three times in this passage—all the earth has to offer without ever leaving his "warme studie or perler." While maps have most commonly been discussed in terms of their role in both representing and constructing city, county, or nation, accounts such as Elyot's also foreground the map's efficacy in shaping the spaces of its consumption. The two spaces are dialectically and mutually defining; the study is made all the cozier by the reviewing of information normally available only as the product of "longe and paynfull iournayes," and all that the world contains is that which lies outside the safe confines of one's parlor. However, there is also a sense in which that world lies squarely inside the parlor, for Elyot fails to distinguish between representation and reality. Elyot's map reader "beholds" the world's bounty, as if he has traveled across the globe depicted in the map; the map brings to its reader the knowledge usually gleaned from travel, from experience. In this regard, the word "behold" retains much of its etymological force, suggesting not only looking at, but actually "holding by" or "keeping," that which one observes (OED I).[8]

And yet, to talk here of the consumption only of maps is misleading. The map Elyot's narrator reads is part of a geography text, Ptolemy's *Geographia*. His rhapsodic account must be understood in terms of broader conventions recognizable as those helping to govern reading in general;[9] this description resembles certain period accounts of the effect of reading on the education of a gentleman. Consider Thomas Nashe's discussion of the relationship between travel and the acquisition of knowledge:

Some alledge they trauell to learne wit, but I am of this opinion, that . . . [it is] not possible for anie great man to attain anie great wit by trauell, except he haue the grounds of it rooted in him before. . . . What is here but

we may read in bookes, and a great deale more too, without stirring our
feete out of a warme studie?[10]

Books are sources of wit that give the gentleman access to a world
larger than his study without his ever having to stir his feet. What
distinguishes this account from Elyot's, though, is the rhetoric of
beholding. Both Elyot's and Nashe's narrators speak of the power
of books in acquiring knowledge of the world, but it is the inclusion of the map that allows Elyot's narrator to witness all that
Nashe's can only read about. It is this "beholding" that raises the
epistemological stakes and lends the map its power.

This brief discussion of Elyot and Nashe is designed to intro-
duce some interrelated topics and issues central to an understanding of the social significance of maps at the turn of the seventeenth
century. First, the map is an elite document that is consumed in a
restrictive social space that it helps define through the act of being
consumed. Second, the map purports to provide a certain kind of
transparent and scientific knowledge; words may be more or less
opaque, but the map allows one to "behold" what other texts may
obscure or incompletely represent. Third, the map blurs the boundaries between representation and represented; it appears to present
things "as they really are."

We have already seen the way in which Elyot's map discursively
invokes the parameters of the aristocratic study. It is important to
note, however, both that maps defined the boundaries of the domestic spaces of gentry and aristocrats in a more material and palpable fashion, and that they are multiple in design and use. Cartographic images in this period do not exist only as appendixes to
books; they also appear in paintings, tapestries, atlases, wall maps,
and even on the backs of playing cards.[11] Some of the different uses
of maps are famously delineated by John Dee:

While, some, to beautifie their Halls, Parlers, Chambers, Galeries, Studies,
or Libraries with: other some, for thinges past, as battels fought, earth-

quakes, heauenly fyringes, & such occurentes, in histories mentioned: and such other circumstances. Some other, presently to vewe the large dominion of the Turke: the wide Empire of the Moschouite: and the little morsell of ground, where Christendome (by Profession) is certainly knowen. . . . Some, either for their owne iorneyes directing into farre landes: or to vnderstand of other mens trauailes. To conclude, some, forone purpose: and some, for an other, liketh, loueth, getteth, and vseth, Mappes, Chartes, & Geographicall Globes.[12]

Dee's description reminds us that in this period cartographic representations are understood in terms quite different from those to which we are accustomed. Cartographic images in the form of paintings, tapestries, or wall maps function to beautify and to define the social spaces of the wealthy; they are objects that signify the wealth and prestige of their owners, while also literally marking the perimeters of "Halls, Parlers, Chambers, Galeries, Studies, or Libraries." In addition, they serve as graphic representations of "thinges past," and as visual reminders of the precarious state of a Christendom that, in contrast to the "large dominion of the Turke," occupies only a "little morsell of ground." Objects that "beautifie," maps are also desirable commodities that many "liketh, loveth, getteth, and useth," but that use accommodates more than just the reading of cartographic information. Dee's account understands the social utility of maps emerging not only from the way in which they make information available, but from the kind of cultural capital that accrues to those owning them. In a sense, both the reading and the ownership of maps help to fashion a gentleman and the spaces of his home.

Maps are associated with gentlemen on yet another interpretive register, however, for English cartographic images came into being in part because of the requirements of a centralized government; we must remember as well "the administrative use of maps, which eventually covered almost all aspects of state activity."[13] Both Sir Humphrey Gilbert and Sir Thomas Elyot advocated that gentle-

men learn how to draw maps because of their administrative utility,[14] and the map collections of Lord Burghley and Sir Francis
Walshingham reveal, through both what is included and how those
inclusions are annotated, the importance of maps in issues of local
and regional administration, tax collection, and civil and national
defense.[15] Walshingham said in 1573 that "A Secratarie [of State]
must likewise have the booke of Ortelius's Mapps, a booke of the
Mappes of England . . . and if anie other plottes or mappes come
to his handes, let them be kept safelie."[16] In short, map reading and
ownership were prerequisites for those gentlemen with political
ambitions or responsibilities.

While they appear only in muted form, some of the cultural assumptions about the efficacy of maps that we have discussed above
can be recognized in Dee's description: through the map we view
the land of the Turk, not its representation. Arguably Dee is just
being imprecise, as we might be similarly imprecise in saying we *see*
the United States on a map of the world. However, it is important
to realize that such imprecision signifies quite differently in the late
sixteenth and early seventeenth centuries than it does today. I have
addressed in Chapter One the way in which the estate map functions as a substitute for the land it represents because of the way in
which, in J. B. Harley's words, "the acceptability of the cartographic message began to be coloured by a perception of its detailed accuracy in representing what was believed to be scientific or
geographical truth."[17] What remains to be discussed more fully is
the role of maps and of "beholding" in constituting what this period understands as "scientific truth."

Patricia Parker has recently written of the intriguing conceptual
links between the acquisition of scientific knowledge, the exploration of distant territories, and what she calls the "ocular impulse";
she discusses "a characteristic early modern preoccupation with the
ocular, an appetite which . . . involved the hunger to 'know' as a
desire to 'see.'"[18] This preoccupation is evident in the work of

Francis Bacon, who asserts that

all depends on keeping the eye steadily fixed upon the facts of nature and so receiving their images simply as they are. For God forbid that we should give out a dream of our own imagination for a pattern of the world; rather may he graciously grant to us to write an apocalypse or true vision of the footsteps of the Creator imprinted on his creatures.[19]

Bacon's statement provides us with a good example of what Timothy Reiss has described as "analytico-referential discourse," a discourse increasingly dominant in this period and in part inaugurated by Bacon.[20] As Elizabeth Hanson concisely defines it, "analytico-referential discourse" is "discourse that assumes that truth is an objective condition, external both to the mind that perceives it and to the language that describes it. . . . [T]he encounter with truth depends on a separation between the knowing mind and the object of its knowledge."[21] This assumption certainly undergirds Bacon's statement, but in the same passage in which he asserts that one should generate knowledge by keeping one's "eye steadily fixed upon the facts of nature," he also attests to the unsettling possibility that we might "give out a dream of our own imagination for a pattern of the world."[22] In describing the proper role of the scientist, Bacon neatly and unwittingly captures the contradictions both of "analytico-referential discourse" and, more importantly to us, of the map in this period: is it an empirical representation of the geographical facts of nature "simply as they are," or is it "a dream of our own imagination" standing in for "a pattern of the world"? As we have seen, early modern thinkers tended to opt for the former possibility, perhaps in part because, after Ptolemy, cartographic production depended upon the "theoretical linking of terrestrial locations to astronomical observations, thereby generating a theoretical spatial grid and locational coordinates for any place on earth."[23] The construction of this grid placed mapped space into a conceptual context that boasted the inevitability and unerringness not only of mathematics but also of an underlying cosmographical order, and while the graphic content of the map might change over time, its context seemed natural, immutable, "a pattern of the world."[24] It is perhaps this that Shakespeare is spoofing in the Hotspur episode, for, as we have noted, Hotspur imagines the map's partitioning of space to be more natural and immutable than the land itself.

We need not end our discussion of the social role of maps by definitively asserting that in this period map readers always took representation for reality, always took the cartographic terms to be natural ones. One must be careful not to discount the multiple ways in which maps could (and can) be used and understood. As Graham Huggan puts it, "The accuracy of a map obviously depends on its precision of detail and refinement of delivery, yet it also depends on explicit or tacit perceptual conventions that differ widely from culture to culture [and, I argue, even within single cultures]. Maps, in this sense, are the unstable products of social, historical and political circumstance."[25] In Elizabethan and Jacobean England this is especially so, for it is only in the late sixteenth century that England first encountered what has been called the "new geography."

For much of the first Elizabethan era, England was in many, probably in most, respects behind the Continent and mapmaking was no exception but during the last quarter of the sixteenth century the English made rapid progress in a number of fields. There was a surge of activity not to be disassociated from the accumulating wealth acquired from overseas activities and the valuable input into the English treasury of gold stolen from Spanish ships. Cartography was one among the many activities of the time which surged forward, and the outstandingly successful enterprise was the mapping of England and Wales by Christopher Saxton.[26]

We shall soon return to Saxton's work, but for now it is important to stress that the new geography, fueled by technological advances in surveying and an increase in information made possible by voyages of commerce and exploration, must only have enhanced the belief that maps were objective and transparent representations of the natural world. At the same time, however, the new geography's hegemony was far from total, and the conventions governing the production and consumption of the old geography collided with those of the emergent new.[27] This collision arguably helped make possible a range of interpretive responses to maps, some of which we have discussed above, and not only ones that collapsed representation into represented. There is, for instance, Samuel Daniel's following assertion: "Nor must we thinke, viewing the superficiall figure of a region in a Mappe, that wee know strait the fashion and place as it is."[28] Daniel rejects the kind of thinking offered up by Elyot, Nashe, and Dee, and suggests another possibility, one that may seem more suited to what we think of as "correct" cartographic reading practice. And yet, it is important to stress again that the conventions of "correct" map reading were not firmly in place in this period, and that maps were often "misunderstood," on occasion in ways that led to significant material difficulties. Consider Victor Morgan's discussion of an important governmental misreading of maps:

[A]s the burden of *ad hoc* forms of taxation increased under Elizabeth, especially for military purposes, it was often important . . . to have means of assessing the impositions placed on individual counties in matters such as levies for the wars in Ireland. Certainly, in [the Welsh cartographer] George Owen's opinion, one of the reasons why Pembrokeshire was unduly burdened with royal demands compared with its neighbouring counties was that councillors sitting in London were using Saxton's maps, and unfortunately Saxton had devoted a whole sheet to Pembrokeshire, but had crowded the other four Welsh counties, with which comparisons were made, on to one. . . . [T]he councillors, not being properly trained in the reading of maps, had failed to consult the different scales on the two maps, and had proceeded in their allocation of burdens according to the superficially similar areas depicted on the two sheets.[29]

Morgan's account of the disastrous role of the map in the levying of Welsh county taxes for the nation's wars in Ireland will have a particular resonance for my reading of *Richard II* (and, in a later chapter, of *Cymbeline*), but for now I want only to draw our attention to the way in which this account recapitulates much of what we have seen so far. Maps are read by gentlemen, on this occasion ones occupying elite positions in government, who in a significant way take for truth that which they see in front of them. What is suggested by this anecdote, reminiscent as it is of Richard's efface-ment of Kent's customary landscape in *Woodstock*, are the political effects of the cartographic representation of land, and the costs of a cartographically enhanced bureaucratic control of the spaces of the nation—the costs, that is, of a landscape of sovereignty. Such ef-fects and costs are explored in a text of a very different nature: Shakespeare's *King Lear*.

"GIVE ME THE MAP THERE," Lear famously orders, and he then proceeds to explain how "we have divided / In three our king-dom."[30] As with the case of Hotspur, it soon becomes clear that such divisions are not as straightforward as they appear to be. While the portions are of the same size, their equality is uncertain. The play between boundaries and boundlessness that governs the opening action of *King Lear*—Regan and Goneril speak a love that is, in the words of the latter, "Beyond what can be valued rich or rare" (1.1.56), while Cordelia "love[s Lear] / According to my bond; no more nor less" (91–92)—is cartographically and geographically inscribed in Lear's partitioning of space. On the one hand, Lear gives Regan an "ample third of our fair kingdom, / No less in space, validity, and pleasure, / Than that conferr'd on Goneril" (79–81). On the other, he urges Cordelia to speak her boundless love so that she might gain "A third more opulent than [her] sisters" (85). In doing the latter, Lear unwittingly suggests what seems to be a dis-junction between the equal partitioning made possible through cartographic representations of space and the unequal nature of the space being represented. Moreover, this disjunction is arguably also evident in the gap between the thirds equal in "space, validity, and pleasure"—terms that operate on different interpretive registers— and the elaborate descriptions of the land itself: Goneril's portion, for instance, is filled "With shadowy forests and with champains rich'd, / With plenteous rivers and wide-skirted meads . . ." (63– 64). The portions of land are read in terms not only of size, but of presumably varied natural resources, and of "validity [i.e., value], and pleasure." What is missing in all of these descriptions, however, is what is largely missing from maps themselves: a sense of the land as social site. As Francis Barker has recently argued, "[While] the land is a place of fulsomeness and abundance, it is at the same moment one of ideal emptiness, a depopulated landscape. No one lives or works in the countryside of Lear's map . . ."[31] Lear divides the kingdom as if it is a unified and homogeneous entity, and in so doing he effaces social activity and local differences. In that regard, Lear follows the logic of the map, for he erases the social in the name of a partitioned land that can be readily distributed to the heirs to his throne. At the same time, however, Lear's own rhetoric suggests the inequivalence and incommensurability of portions of land even when divided into thirds: one portion is "more opulent" than the others.

As is evident in the work of Christopher Saxton, the first Englishman to produce an atlas (1579) and wall map (1583) of England and Wales, the sixteenth-century map provides us with a model not only for *Lear*'s cartographic representation of his kingdom, but also for Lear's geographic descriptions of the land. Consider what surrounds the image of England and Wales on Saxton's wall map:

A fretwork cartouche, top right, surmounted by the Queen's arms with supporters, contains a summary of English history from Caesar to the Tudors, ending with the dedication in which Thomas Seckford, Master of Requests [and Saxton's master], presents 'this laborious and costly work' to the Queen. . . . Two panels in similar cartouches at the left-hand edge contain, respectively, an account of the legal system and courts of England . . . and a geographical description of the country, ending with a recommendation to the curious reader to seek further information 'in our geographical maps.'[32]

I do not want to discuss here the professional and monarchical hierarchies within which language such as this places Saxton; that topic has been admirably explored by Helgerson. Instead, I want to direct our attention to the number of contexts within which the land is read: not only in terms of patronage relations, but also of the disciplines of history, law, and geography.[33] However, it is the geographical description that is most important here, for it is this type of description that both accompanies and complicates the mathematical rigidity of the partitioning of space in *King Lear*. While division and description are made to complement one another, Saxton's surveying activities involved subordinating geographical details to the demands of a political partitioning of space. As R. A. Skelton has noted, Saxton created his atlas not by doing what surveyors would normally do—that is, "be guided by physical boundaries [such as] those of a river basin or watershed"—but by adhering to political boundaries, those defining the borders of the counties.[34] However, as we have seen, in Saxton's maps the delineation of these boundaries exists side by side with a description of the land designed to give the county a distinctive character; political boundaries are naturalized through geographical description.

With this in mind, consider the period's oddest cartographic products of all: the playing cards based on Saxton's county maps. Like the wall map discussed above, these playing cards provide information to be read in varied interpretive registers. The card for "WARWICK[SHIRE]," for instance, includes the county's mathematical dimensions ("In Quantitie Supficiall 555 In Circuite 122"), its place in relationship to other counties ("In Length from Staffordshire to Oxford 37 / In Bredth from Lecestershire to Worcester

28"), a catalogue of important cities and towns ("Hauinge Lecester & Northap: East Worcest: West / Lecester & Stafford"), and a geographical description ("one pte champia, the other woodlad / Aboundinge with corne & grasse, well Inhabited").[35] As in *Lear*, geographic description and mathematical partitioning coexist; both *Lear* and period maps present as complementary different ways of understanding the land. Moreover, especially given the scientific authority ascribed to cartography that we have discussed above, these multiple ways of representing and measuring the land can appear to exhaust its meaning, to sum up its significance. And yet, what the above scene from *King Lear* suggests is both the inadequacy of these conceptions and the tension between these ways of construing land. The yoking of the division of the land to the drama of filial obedience foregrounds the arbitrariness of the very divisions a map would seek to render permanent—the kingdom exists first as one, then as three, finally as two—and the particularized descriptions of the land reduce it to "opulent" jewels to be allocated at will. At the same time, the inequality of the pieces of land (one-third is more opulent than others) problematizes the cartographic processes by which land is rendered homogeneous or alienable. *King Lear* gestures toward twin processes of construing land and suggests their fundamental incompatibility, and thereby raises questions about cartographic modes of perception that both unintentionally register that incompatibility and simultaneously deny it. At the same time, however, Lear's kingdom, unlike Warwickshire, is never understood to be "well Inhabited"; what Helgerson describes as the map's potential ability to "[strengthen] the sense of both local and national identity at the expense of an identity based on dynastic loyalty"[36] is nowhere in evidence. Instead, the kingdom is the space across which the drama of Lear's and his dynasty's dissolution is performed, and it is the map that helps make this performance possible.

Of course, on another interpretive level, the division of the kingdom into three political units in both *1 Henry IV* and *King Lear* evokes the national divisions of Britain: England, Scotland, Wales. In the case of *Lear*, Cordelia's "third more opulent" is England, compared with Goneril and Albany's Scotland and Regan and Cornwall's Wales, and Lear's granting of England to his favorite daughter may suggest a political shrewdness his later actions belie—that is, it may indicate his (unfortunately soon forgotten) uncertainty about his pelican daughters, a reading confirmed by his granting to them of regions removed from the political center of Lear's formerly integrated realm.[37] Most significantly, Lear's partitioning engenders, as Hotspur's evokes, the national divisions that, at the moment of the play's production, James worked hard to efface through his attempts to unify the kingdom.[38] At the same time, this partitioning is accomplished by monarchical fiat, with no attention paid to the people affected by these divisions—while regions are granted a certain geographical specificity, they are seen as culturally vacant. While the geography of a particular region may add to that region's allure, it also remains divorced from the customary practices that render a given area incommensurable with others and offer one alternative to a landscape of sovereignty.

Customary practice suggests the incommensurability of one region with both other regions and a homogenized conception of the nation as a whole; in turn, such a homogenized conception effaces what is particular about certain regions. In dividing kingdoms into three, Lear and Hotspur produce landscapes of "ideal emptiness" in which the local and customary disappear. As in *Woodstock*, we see that the construction of a landscape of the nation, in these cases landscapes of sovereignty, poses a threat to regional identity and practice, whether that region is a village, a town, or, in the case of Wales and Scotland, a nation. And yet, both Shakespeare and the author of *Woodstock* realize that national landscapes need not be produced at the expense of the regional. In *Woodstock* Richard's abuse of customary practice is countered by "plain Thomas's" idealized negotiation of the imperatives of the local and national. In the case of Shakespeare, one need only turn to *Henry V* in order to witness the integration of peoples of varying regions, ranks and nations into Henry's relatively inclusive British army, an army (and vision of Britain) in which difference is registered and accommodated. Certainly such an integration is incomplete and uneven: on the eve of war with France Henry and his advisers fret about the possibility of a Scottish invasion; there exists within Henry's army a hierarchy of nations, with the (aristocratic and yeomen) English at the top and the Irish, represented by MacMorris, at the bottom; and finally there is little room in the martial world of *Henry V* for representatives of the tavern world represented by Falstaff. Nevertheless, Henry's inclusion of the three nations that inhabit what *Richard II*'s John of Gaunt calls the "sceptred isle," not to mention Ireland, stands in stark contrast to the eagerness of Hotspur, Henry's onetime foil, to divide the island into three. Henry V, like Woodstock, maintains and forges alliances not out of the suppression of the customary but out of its extension, integrating regional difference into an inclusive conception of Britishness. As we shall now see, in *Richard II* we encounter something else altogether, a landscape of sovereignty in which the monarch fails to recognize the (often geographical) limits of his authority.

'I HENRY IV' PARODIES the truth claims of the map and examines the confusion of representation and represented made possible by those claims; *King Lear* reveals the inadequacies of and contradictions within cartographic conceptions of the land. It is *Richard II*, however, that stands as both the most sustained and most elliptical of all Shakespearean explorations of the meaning of early modern maps. We will start where so many others have: John of Gaunt's famous evocation of a Britain threatened by Richard's "farming out" of the kingdom. Michael Neill has recently shown that "Gaunt's patriotic oratory is ultimately dependent on developments in sixteenth-century mapmaking . . ."[39] That is, Gaunt's imagining of England, his depiction of the country as if he were beholding it from some undefined point above, is made possible by its representation on the map. Neill does not develop the implications of this point, and it is my aim to trace further the connections between cartography, landscape, and both this speech and the play as a whole. The proliferation of metaphors used to describe England—Eden, walled fortress, house, womb, throne, jewel—is well known, and the metaphors attest not only to the force of Gaunt's conception, but also to his conceptual confusion.[40] Gaunt's famous description of the "royal throne of kings" (2.1.40), the vision of "a prophet new inspir'd," comes immediately after a series of clichés that are also a part of Gaunt's prophecy: "For violent fires soon burn out themselves; / Small showers last long, but sudden storms are short; / He tires betimes that spurs too fast betimes," and so on (31–36). These clichés are of a piece with the rest of the speech, which is largely comprised of a string of related but unequal metaphors for England that, despite their undeniable evocative power, are less deathbed profundities than a potent muddle of conflicting conceptions of the nation.[41] And yet, it is this muddle that has often been seen as a founding moment in England's vision of itself. Gillian Beer has suggested that this speech "provide[s] the initiating communal self-description [of England], alluringly emblematic and topographical at once." She discusses the legacy of this description:

The identification of England with the island is already, and from the start, a fiction. It is a fiction, but an unwavering one among English writers and other English people, that England occupies the land up to the margins of every shore. The island has seemed the perfect form in English cultural imagining . . . Defensive, secure, compacted, even paradisal . . .[42]

Moreover, as Neill has suggested, the creation of this perfect form has been enabled by cartographic representations of the country, with Saxton's wall map providing the clearest model. Gaunt's speech acknowledges his debt to the map through the cartographic pun apparent in the reference to England as a "blessed plot" (50). As I suggested in the first chapter, "plot" suggests both a portion of land (OED 2) and a map (OED 3). In its reference to a parcel of land, the plot metaphor is puzzling, for a plot refers to a small portion of land, not a kingdom. Moreover, to talk of England as a plot of land is unwittingly to evoke Richard's vices; he is the one who, as we shall discuss and as we saw in *Woodstock*, is less king than bad landlord, who understands the nation as an aggregation of plots. However, one might understand the second definition of plot (as map) as solving the problem of the first (as piece of land); Richard's reduction of England to plots of land is answered by a rhapsodic account of the nation as a blessed plot, as a cartographically defined sacred space untouched by the king's machinations. The blessed plot, then, is the cartographic image of England that seems to stand outside of history and beyond Richard's reach.

There are problems with this reading, however. One is the air of nostalgia that envelops Gaunt's speech. The England he describes is ironically both of a different time and made possible by sixteenth-century cartography. In that sense, the map represents an idealized vision of the country and a faded one, England as sacred space and lost island. (As Phyllis Rackin puts it, "Longing for a lost past, Gaunt imagines it as an unchanging ideal.")[43] This attests to the power of maps to construct a nation that seems timeless and impervious to change, like an unyielding scientific fact. The second problem, however, lies in a major use of maps in this period. While a cartographic representation of England might suggest the nation's timelessness, maps themselves were employed for particular political ends, such as Richard's leasing out of his kingdom. As *Woodstock* makes clear, such uses also offer a vision of the nation not as idealized organic unity but as a collection of exploitable economic resources; as Alexander Leggatt shrewdly notes, "a king who is simply a tax-gatherer will get funds only by losing allegiance. . . . This is an unfortunate kind of national unity."[44] Most immediately, though, cartographic texts such as Saxton's wall map represent England in a way crucial to understanding Richard's inability to recognize the metaphorical and geographical limits of his power.

Richard II explores the relationship of the map's construction of a nation to the issue of the nature and limits of Richard's authority. Beer has suggested the simple conceptual problem with Gaunt's originary fiction—England is *not* an island. While Lear and Hotspur divide the kingdom, *Richard II*'s image of national, geographic unity is predicated upon a false organicism that poses its own problems. Where do Gaunt's England and Richard's authority end? What of the relationship of England to Wales and Scotland?[45] (Saxton's wall map includes Wales, but Scotland is represented only by a blank fragment at the top of the map.) More troublingly, what of Ireland, given that, as one historian puts it, "The history of Ireland under Elizabeth is essentially the story of the forcible imposition of English authority over the whole island . . ."[46] We shall see that certain national boundaries and the problems they pose are effaced not only in Gaunt's speech but in Richard's actions, and the false conception of unity supplied by Gaunt's nationalistic rhetoric is partly what leads to Richard's demise. In *Richard II*, the cartographic conception of the nation contributes to the fall of the king. At the same time, as we have seen, that conception as it informs John of Gaunt's speech serves as a crucial site of identification with the "imagined community" of England. Map and speech suggest landscapes both of sovereignty and of imagined community. This is illustrative of a dynamic crucial to the play, for, as we shall see, different characters appeal to different conceptions of the nation in order to shore up their authority and identity.

The question of the nature and limits of Richard's authority is repeatedly raised in the first act of the play through Richard's attempts to exercise control over the conflict between Bolingbroke and Mowbray. Each of the two enemies accuses the other of treason, thereby seeming concerned with the threat the other poses to the state, but it is the honor of each that is primarily at stake, and the rivals insist that in such cases only trial by combat can ensure the loyalty of the victor; as Bolingbroke puts it, "What my tongue speaks my right drawn sword may prove" (1.1.46). Richard denies them such a trial in a way that reveals the arbitrary imposition of his authority. At the very first Richard seems prepared to judge the two enemies without benefit of trial by combat ("impartial are our eyes and ears," he asserts [115]), but soon thereafter he demands that Bolingbroke and Mowbray forget their quarrel: "Forget, forgive, conclude and be agreed" (156). The combatants refuse, asserting the primacy of honor over even loyalty to the king's dictates. "My life thou shalt command," Mowbray says, "but not my shame: / The one my duty owes, but my fair name . . . / To dark dishonour's use thou shalt not have" (166–69). In the face of their resistance, Richard capitulates and schedules their trial, only on the day of their combat to stop the fight before it begins. At that point Richard banishes both Mowbray and Bolingbroke for different periods of time, and then reduces the length of the latter's sentence at the behest of his aged father, John of Gaunt. I run through this much of the plot both to make clear the fickleness of Richard's rule and to suggest the limits that honor places on the king's authority, limits that are also made clear by Bolingbroke's return to England in the name of "rights and royalties" that do not fall under the monarch's sway (2.3.119) and that gesture toward an alternative conception of the nation.

What is most important for our purposes, though, is that honor is geographically inscribed in a way that provocatively echoes both the process of mapmaking and the details of Mowbray's and Bolingbroke's banishment. To prove Bolingbroke's cowardice, Mowbray says that he would be willing to "meet him were I tied to run afoot / Even to the frozen ridges of the Alps, / Or any other ground inhabitable / Where ever Englishman durst set his foot" (1.1.63–66).

Similarly, Bolingbroke pledges to "in battle prove [his honesty] / Or here, or elsewhere to the furthest verge / That ever was survey'd by English eye" (92–94). Each seems to pledge to go to the ends of the earth to fight the other, but that pledge is qualified by their Englishness: they will travel no farther than Englishmen have before. Even the negotiation of foreign terrain is subordinated to an English identity constituted here in terms of a history of English travel. For Mowbray and Bolingbroke honor is inextricably linked with their conception of nationhood; in denying them the right to fight, Richard strikes at not only their aristocratic but their national identities, identities asserted through their identification with what past Englishmen have done. Intriguingly, though, at least one of those identities is understood in cartographic terms. In referring to "the furthest verge / That ever was survey'd by English eye," Bolingbroke understands Englishness in terms of surveyed boundaries. The surveyor goes beyond the nation's limits, and yet the furthest verge, the edge of the measured world, emerges only through its dialectical interaction with the English eye. This play between alien spaces and English subjectivities ironically foreshadows the expulsion of the rivals, both of whom are sent beyond the scope of most English eyes.[47]

Given the play of national identity and geographical boundaries, the act of banishment is particularly intriguing. While the rivals had asserted their claim to an English identity through the promise to pursue honor beyond the confines of their country, Richard exercises his authority by forcing them to do what they had earlier volunteered to, though no longer in the name of honor. In Mowbray's case, however, banishment means being stripped of his national identity, an identity constituted by language: "The language I have learnt these forty years, / My native English, now I must forgo . . ." (1.3.159–60); Richard's sentence he describes as "speechless death, / Which robs my tongue from breathing native breath" (172–73). What I want to focus on, though, is Richard's role in this.

Richard asserts his authority as king by attempting to regulate the behavior of Mowbray and Bolingbroke once they pass *beyond* English borders. Richard makes each swear that "You never shall, so help you truth and God, / Embrace each other's love in banishment, / Nor never look upon each other's face, / Nor never write, regreet, nor reconcile / This louring tempest of your home-bred hate . . ." (183–87). Of course they swear in the name not of Richard but of "truth and God," but they do so by laying their hands on Richard's "royal sword" (179); it is to the king they finally make their oaths. At the same time they are set up in explicit opposition to both king and country as they are made to promise not to act "'Gainst [Richard,] our state, our subjects, or our land" (190). It is of course a Tudor commonplace to conflate the interests of king, state, subjects, and land, but *Richard II* dismantles this commonplace. The play makes clear that the interests of the nation and its subjects are not identical with those of the king; it suggests that different conceptions of nationhood are held by different persons. As we noted above, Bolingbroke disobeys Richard in the name of *his* rights and royalties. "I am a subject," he insists, "And I challenge law" (2.3.132–33).

The relationship between the physical limits of the nation, English identity, and the limits of Richard's authority is played out geographically through Richard's disastrous relations with Ireland. It is while Richard is in Ireland that Bolingbroke returns to claim his "rights and royalties." Moreover, Richard's fight against the Irish is understood by the play as reflecting his unawareness of the proper limits of his power and his kingdom. As York says to the queen, "Your husband, he is gone to save far off, / Whilst others come to make him lose at home" (2.2.80–81). We might understand Richard's journey "to save far off" in light of England's conflicting impulses toward Ireland. As Michael Neill puts it, "while the ideology of national difference required that the Irish be kept at a distance and stigmatized as a barbaric Other, the practicalities of

English policy more and more pressingly required that Ireland be absorbed within the boundaries of the nation-state."[48] This absorption was to be effected in part through the process of surveying and regularizing Irish land:

The energetic English insistence on surveying, mapping, and shiring, and on reducing wilderness to the ordered topography of gardens, orchards, parks, ploughlands, and townlands had its obvious practical value, but it functioned equally powerfully as a symbolic translation of the colonized landscape—an Englishing of Ireland . . .[49]

This "Englishing" was in part an attempt to eradicate that which was customarily Irish. It was largely a failure, though, and, as Ann Rosalind Jones and Peter Stallybrass have shown, Ireland was commonly associated with bogs and woods, the Irish with nomads and barbarians: land and people resistant to the surveying and ordering gaze of the English.[50] Richard's failed mission to Ireland evokes the futile English attempt "to save far off" by incorporating Ireland into England, to turn that "wilderness" into one of the lands "survey'd by English eye."

Richard returns from "far off" and states, "I weep for joy / To stand upon my kingdom once again" (3.2.4–5); "weeping, smiling, greet I thee, my earth . . ." (10). He commands "[his] gentle earth" to resist his foes, to "Throw death upon thy sovereign's enemies" (12, 22). However, the portion of his kingdom upon which Richard has landed is Wales, and two scenes earlier the Welsh captain, believing Richard's absence to indicate his death, informs the earl of Salisbury that the Welsh soldiers supposed to aid Richard will "disperse [them]selves" (2.4.4). The Welsh captain in no way interrogates Richard's authority, but his reasons for disbanding the army foreground both Wales's separateness from and its incorporation into England, a topic I take up in some detail in the next chapter. In fifteen lines of text the captain refers once to "our country," twice to "our countrymen"; most significantly he says that "The bay-trees in our country are all wither'd, / And meteors fright the fixed stars of heaven . . . These signs forerun the death or fall of kings" (8–15). The natural upheaval that presages Richard's fall certainly suggests that Wales and England might be conflated under the rubric of Richard's kingdom, but at the same time Wales is established as a country with its own identity and imperatives: it is only "in our country" that "meteors fright the fixed stars." Richard collapses England and Wales into one another—both are understood in terms of "[his] gentle earth"—but his doing so has been rendered ironic by both the departure of the Welsh forces and this (admittedly sketchy) delineation of the imperatives of a Wales separate from England. Such a delineation is of course a statement of the obvious—after all, Wales *is* a different country from England—but the point is that Richard forgets the obvious in his rhapsodic account of "his" earth. Moreover, Richard's mystification of the land stands in stark contrast to his earlier decision to "farm our royal realm" (1.4.45), to "leas[e] out [the kingdom] . . . / Like to a tenement or pelting farm" (2.1.59–60),[51] and at the same time such mystification goes hand in hand with the exploitation of the land's resources and inhabitants: both suggest a landscape of sovereignty, and both entail at most the effacement of customary and regional difference, or at least the failure to attend fully to them.

Arguably Richard's contradictory constructions of his realm as sacred land and farmed-out kingdom are both map-enabled. The mystification of nation and land evokes John of Gaunt's cartographically inspired, idealized vision of the country, while, as discussed in relation to *Woodstock*, the effective farming out of the kingdom depends upon the way in which map and survey reduce it to "plots" of land. In Richard's formulation of his gentle earth, his kingdom is imbued with the same kind of mystified potency as is John of Gaunt's "royal throne of kings." However, while we have discussed John of Gaunt's speech as a locus of identification crucial to the creation of an "imagined community," Richard's appropriation of Gaunt's rhetoric is in the service of a landscape of sovereignty. His account speaks to the power of "England," but a power that is for Richard inseparable from his rule: "This earth shall have a feeling, and these stones / Prove armed soldiers ere her native king / Shall falter under foul rebellion's arms" (3.2.24–26). Of course neither earth nor stones offer any resistance, and the vision of land and kingdom that the play finally endorses is the famous one of Richard's England as an untended garden (3.4). The garden image is in implicit opposition to that of the kingdom as pelting farm; it is a carefully maintained and cultivated space, a model for proper landownership. At the same time, it clearly echoes and seems to accept the terms of Gaunt's description of England. One of the gardener's servants asks,

> Why should we, in the compass of a pale,
> Keep law and form and due proportion,
> Showing, as in a model, our firm estate,
> When our sea-walled garden, the whole land,
> Is full of weeds, her fairest flowers chok'd up,
> Her fruit-trees all unprun'd, her hedges ruin'd,
> Her knots disordered, and her wholesome herbs
> Swarming with caterpillars?   (3.4.40–47)

The garden, which keeps "law and form and due proportion," is offered as a model for the nation, "our sea-walled garden." However, as we have seen, neither nation nor kingdom is a sea-walled garden. Moreover, while that metaphor may suggest the nation as organic space, the description of the garden foregrounds both the processes of enclosure required to demarcate boundaries—the references to pale and hedges suggest enclosed spaces—and the labor necessary to keep them up.[52] If the state is a garden, this speech suggests, its political boundaries are not natural, but need to be constructed and maintained, much as county boundaries were in Saxton's survey.

Upon his banishment, Bolingbroke says farewell to "England's ground": "sweet soil, adieu, / My mother and my nurse that bears me yet! . . . Though banish'd, yet a true-born Englishman" (1.3.306–9). The soil "bears [him] yet": Bolingbroke's English identity emerges out of a relationship to the land, which is described as both mother and nurse, as both birthing and nurturing him. This suggests a landscape of imagined community; England is presumably not only Bolingbroke's mother but that of all Englishmen, and the appeal to the "sweet soil" potentially overrides the authority of the king by generating a national identity not dependent upon him. Bolingbroke insists that, even beyond English eyes, he will remain an Englishman, and, as we have said, it is in the name of his rights as "true born" that he returns. Moreover, his return involves a reconceptualization of both land and nation. As Richard puts it in the same scene in which he appeals to his gentle earth, Bolingbroke "Measure[s] our confines with . . . peaceful [i.e., unhindered] steps" (3.2.125). This line evokes the Rogationtide ceremonies discussed earlier in this book. As we have seen, Rogationtide ceremonies work to understand the land within the context of a particular set of social relations; Bolingbroke's passage through the country involves not only the drumming up of support for his cause, but also a reworking of the meaning of land and nation.[53] However, while Rogationtide ceremonies construe the land in terms of customary practice, Bolingbroke finally acts in the name of his own authority; he generates his own landscape of sovereignty. Measuring Richard's confines is Bolingbroke's first step toward making the nation his, a step taken in the name of a "true-born" Englishness nurtured by the very soil he treads. While Bolingbroke claims to act in the name of his rights as subject and as a representative of the people, the landscape of imagined community implied by his trek (and by his reference to English soil as his and his nation's mother) masks his own ambition. Moreover, Bolingbroke's actions culminate in the deposition of the king. While

Bolingbroke measures the nation in his footsteps, Richard's deposition erases for a time his identity: "Think that I am unking'd by
Bolingbroke, / And straight am nothing" (5.5.37–38). In death,
however, Richard reasserts both his kingliness and his claim on the
land: "Exton, thy fierce hand / Hath with the king's blood stain'd
the king's own land" (109–10, my emphasis). This assertion is
poignant and ironic, for it both echoes the hubris of Richard's
claim to his gentle earth and unwittingly underscores that "the
king's own land" is now Bolingbroke's.

Of course in significant ways the land is even less Bolingbroke's
than it was Richard's. While Richard mishandles the duel between
Mowbray and Bolingbroke, suggesting his failure to understand the
limits of his authority, Henry IV's rule is crippled by the near-
comic proliferation of challenges offered among his nobles. "These
differences shall all rest under gage" (4.1.86), Henry decides, but
they do not rest there; instead, they blossom into the Wars of the
Roses, wars in which occur, as the Bishop of Carlisle predicts, "the
woefullest division ... / That ever fell upon this cursed earth"
(146–47). Richard's gentle earth is to be cursed, the country to be
divided not cartographically but by civil strife—strife that will re-
shape the nation. Moreover, the blessed plot is less in evidence than
is the plotting of Henry's overthrow:

> *Aumerle:*   You holy clergymen, is there no plot
>   To rid the realm of this pernicious blot?
> *Abbot:*   My lord, . . . I will lay
>   A plot shall show us all a merry day. (324–34)

While John of Gaunt's "blessed plot" evokes a merry England both
long past and yet cartographically generated, it is the plotting of the
conspirators that now supposedly offers hope for England's restoration. Of course, such plotting really leads only to further division.

Through its visual representation of the country, the map allows its reader to behold England, and that very act of beholding opens up possibilities for interpretation that are both enabling and undermining. If, as Richard Helgerson has argued, the map makes possible certain forms of national identification, it also enables other readings that have important material effects. Richard's failure is in part caused by his understanding of his kingdom both as a mystified space imbued with his authority and as an aggregation of plots to be farmed out. This failure mimics particular effects of the map: it engenders a false but powerfully enabling organicism, a homogeneous nation that the reader can "behold" (both look at and hold by), and simultaneously it, along with the survey, makes possible the mismanagement of land and resources, the transformation of the nation into a pelting farm.[54] While the map purports to offer a transparent view of the land it represents, both its opacity and its peculiar efficacy are explored in a play in which the limits of the monarch's authority are as uncertain as are the geographic boundaries of the "blessed plot" over which he rules. The map aids Richard in the construction of a landscape of sovereignty, and that landscape is finally revealed to be both incoherent and exploitative.

There is another possible reading of the relationship between nation as mystified organic entity and as pelting farm: one can imagine Richard's deployment of the first notion as a political strategy designed to mask the second. In this view, Richard consciously cultivates the kind of vision of nationhood offered by John of Gaunt, crucially molding that vision to insist on his own centrality to it. Thus Richard's "feeling earth," the physical landscape so imbued with his authority that its stones will act as his soldiers, functions as both an adumbration of John of Gaunt's rhetoric and a mystification of Richard's more utilitarian relationship to the land, both of which are, as we have seen, enabled by maps. If this is so, then we encounter a Richard shrewder than *Woodstock*'s, for that Richard declines to cloak his actions in a justifying rhetoric, and the nationalism he offers is only that of the exploitative landlord.

A more important difference between the two plays has to do with *Woodstock*'s conception of the map, however. In that play, the map is crucial to the creation of a conception of the nation as exploitable resource. *Richard II* offers us something in addition to that, a vision of the nation as *Gesellschaft*, as an abstraction that is nonetheless the locus for powerful forms of identification. However, Richard's efforts to yoke that abstraction to his authority are undone by Bolingbroke, who, as we have seen, presents his own enabling (if finally disingenuous) image of the power of the soil in shaping his identity. The abstraction is open to appropriation; Richard is not the only one who can claim a mystified relationship to the land. Thus, even as *Richard II* reveals John of Gaunt's image of England as a geographically confused one, the confusion of which is mirrored in Richard's misrecognition of the scope and limits of his authority, the play also attests to the potency of the mystifications that image promulgates. Nationhood, the play suggests, is both an incoherence, an abstraction that lives in uneasy relationship to the geography of Britain, and a powerful idea open to appropriation and strategic or sincere deployment (or both at once). While the nation can take the form of a landscape of absolute property or of sovereignty, it is not summed up by them, much as the map is not summed up as either a tool for the king's abuse of his subjects or a vehicle for the creation of an imagined community. Nevertheless, while maps can be read in multiple ways, ways dictated not only by their semiotic multiplicity but also by the different purposes to which they are put, their status as authoritative, "scientific" documents means that the specific landscapes they engender can make truth claims that belie the maps' interpretive instability. Moreover, although the national landscapes discussed in *1 Henry IV*, *King Lear*, and *Richard II* are distinct, the three plays have this in common: while critiquing the creation of landscapes of sovereignty, they simultaneously efface the customary life of particular regions.[55] John of Gaunt's articulation of England may, as in the above discussion of *Gesellschaft*, "reinforce [a] sense of membership to the group and the development of a sense of distinctiveness," but the communities imagined in these plays do not leave room for, say, the interpretive community we encountered last chapter in the Dunstable marketplace. In this regard, both the map and Shakespeare's landscapes of nationhood hold out, in Bacon's phrase, "a dream of our own imagination for a pattern of the world." And in that dream the imperatives of the political nation efface the regional landscapes of custom as surely as Hotspur's redirected river would submerge the villages that once rested on its banks.

Where All Roads Lead

LAND, TRAVEL, AND IDENTITY

CHAPTER FOUR

Civilizing Wales

'CYMBELINE,' ROADS, AND THE LANDSCAPES
OF EARLY MODERN BRITAIN

In this chapter I will show how Shakespeare's *Cymbeline* gestures toward the disjunct, if not always conflicting, imperatives of different (conceptual, historical, and national) landscapes. In order to do so, however, I must begin rather far afield, with seemingly simple questions posed by Imogen upon her discovery that her exiled husband Posthumus purportedly awaits her at Milford Haven. Of Pisanio Imogen eagerly asks "How far 'tis thither. If one of mean affairs / May plod it in a week, why may not I / Glide thither in a day?"[1] A few lines later, Imogen echoes her earlier utterance: "how far it is / To this same blessed Milford. And by th' way / Tell me how Wales was made so happy as / T' inherit such a haven" (3.2.59–62). And again, shortly thereafter: "How many score of miles may we well rid [i.e., cover] / 'Twixt hour, and hour?" (68–69). These utterances may seem at first glance identical, but they differ in subtle ways. The first question asks about mileage (how far is it . . .) then links it to rapidity of passage (. . . for one who glides rather than plods), thus registering distance in terms both of miles and, more emphatically, elapsed time. The second statement concerns geographical distance, while the third focuses on the hourly rate of travel Imogen will be able to maintain. Imogen is collecting information necessary to plot her journey: if I travel x miles at an hourly rate of y, then . . . However, only the last of these simple questions is answered; Pisanio says that "One score 'twixt sun and sun, / Madam's enough for you" (69–70), but Imogen vigorously disagrees, stating that "one that rode to's execution . . . / Could never go so slow" (71–72). Pisanio's answer is unsatisfactory to her, and both the distance and Imogen's rate of travel remain unknown. The effect of Imogen's questioning is to suggest the contingency of travel: thanks to her evocation of different travelers and rates of travel, of the variable relationship between distance covered and time elapsed, after her questioning we seem farther away from knowing "how far" Milford Haven is than we did at first.

While contingency is suggested, Imogen's journey is also reduced to two variables: her rate of travel, understood as a constant, and the distance to be covered. What is missing from her calculations is a description of the nature of the terrain to be traversed—a journey over hills obviously necessitates a rate of travel different from that maintained over plains. Reducing the journey to the equation that she does means that Imogen figures the landscape as a frictionless surface to be passed over at a constant rate. Arguably Imogen's questioning represents a witty bit of metatheater. We know that in one sense she could as effortlessly pass from Lud's Town (or London) to Milford Haven as she (or he, the boy actor) crosses the flat stage; Imogen's concern with how to get from one to the other can be seen as laughable in the context of Shakespearean romance, with its easy and fantastic negotiation of far-flung places.[2] However, this only makes the difficulty that Imogen has in locating Milford Haven all the more striking; while that difficulty could be chalked up to the exigencies of plot—for instance, by getting lost she meets Belarius, Guiderius, and Arviragus—more can be made out of the frustration of Imogen's journey. Her questions are eminently practical ones, and it is at the level of their practicality that I will first take them up, with the understanding that, as is always the case, the practical is inseparable from the ideological. Moreover, it is from an analysis of the seemingly prosaic problem of how to get from point A to point B that I will turn to *Cymbeline*'s investigation of the relationship between disparate national landscapes, a relationship articulated in terms of relations between England and Wales in the pre-Roman, Roman, and Tudor-Stuart periods.

IN 1625, JOHN NORDEN produced a text that a traveler could turn to in order to find the distance between points A and B. While Norden is not the first to present information regarding the distance between towns—for principal thoroughfares, such information was a staple of almanacs and calendars from at least the early sixteenth century—*England. An Intended Gvyde for English Travailers* not only includes more complete information than ever before but also provides for the first time tables that allow the reader to determine the distance between a number of possible starting and end points. Unlike in the almanacs, distances are not arranged along the axis of the highways; *England* focuses primarily but not exclusively on the mileage between towns in any given county. While Norden is certainly cognizant of the groundbreaking nature of what he calls his "new inuention," he is also keenly aware of the possibility that he will be criticized because "some errours of necessitie will be committed . . ." The reason for these errors? The most immediate one is the interference of "hills, dales, woods, and other impediments, which intercept the view from station to station. So that the lines of opposition cannot be so exactly directed, as upon a plaine and open horizon." What is important to notice here is the kind of measurement privileged by Norden: miles are measured as the crow flies, not as the wayfarer walks. For Norden, the distance actually covered by the traveler is a corruption of his true measurements: "But were the distances neuer so truly taken, by the intersection of right lines, yet in riding or going, they may seem vncertaine, by reason of the curuing crookednes, and other difficulties of the wayes."[3] The crookedness of the roads, the difficulties of the ways: these are not the conditions governing accurate measurement, but impediments to its actualization. While for Imogen the land's terrain appears only indirectly (through her inquiries about the time it would take to get to Milford Haven), Norden understands it as a force in one sense resistant, and in another irrelevant, to his measurements.

The resistance of the land to measurement, its reluctance to resolve itself always into "a plaine and open horizon," is particularly telling in the case of Wales. Next to the table representing "the distances of the most of the chiefe towns in Wales," Norden writes:

It is to be considered that by reason of the multitude of Hilles, Mountaines and Dales, and the bending of the Sea, betweene *St. Dauids* and the point neere *Bradsey* Iland, causing passages and highwayes in many places so to curue and crooke, that the distances betweene the Townes, may be something differing from this Table: But not so, but that good vse may be made of it.[4]

This passage is somewhat equivocal. It is torn between articulating the above viewpoint—the curved and crooked highways again suggest the terrain's deviation from its own "accurate" measurement— and foregrounding the utility of the table, which would seem to depend upon its conforming to a traveler's experience of the landscape. However, what is clear is that Wales poses a potent problem for Norden's text; after the proliferation in this passage of impediments to proper measurement, the final assertion of the table's "good vse" as a traveler's aid seems timid and unconvincing. In addition, while Wales itself is difficult to measure, so is the passage from England: "by reason of the Seuerne, that diuides *Wales* [from] *Cornewall, Somerset,* &c. . . . the distances betweene the Townes of either side, cannot be precisely set downe, for that there is great difference, between the land trauaile[d], and passages by water . . ."[5] Even entry into Wales defies easy and accurate measurement.

Were Wales composed only of "plaine and open horizons," there would still be a crucial disjunction between Norden's measurements and the miles covered by a traveler, a disjunction that emerged out of the unit of measurement itself. It was only in 1593 that the mile was standardized, importantly in a statute whose aim was to prohibit new building in London's suburbs (35 Elizabeth I c 6 1592/3). However, the statute mile was only "adopted gradually throughout the kingdom, the adoption being nearly complete by the end of the eighteenth century, but only becoming of universal application through the all-encompassing Act of 1824 (5 George IV c 74)."[6] As the purpose of Elizabeth's statute suggests, the immediate locus of relevance for this standardized mile was London; throughout the rest of the kingdom customary miles held sway. Such customary miles are usually understood as evidence of prescientific imprecision, as archaic units of measure that needed to be abandoned in the name of greater rationalization. This viewpoint is recorded in J. B. Harley's discussion of John Ogilby's landmark road atlas, *Britannia* (1675), one achievement of which was to survey roads, via a perambulator, in statute miles. As Harley puts it, "The statute mile of 1760 yards . . . was adopted only in parts of London and its environs, so that in Ogilby's day 'Vulgar Computations' [i.e., customary miles], as he termed them, with 'Erroneous and Irregular Consequences,' were still widely employed, and were predominantly longer than the statute mile measured by [Ogilby's] perambulator."[7] Ogilby's language attests to the disdain in which customary miles were held, but it is worth noting that these "vulgar computations" were still enough of a fact of life in 1675 that *Britannia* included them side by side with Ogilby's "dimensurations," his "accurate," perambulated measurements. (Ogilby also listed "horizontal distance," the distance as a crow flies, "from station to station.") Thus, while he dismisses customary miles as erroneous and irregular, Ogilby must still take them into account. With that in mind, it is worth taking seriously their status as customary, a status that situates regional measures in terms of customs that, as we have seen in earlier chapters, help articulate local conceptions of landscape. The customary mile attests to the ir-reducibility of the region, the incommensurability of its landscape with other landscapes. While the statute mile seeks to make the mea-sure of London the measure of all England and Wales, the custom-ary mile insists on its own and its region's specificity.

Ogilby, then, can be understood in part as a promoter of the stat-ute mile, and such promotion necessitates the denigration of custom in the name of a rationalized and uniform landscape. Moreover, in Norden's case such a landscape reveals a conception of measurement divorced from the exigencies of travel—as we have seen, the crooked or difficult highway is not a condition of but an impediment to "ac-curate" measurement. This formulation bespeaks several conceptual assumptions of the early modern period—a neoplatonic emphasis on form or ideal rather than the "accidents" of the material; the privi-leging of geometric or mathematical over experiential knowledge—but the one I want to emphasize here is perhaps the most counterin-tuitive. Norden and Ogilby's texts, both of which are understood as traveler's aids, function primarily as compendia of knowledge that exist in an uncertain relationship to the topography they describe. That is, each text has a value that exists independently of its status as a "traveler's aid." This is clearer perhaps in the case of Ogilby, whose *Britannia* was part of a much larger project designed "to cover the entire world" through a series of volumes devoted to Africa, America, Asia, Europe, and Britain, each volume comprised of travel accounts, engravings, and maps.[8] Moreover, the atlas of strip maps was sup-posed to be only one part of a multivolume *Britannia* that would also include travelers' accounts and "The Description of the British Monarchy."[9] Given this broader purpose, one can see how the accu-racy of Ogilby's survey of the roads has a value and ambition that ex-ceeds that of a traveler's aid; it is part of a larger empiricist project to collect and catalogue information, the immediate utility[10] of which is, in the case of the strip maps, arguably less significant than is the encyclopedic impulse motivating the project.[11]

While Norden's text is not the outgrowth of such an elaborate and ambitious endeavor, we have already seen that his tables are suited more to an abstract idea of the land than they are to actual topographies. When Norden imagines others censuring him for *England*'s inaccuracies, he suggests that they will do so because his text does not betray evidence of "deepe *Diuinitie*, high *Astrologie*, or intricate *Geometrie*," that it is instead "so vulgar, and so plaine, that euery *Eye*, may see it, euery *Minde* may conceiue it, & euery *Tongue* may censure it."[12] However, through his tables Norden works to supplant the evidence of individual eyes with the rules of geometry—to ground his measurement not in perambulations but in the view from station to station, hilltop to hilltop. It is geometrical knowledge that he obtains, and when his miles do not match those covered by a traveler, the problem lies in the land and its failure to conform to mathematical abstraction. Norden's tables exist less to provide the traveler with a precise sense of how far s/he has to go, a difficult enough task given the question of how to accommodate regional and statute miles, than to testify to the power of a surveyor to produce and display knowledge that is understood as having value in its own right. In this sense, the "good use" that can be made of *England* exceeds its status as a traveler's aid.

BY NOW WE SHOULD have a sense of how difficult it would be in the seventeenth century to produce satisfactory answers to Imogen's questions.[13] However, that difficulty is less important than the way in which travel, landscape, and the production of knowledge are construed in these two seventeenth-century "traveler's aids." Ogilby's and Norden's texts reveal the problematic rift between what we might (somewhat imprecisely) call a perspective on and an experience of the land,[14] a rift that conforms to Michel de Certeau's distinction between a panoramic view and a set of practices "that are foreign to the 'geometrical' or 'geographical' space of visual, panoptic, or theoretical constructions."[15] De Certeau's emphasis is on the relationship between the rationalized spatial order of the modern city, which is easily reconciled with the imperatives of the panoramic view, and the resistance of everyday practice to that order, but his insight is instructive here, especially given the conceptual centrality of the visual to knowledge production in the early modern period.[16] Moreover, de Certeau's opposition can be fruitfully yoked to our discussion of custom and landscape, both of which can be construed in terms of practice. In Ogilby, the customary mile is registered only as vulgar and inaccurate, while in Norden topography functions as impediment. For each the road is "the 'geometrical' or 'geographical' space of visual, panoptic, or theoretical constructions," and to each one might oppose a notion of the road as an integral part of a customary landscape defined by practices that exceed or evade panoramic scrutiny.[17]

De Certeau understands the panoramic view as existing at the expense of practice: "The panorama-city is a 'theoretical' (that is, visual) simulacrum . . . whose condition of possibility is an oblivion and a misunderstanding of practices. The voyeur-god created by this fiction . . . must disentangle himself from the murky intertwining daily behaviors and make himself alien to them."[18] Crucially, the panoramic view presupposes a subject position, albeit a false or alienating one, that is divorced from practice and from the customary. The "oblivion" of this position, its alienated singleness, is implicitly contrasted with the identity that emerges out of "murky *intertwining* daily behaviors," an identity predicated not only on practice but on intersubjectivity. And yet, a panoramic view offers something important to its viewer: it locates him or her in space and in clear relation to the landscape s/he views. Practice, emerging out of a murky intersubjectivity, is not the antithesis of this—it too presupposes a social location, albeit a shifting and regularly renegotiated one—but it is more complicated. A landscape of custom, understood in terms of both intersubjectivity and the collective negotiations inherent in custom, constitutes a theory of location and identity that exists as and at the nexus of practice and topography. On the other hand, the panoramic view, like the survey, brings the land into knowledge in a way that fails to coincide with, and threatens to commit (an at least conceptual) violence against, the landscape of custom and practice.[19] At the same time, it offers an identity that presupposes the visual mastery of the land—not lived landscape but a panorama.

I will consider Imogen's journey in light of de Certeau's analysis, but first I want to talk in greater detail about Milford Haven itself. The significance of Milford Haven has been largely neglected in criticism of the play; when it has been discussed, scholars have followed Emrys Jones in seeing the meaning of the place as summed up in its associations with Henry Tudor's triumphal arrival into England and the monarchy via Milford Haven.[20] This viewpoint is confirmed by reference to Michael Drayton's chorographical description of Milford Haven in *Poly-Olbion* (1612),[21] and to John Speed's 1676 map of invasions of England and Ireland "with al their Ciuill Wars Since the Conquest," on which the harbor is identified as where "Henry Earl of Richmond at milford hauen ariuet against R. 3 in august 1485."[22] William Camden talks of it as a haven

[like] which there is not another in all Europe more noble or safer, such variety it hath of nouked bayes, and so many coues and creeks, for harbour of ships, wherewith the bankes are on every side indented. . . . Neither is this haven famous for the secure safenesse therof more, than for the arrivall therein of King Henrie the Seventh a Prince of most happy memory, who from hence gave forth unto England then hopelesse the first signall to hope well, and raise it selfe up, when as now it had long languished in civill miseries and domisticall calamities within it selfe.[23]

Camden reads Henry's landing as the catalyst necessary for England to "raise it selfe up"; it is an end to England's languishing illness, its miseries and calamities. Speed's map, however, suggests an alternative: while it innocuously enough refers to Henry's "arrival," the map is one of civil wars and armed incursions. The potentially equivocal nature of Henry's landing is made clear by the context within which it appears; it is from one perspective a triumphal entry, from another an invasion. This equivocality is suggestive when considering Camden's description of Milford Haven itself. This safe and noble haven, replete with "coues and creeks, for harbour of ships," offers sanctuary as easily to invaders as it does to natives. It is this accessibility that worries many period accounts of Milford Haven and its significance.

Sixteenth- and seventeenth-century government officials thought about Milford Haven less as the site of Henry Tudor's historic arrival than as a potential point of penetration into England by Spanish invaders. This is made clear by a letter that on November 1, 1595, the earl of Pembroke, Lord Lieutenant of Wales, wrote to the Welsh cartographer George Owen:

My Good Cousin, I have long expected to have received from you a map of Milford Haven. There is now great occasion to use it and therefore . . . I most earnestly desire you with all possible speed to send it . . . I pray you be very careful to make your scale perfect for thereby shall I be able to know the true distance of places . . . First take truly the breadth of the entrance of the haven. Secondly the distances of one place to be fortified from another. Thirdly what place every fortification may annoy. Forget not to note in how many places you shall conceive fortifications to be needful and set down everything you shall think in this case meet to be considered of and provided for. . . . Your plots shall be shown to Her Majesty for as I know you can better any that I have yet seen, so shall Her Majesty know both what you can do and what you will do.[24]

Owen completed his map shortly thereafter, thus providing Elizabeth and her court with the dimensions, clearly yoked to the specific needs of defense, of Camden's safest of all European havens—here the land is measured (in customary miles?) not to aid but in the hopes of hindering "travelers," invaders of England. However, fears regarding such an invasion of Milford Haven did not subside with the production of this map; in 1759 one writer still spoke of Milford Haven as "the most convenient and natural landing-place in all Great-Britain for a descent or invasion with a few troops," an opinion evidenced by the "history of Henry earl of Richmond, who, by means of a small army brought into this harbour, made himself master of the crown of England. . . ."[25] The significance of Henry's actions was not lost on Guy Fawkes, who as late as 1603, two years before the exposure of the Gunpowder Plot, traveled to Spain to attempt to convince King Philip to land an invasionary force at Milford Haven.[26] In that same year, rumors circulated that supporters of the Main Plot, a Catholic scheme to seize control of the government and, if he did not accede to their demands, replace James with Arabella Stuart, had "captured Milford and were awaiting the arrival of Spanish soldiers."[27] The capturing of Milford had broad implications, as George Owen understood:

. . . the havon yt selfe . . . is a sufficient harborowe for an infinite number of shippes, which havon being once gotten by the Enymye may drawe on such fortification at Penbroke towne and castle . . . as infinite numbers of men, and greate expence of treasure will hardly in a long tyme remove the Enymye, during w[hi]ch tyme her Ma[jes]tie shall loose a fertyle Countrey . . .[28]

Moreover, once in possession of Milford that enemy "may make along [the river] Seaverne in both sydes even to Bristowe . . . And if he (w[hi]ch god forbidd) should enjoy Britayne withall, our English Marchantes can have noe trade, which will decrease her highenes Customes, and decaye the Navye . . ."[29] In short, Milford Haven, in which there were "many places where [an enemy] may easyly lande,"[30] signified not only as the celebrated point of entry for Henry Tudor, but also as a locus of national vulnerability.

LET US RETURN to Imogen. The scene in which she talks to Pisanio about the distance to Milford Haven ends with Imogen insisting that her present time and location "have a fog in them," and that "Accessible is none but Milford way" (3.2.80–83). Despite the supposed accessibility of the "way"—the word can refer both to her itinerary and to a specific road—she does not exactly glide either to Milford Haven or to her rendezvous with Posthumus. Instead, somewhere near Milford Haven she learns of Posthumus's murderous designs, and Pisanio suggests she seek out Lucius, who is to meet the Roman troops at the harbor. However, she gets lost, and this after a view of the area: "Milford," Imogen states, "When from the mountain-top Pisanio show'd thee, / Thou was within a ken [i.e., in view]" (3.6.4–6). On the ground, however, Milford is not locatable, even though "Two beggars told me / I could not miss my way" (8–9). Consider the two kinds of assistance Imogen is offered: a panoramic view, in which she can precisely, if finally not usefully, locate herself in distant relation to the land she plans to traverse; and directions that situate her in terms of the landscape in which she finds herself. However, her "way," perhaps both physical path and personal itinerary, brings her not to Milford Haven but to the cave of Belarius, Arviragus, and Guiderius. Viewed panoramically, Milford Haven is apprehendable, but from the ground it becomes elusive. When the Roman army finds her, she seems to be both at and away from Milford Haven. The Romans name it as their location (4.2.335), but Imogen is outside the cave, a place earlier clearly designated as distinct from Milford Haven (3.7.30–31). Moreover, it is a location that is at one point identified by Imogen as other than Milford. She awakens from her drugged sleep as if in midconversation and says: "Yes sir, to Milford-Haven, which is the way? / I thank you: by yond bush? pray, how far thither? / 'Ods pittikins: can it be six mile yet?" (4.2.291–93). Psychic and geographic disorientation are inseparable here, and they are oddly underscored by the ensuing misrecognition: she takes Cloten's headless trunk for Posthumus's—this in spite of her earlier insistence on the complete incommensurability of the two (e.g., 2.3.123–35). For Imogen, Milford Haven is both unlocatable and a site of dislocation, a place that not only is hard to get to, but is also marked by the confusion of identity and allegiances.[31]

I have focused on Milford Haven and the problems of location: locating it, locating oneself in relation to it. The historical accounts of the harbor that I adduce above suggest that Milford Haven functioned in the English cultural imagination as the site of either triumphal entry or martial invasion—in either case, as a point of disembarkation and a way into England. That is, Milford Haven was understood as a focal point for anxieties about or the celebration of military incursions. However, in dwelling on Milford Haven and on *Cymbeline* as a text that engages with the harbor's historical, geographical, and cultural specificity, I have not attended to the country of which it is a part. It is my contention that Milford Haven can also stand in for all of Wales, and that the play concerns itself with the position of Wales in relation to English culture.[32] Moreover, to understand why Milford Haven would be difficult to locate, we need to consider its status as a part of the Welsh landscape. As we have seen, it is the Welsh landscape in particular that defies measurement. This is true in the narrow sense of Norden's tables and in a larger conceptual sense, for Wales figures for early modern England as that which is both familiar and strange, both a part of (and a way into) England and an alien land on the other side of the Severn.

Later I will take up the play's conception of Anglo-Welsh relations in the Roman period; for now my focus will be on the sixteenth and seventeenth centuries, a time characterized by the placid integration of the English and Welsh political nations. This integration has led critics to assume that the two countries are broadly indistinguishable in this period, an assumption that has also led to the nearly total effacement of Wales from discussions of the play.

While Leah Marcus stands as a partial exception to this trend, her comments on England and Wales in the play are instructive in light of my argument: "In the Britain of *Cymbeline*, unlike the Britain of James I, Wales, or Cambria, is a separate country. The Roman ambassador to the court of Cymbeline is escorted only as far as its border at the river Severn; British law is not applicable beyond that point."[33] Marcus's contention that in the logic of the play Wales is a separate country is a shrewd one that, as will become clear, this chapter partly endorses. Its separateness also requires that we see that Britain really refers to England, that the court of Cymbeline is seen as an English one. However, her assertion that Wales is not separate in James's time is problematic insofar as this view requires seeing Wales's administrative and political integration into Britain as the only index of its status as country. My argument is that in cultural and, if we believe Norden, geographic terms, Wales often either maintains its separateness or has its separateness forced upon it.[34] At the same time, that separateness does not obtain at every level, even within the world of *Cymbeline*. On the one hand, Wales is a country distinct from a Britain suggestive of England; on the other, it is where "British" battles against Roman troops take place. Thus, within the logic of the play Wales is simultaneously other than, and conceptually annexed by, Britain.

For many of the Welsh people, cultural separatism did not register as antithetical to allegiance to Britain. Historians agree that during the period following Henry VIII's Acts of Union between England and Wales (1536, 1543) most members of the Welsh gentry simultaneously held feelings of Welsh nationalism and of fervent loyalty to the Tudor and Stuart governments into which they were administratively integrated.[35] These feelings were initially made possible by the strong connections between the Tudors and the Welsh. Many Welsh understood Henry VII as a figure who would restore Wales to its former greatness, that of the ancient Britons; Henry himself even went so far as to promise that he would release the Welsh from "such miserable servitude as they have piteously long stood in,"[36] a reference to the fact that, after Saxon invasions and Norman Conquest, the Britons who had once ruled the entire island were driven to Wales and Cornwall. Later, ties between the Welsh gentry and the courts of Elizabeth and James had developed to such a degree that even early in Elizabeth's reign Humfrey Lhuyd noted that "you shall finde but few noble men in England, but that the greater parte of their retinew (wherin Englishmen exceede al other nations) are welsh men borne."[37] That Owen produced his map for the earl of Pembroke, Lord Lieutenant of Wales, who planned to share the map with the queen, attests to the interconnections between court and Welsh gentry. These interconnections were ideologically underwritten by "the belief that the Stuart as well as the Tudor royal dynasty was derived from a common British stock, a source of pride for the Welsh *uchelwr* class [i.e., the nobility active in administrative services at home and court] so closely attached to a new concept of British citizenship."[38]

I will return to this notion of a common British stock in my discussion of *Cymbeline*'s Roman context; for now it is only necessary to note that Welsh assimilation into English political life was not always greeted with unadulterated enthusiasm. Consider the equivocality of Lhuyd's account of the effects of the Acts of Union, an account that immediately precedes his comment regarding the predominance of the Welsh in noble English households:

[Henry VIII] deliuered [the Welsh] wholy from all seruitude, and made them in all poynets equall to the Englishmen. Wherby it commeth to passe, that laying aside their old manners, they, who before were wonte to liue most sparingly: are now enritched and do imitate the Englishmen in diet, & apparell, howbeit, they be somedeale impatient of labour, and ouermuch boastying of the Nobilitie of their stocke, applying them selues rather to the seruice of noble men, then geuynge them selues to the learnyng of handycraftes.[39]

This supposed deliverance from servitude leads in Lhuyd's account to the transformation of the Welsh character, a transformation that takes place because the Welsh are now free to act in ways apparently detrimental to themselves. This transformation might more precisely be called an assimilation, for the Welsh both abandon their traditional labors and become indistinguishable in diet and apparel from the English. Their "boastying of the Nobilitie of their stocke" seems to suggest less their commonality with the English through shared British roots than their indistinguishability from them. For Lhuyd, it is this uneasy sameness to the English that marks, for worse more than better, the Welsh gentleman.

What many, perhaps most, members of the Welsh political nation seemed to desire was both political integration and cultural independence, as is borne out by the case of William Salesbury, who could both applaud that after the Acts of Union "there shall hereafter be no difference in laws and language" and worry that the Welsh language, often called British, would become "full of corrupt speech and well-nigh completely lost."[40] Lhuyd suggests, however, that *British* citizenship, the supposed return to an integrated British culture, largely means the adoption of an *English* identity. More broadly, Lhuyd betrays a suspicion about the social and political ends of the reunification of Britain—that it is finally in the service of the cultural annexation of Wales by England. I would argue that this fear is borne out in slightly different form in *Cymbeline*, a play in which the political nation of pre-Roman Britain is figured only as English. (I am speaking anachronistically, of course; the world of the play predates both the division and the reunification of England and Wales. And yet, the play's obvious topicalities and its own adducement of a divided Britain—we began this chapter with Imogen referring to a Wales so happy as to have Milford Haven in it—forces us to examine its articulation of early Stuart Anglo-Welsh relations.) We can see confirmation of this fear by considering that, with the possible exception of the two beggars who give Imogen directions, there are no Welsh in the play. More pointedly, Wales is occupied by invaders or court figures in temporary exile and/or disguise: Pisanio, Imogen, Cloten, Posthumus, Belarius, Arviragus, and Guiderius. These last three, attired as rude mountain men who defeat the invading Romans with the aid of (the also disguised) Posthumus, are as close as we get, but they, of course, are finally and fully reintegrated into the world of the court from which they came. As it happens, by play's end Wales is vacated, and the cultural centrality of the court is reaffirmed. Moreover, we have seen that this "British" court is by and large an "English" one. While Lhuyd worries about the Welsh becoming English, Shakespeare suggests that Wales is a geographical site across which English cultural struggles take place. Thus, both Milford Haven and Wales are landscapes across which English concerns of invasion and identity are articulated. Wales is constituted here in terms of a landscape of sovereignty, characterized as it is by its conceptual annexation into England.

But if for Shakespeare Milford Haven signifies as point of access to England, and if Wales is the site of English cultural struggles, then what specifically can we say about these two places? Above I follow de Certeau in drawing a distinction between panorama and practice, between viewed and customary landscapes. My argument suggests that in this play Wales is like the object of de Certeau's panoramic view insofar as it presents us with a landscape divorced from the imperatives of custom and practice. Intriguingly, Imogen's panoramic view of the landscape is not the only one in the Wales section of the play; it is mirrored by the view to be offered Guiderius and Arviragus from atop a mountain. Belarius frames that view as follows:

> Now for our mountain sport, up to yond hill!
> Your legs are young: I'll tread these flats. Consider,
> When you above perceive me like a crow,
> That it is place which lessens and sets off,

> And you may then revolve what tales I have told you
> Of courts, of princes; of the tricks in war.
> This service is not service, so being done,
> But being so allow'd. To apprehend thus,
> Draws us a profit from all things we see:
> And often, to our comfort, shall we find
> The sharded beetle in a safer hold
> Than is the full-wing'd eagle. O, this life
> Is nobler than attending for a check:
> Richer than doing nothing for a robe,
> Prouder than rustling in unpaid-for silk.   (3.3.10–24)

As described here, this panorama offers Guiderius and Arviragus both a view of a landscape peopled only by the man they believe to be their father, who because of his distance from them appears to be a bird, and an opportunity for reflection on life at court, understood here as existing in explicit opposition not only to the lives they lead but to the landscape they inhabit. While the opposition between rural purity and courtly corruption is hardly a startling one in Shakespeare,[41] what is important here is that the Welsh landscape is figured only as the vehicle and opportunity for an object lesson about the court that Belarius has fled; the profit the two boys are to draw "from all they see" will supposedly drive home that lesson.[42] This assumption about the landscape finds its analogue at the beginning of the scene, in Belarius's following lines:

> A goodly day not to keep house with such
> Whose roof's as low as ours! Stoop, boys: this gate
> Instructs you how t'adore the heavens; and bows you
> To a morning's holy office. The gates of monarchs
> Are arch'd so high that giants may jet through
> And keep their impious turbans on, without
> Good morrow to the sun.   (1–7)

Belarius refers first to the fact that they have left their low-roofed cave; that they stoop in exiting from it reminds Belarius of stooping in prayer, and the roof of the cave suggests to him the roof of the heavens. However, the heavens are then compared with a king's arched gates—even in the act of performing "a morning's holy office" Belarius evokes the court. While his aim is presumably to suggest the hubris of kings who aspire to produce gates as lofty as the sky above, it remains that the court structures Belarius's apprehension of his wilderness environment.

Unsurprisingly, the court also structures both Guiderius's and Arviragus's desires and their sense of the landscape, as is made clear in Guiderius's complaint to Belarius that

> Haply this life is best
> (If quiet life be best) sweeter to you
> That have a sharper known, well corresponding
> With your stiff age; but unto us it is
> A cell of ignorance, travelling a-bed,
> A prison, or a debtor that not dares
> To stride a limit. (29–35)

While in the preceding passage the roof of the cave suggested that of the heavens, here it is yoked by Guiderius to his sense of his restricted life, which is compared to a cell and a prison, the site of only imaginary travel ("travelling a-bed"). Implicitly in opposition to this is experience of the court, as is revealed by Belarius when he reflects that the princes, unaware of their true identities, "[from within] th' cave wherein they bow, [think] thoughts [that] do hit / The roofs of palaces . . ." (83–84). In this complex conflation of the images we examined above, Belarius metaphorically renders indistinguishable cave, court, and heavens; the cave within which they bow suggests both their aristocratic origins and the homage paid beneath the roof of the heavens. However, the brothers' thoughts lead them only to "the roofs of palaces"—the landscape of either cave or countryside unwittingly brings them back to that of the court. Of course these scenes work to suggest the inevitability and naturalness of Guiderius's and Belarius's royal identities. However, it is worth noting that Wales is both where those identities have been shrouded (and admittedly where they will be most spectacularly enacted, in the battle against the Romans), and the obstacle that must be cleared in order for them to become princes again.

"It is place which lessens and sets off": Belarius's statement tells us that it is location, the place from which one apprehends one's environment, that either diminishes or enhances what one sees. Intriguingly, in these scenes it is the conceptual proximity of the court that is always made plain, reducing the Welsh landscape to the stage across which the drama of a distant kingship is performed. Those who inhabit that landscape—again, there are no Welshmen, only disguised and exiled courtiers—nonetheless finally exist in relation to it in a way exemplified by the panorama's imposition of a false order on what is apprehended visually. For them, the landscape is brought into knowledge and representation in terms of the cultural centrality of the court. However, while de Certeau's account of the panorama understands it as existing in opposition to practice, *Cymbeline* offers us no customary world to which the panorama can do a violence. All we have is a shadow Wales that exists to promote the cultural centrality of London and the court. Moreover, we should be able to see by now the affinities in this play between the panorama and the landscape of sovereignty: the viewed landscape that takes shape in accordance with the imperatives of the court makes clear the conceptual and cultural annexation of Wales, its subsumption into British (or English) monarchical culture. However, that does not mean that we need not consider the specificity of Shakespeare's inclusion of Wales—this shadow Wales reinforces and enacts Lhuyd's fears about England's conception of Britishness, that it involves not the confirmation but the eradication of a distinctive Welsh identity.

OVER THE LAST few pages I have stressed the conceptual integration of Wales into England, an integration that takes place at the expense of Welsh identity. And yet, earlier in this chapter I emphasized the cultural and geographic incommensurabilty of Wales and England. This seeming contradiction is crucial to Anglo-Welsh relations. For whereas one strain of English thinking about Wales downplayed the differences between the two cultures, even subsumed them in a notion of Britishness, another figured the Welsh as difficult to assimilate, much as Norden found their land difficult to measure. This paradoxical relationship is instantiated in the very name of Wales, as Lhuyd makes clear:

Cambria, called Wales . . . wee in our mother tongue doo terme *Cymbri.* This . . . the Englishmen, after the fashion, and maner of the Germans [i.e., the Germanic tribes that invaded Britain]: haue called Wallia, that is Wales. For when the auncient Almaines had sometime ioynyng next unto them of Forreyners, the Frenchmen, whom they called Walli: it came to passe, that afterwarde they called all straungers, and those whiche dwelt in other prouinces: Walli, and Wallisei. . . . & al thinges that come foorth of strange countries: *Walshe.*[43]

The name of Wales inscribes the perceived alienness of that country's inhabitants, an alienness that exists side by side with its opposite, the sense of Wales as familiar, as assimilable into narratives of Britishness.[44] As Glanmor Williams puts it in describing the Welsh who came to England, "[They] seemed to their English hosts to be readily recognizable: the closest and most familiar of foreigners, and also the most distant and outlandish of provincials."[45] Williams's pithy articulation of Anglo-Welsh relations precisely isolates the problem of Wales and the Welsh for England: is it a foreign country or a distant province? Are they familiar outsiders to England or strange co-inhabitants of Britain?

What I have suggested so far is that *Cymbeline* is true to the paradox embedded in the first of the above two questions: it annexes the Welsh landscape for the purpose of staging a drama focusing on the fate of a throne seen as English, while it also reads that landscape as alien, as resistant to integration into English schemes of measurement. Moreover, as the example of Ireland in this period makes clear, the measurement of alien lands is a necessary precondition for their colonization, and yet the inscrutability of the Irish landscape, linked to that of the Irish themselves, constituted an impediment to England's imperial ambitions.[46] While the position of Wales vis-à-vis England is obviously not easily made analogous to that of Ireland, the political significance of measurement obtains in both situations. The extension throughout Wales of the statute mile, a standard whose inauguration is linked literally to the expansion of London into the surrounding countryside, would mark the conceptual and symbolic integration of Welsh territory into England. In neither Norden nor Shakespeare is that integration fully achieved, just as it was not in fact. In his discussion of different measures, Holinshed declines to say much of "the olde Brytishe myle," asserting that there is

not greatly néede to make any discourse of it, & so much the lesse, sith it is yet in use and not forgott[en] among the Welch men, as Leland hath noted in his commentaries of Bryteine: wherfor it may suffice to haue saide thus much of the same, and so of all the rest, beyng mindfull to goe forwarde and make an ende of this treatise.[47]

Like Ogilby with his "vulgar computations," Holinshed registers a different form of measurement, in this case one explicitly linked with Wales, only to assert its marginality: there is no great need "to make any discourse of it." At the same time, this need is not felt partly because the standard is still customary, still in use "among the Welch men." This simultaneous inclusion and exclusion of a customary mile used by the Welsh marks the end of Holinshed's section on measurement, eager as he is to "make an ende of this treatise." The haste with which Holinshed passes from a mile not worth discussing to the end of his treatise betrays the position of Wales in his chronicle. Wales is both present and absent, discussed here and elsewhere but not granted a space or a section of its own in Holinshed's *Chronicles of England, Scotlande, and Irelande.*[48]

We have seen that Wales is both symbolically incorporated into and displaced from the Anglocentric world of Shakespeare's *Cymbeline*. However, to talk of early modern Wales is to focus on only half of the story, given that the play also concerns itself with the prehistory of England and Wales—that is, the period of struggle between the ancient Britons and the invading Romans. It is my contention that the play simultaneously draws upon discourses governing contemporary Anglo-Welsh relations and takes up the history of Roman Britain in order to shape an early modern fantasy of a completely integrated British landscape, one that incorporates not simply Wales but also Scotland. The play looks both backward and forward to two united kingdoms, the former of which is unified by, among other things, roads.

WE SAW IN MY earlier discussion of John of Gaunt's "royal throne of kings" speech the way in which the rhetoric of nationalism both emerges out of and is complicated by a cartographically enabled image of England as an island. A similar speech occurs in *Cymbeline*, but with quite different implications. As part of a successful effort to convince Cymbeline to resist Roman demands for tribute, the Queen speaks of

> The natural bravery of your isle, which stands
> As Neptune's park, ribb'd and pal'd in
> With rocks unscaleable and roaring waters,
> With sands that will not bear your enemies' boats,
> But suck them up to th' topmast. (3.1.19–23)

With a hubris belied by the vulnerability of Milford Haven, which is soon to be occupied by "the legions garrison'd in Gallia" (4.2.333), the Queen speaks of the invulnerability of this island. Whereas John of Gaunt's patriotic rhetoric required collapsing Wales and Scotland into England, the Queen is referring to the reign of the ancient Britons, which was of course to end with the Roman occupation. Jodi Mikalachki has identified what is most striking about this speech, that the language of patriotism is be-smirched by its association with the evil Queen, and that the play's happy ending involves "A Roman, and a British ensign wav[ing] / Friendly together" (5.5.480–81).[49] Thus the rhetoric of ancient Brit-ish patriotism, which is importantly associated with resistance to the Romans, is denigrated.[50] Moreover, we have seen that rhetorics such as this one provided a crucial framework for the integration of the early modern Welsh into a revivified British culture. What does it mean, then, that the strongest nationalist language that the play proffers is associated with societal disruption and the malign intel-ligence of *Cymbeline*'s unnamed queen?[51]

To answer this question, we might think about the role of the Romans in this text. Readers who have been nurtured on a steady diet of Shakespearean English history plays are often puzzled by not only the play's denigration of the Queen's nationalism but also its simultaneous endorsement of the Roman occupation. However, just as in this period Milford Haven registered as both a site vul-nerable to invasion and a staging ground for Tudor triumphs, the appearance of the Romans could be read as either catastrophe or boon; when seen as the latter, British chauvinism such as the Queen's can signify provincial resistance to "the civilizing process." Consider William Camden's account of the Roman influence on the ancient Britons:

This yoke of the Romanes although it were grievous, yet comfortable it proved and a saving health unto them: for . . . the brightnesse of that most glorious Empire, chased away all savage barbarisme from the Britans minds, like as from other nations whom it had subdued. . . . For . . . the Romanes, having brought over Colonies hither, and reduced the naturall inhabitants of the Iland unto the society of civill life, by training them up in the liberall Arts, and by sending them into Gaule for to learne perfectly the lawes of the Romanes . . . [who] governed them with their lawes, and framed them to good maners and behaviour so, as in their diet and apparell they were not inferior to any other provinces.[52]

While Lhuyd is uncertain about the impact on the Welsh of their adopting the diet and apparel of the English, for Camden the Britons are civilized thanks to the transformations enforced upon them by the Romans.[53] Significantly, the civilizing process is implicitly linked to, among other things, the Roman construction of roads, a topic addressed immediately following this account of the remaking of the Britons. From among the many Roman works, Camden mentions "the Picts wall" and then passes on to

those Causeies [i.e., causeways] . . . [which were] a wonderfull peece of worke, what with dreining and drying up the meres in some places, and what with casting up banks where low vallies were, in others: so fensed and paved with stone, and withall of that breadth, that they can well receive and with roome enough, waines [i.e., wagons] meeting one the other.[54]

Camden continues his discussion of the alteration of the topography of ancient Britain by quoting from Galen, who states that

Trajanus repaired, by paving with stone, or raising with banks cast up such peeces of them as were moist and miry; . . . where the way seemed longer than needed, by cutting out another shorter: if any where by reason by some steepe hill, the passage were hard and uneasie, by turning it aside thorow easier places: now in case it were haunted with wild beasts, or lay wast and desert, by drawing it from thence thorow places inhabited, and withall, by laying levell all uneven and rugged grounds.[55]

As the Romans civilized the Britons, so did they tame the ancient British landscape, altering the topography of the land in a way similar in spirit to the principle underlying Norden's measurements: both turn the crooked into straight, the Romans literally and Norden figuratively through his adherence to geometric absolutes.

For the Romans, roads were an essential prerequisite for military control and imperial expansion; they "fulfilled the most essential requirement of a military commander—mobility of men and supplies . . ."[56] These roads also linked disparate regions in Britain, again through the alteration of the topographical landscape: "It was one of the most outstanding contributions of Rome in Britain that she broke through the successive belts of forest with her new main roads, and for the first time knit together the various habitable belts in one unified transport network, which for the most part radiated from London."[57] We should remind ourselves that such a "unified transport network" is hardly politically neutral. The Romans understood only too well that roads were crucial to the creation and management of a colonized nation: roads served to connect and bring disparate tribes and regions under military control, just as Roman efforts to "civilize" the Britons worked to bring them under ideological control.

An area where the Romans met resistance to their efforts was ancient Wales. Both this resistance and Roman efforts to combat it are registered in the roads, as David Johnston makes clear:

Look at the road pattern west of the Foss Way [one of four major Roman highways] into Wales and you will see that it looks incomplete. . . . On the whole it is because—for geographical as well as political reasons—the initial military penetration was not followed up by the civilian development which produced so complex a pattern elsewhere. The political picture is one of Celtic [i.e., ancient British] tribes which refused to give in. After 50 years or so of military resistance they could be said, as far as the government in Rome was concerned, to have been 'conquered'. However, they had sheltered the British prince, Caratacus, as a refugee, their resistance had occupied much of the time of several governors in succession, and they had even succeeded in causing the death of one through sheer exhaustion. They never fully accepted all that was offered to them as 'Romanisation' . . .[58]

While the incomplete expansion of a road system into Wales indicates the extent of native resistance, the roads that were built were central to local military responses to this resistance. Frequently the ancient British would evade the Romans by sequestering themselves in the hills. In order to prevent groups of resisters from making contact with one another, the Romans cordoned off the hills by building roads in the valleys below and constructing forts no more than a day's march apart from one another. Roads were built to facilitate the movement of the Romans while restricting that of those who rejected their authority.[59] The hills, so frequently linked in the popular imagination with Wales and the Welsh,[60] were loci of resistance, encircled but not traversed by those agents of Romanization, the roads.

WHAT WE HAVE SEEN is that the Roman conquest of ancient Britain involved the "civilizing" of both native peoples and the landscape. Despite these efforts, however, much of Wales successfully resisted assimilation into the Roman empire. At first glance it may seem that this resistance is evoked in *Cymbeline* through the actions of the cave dwellers Belarius, Arviragus, and Guiderius, who by blocking Roman passage through "a strait lane" (5.3.7) inspire Cymbeline's soldiers to victory. However, just as the three men are not really Welsh, so their heroic actions point to a conception of armed resistance that distances them from those who rejected Romanization by taking to and fighting from the hills. Belarius at one point recommends that the three of them "[travel] higher to the mountains, [and] there secure us" (4.4.8). This plan is articulated in opposition to a sentiment expressed by Guiderius, whose views finally dictate the men's actions: "Nay," he says,

> what hope
> Have we in hiding us? This way [i.e., if we hide], the
>   Romans
> Must or for Britons slay us or receive us
> For barbarous and unnatural revolts
> During their use, and slay us after. (3–7)

Guiderius assumes an opposition between Britons who stand up against the Roman invasion and "unnatural revolts," or rebels. This opposition leaves unanswered an important question: against whom would these "revolts" be rebelling—the Romans who would "slay [them] after," or the Britons to whom they are here negatively compared? That is to say, if they are to act as either rebels or British, then their rebellion would situate them in opposition to the British as well as the Romans. This ambiguity is telling, suggesting as it does a conceptual alliance between noble, martial Britons and the Romans, two groups worthy of fighting one another.[61] In terms of this schema, the rebels, who are most suggestive of the resistant Welsh, are displaced from the ranks of the valorous. Moreover, Belarius, Arviragus, and Guiderius also distance themselves from them by eagerly entering the fray. The way they finally follow leads them not to the mountains, implicitly repudiated as home to barbarous rebels, but to a narrow lane.[62]

This narrow lane receives a surprising amount of attention in the play, and it becomes an integral part of the narrative of the heroism of Belarius, Arviragus, and Guiderius: "This was a strange chance," a lord says, "A narrow lane, an old man, and two boys" (5.3.51–52); Posthumus incorporates the lane into a rhyme: "Two boys, an old man twice a boy, a lane, / Preserv'd the Britons, was the Romans' bane" (57–58). While Posthumus's rhyme is shaped in bitter repudiation of the lord's idle wonder at these heroic exploits, its terms are significant. The lane is an agent in the rhyme's narrative, as it along with the old man and two boys exists as a bane to the invaders. Moreover, the strait lane, "ditch'd, and wall'd with turf" (14), is emphatically not a paved Roman road. Its centrality to this narrative of ancient British valor indicates the land itself here resists the civilizing process of Romanization, the subduing of both the landscape and its inhabitants.

And yet, it is important to remember one of the play's central paradoxes, that those who reveal their heroism by fighting the Romans end up among their allies and tributaries. The actions of the "old man, and two boys" serve not to secure their (and the culture's) dominance over the Romans, but only to reveal their intrinsic meritoriousness; that is, what matters is not the defeat of the Romans but the display of valor, which reveals them as worthy both of the court and of the Romans. In one sense, then, the play greets the arrival of the Romans as warmly as Camden did. Traffic throughout the play between the world of the Romans and that of the Britons reveals that the two cultures are more integrated than oppositional. Consider that Imogen, disguised as Fidele and at Pisanio's suggestion, for a time serves a Roman master; or that Posthumus travels among the Roman soldiers as a member of "th' Italian gentry" (5.1.18), then disguises himself as a British peasant, and finally lets himself be taken captive as a Roman. Posthumus's case is suggestive. While he deploys the language of patriotism and fights in the name of Britain, a country from which he has been exiled, no stigma attaches to his involvement with the Romans. Similarly, Imogen's actions seem most suspect not when she serves a Roman master, but when she shows indifference to his fate at a time when she might better it—as she starkly puts it to Lucius upon being granted the power to pardon one prisoner, "your life, good master, / Must shuffle for itself" (5.5.104–5). Only here, and temporarily (see 404–5), do we see a disjunction in the identity of "Fidele," who has up until now been able to serve two masters, one Briton and one Roman. In short, the final alliance between the two nations has been anticipated by an easy exchange between their cultures that has been evident as early as Posthumus's journey to

Rome.[63] Even when Posthumus is exiled, there is little sense in the play that he journeys to the alien world of his country's enemy. Instead, he reenters a social milieu familiar to him from previous travels. Rome here seems a site for cosmopolitan exchange.

Of course, Iachimo poses a problem, as he stands in stark moral contrast to other Romans such as Lucius. Leah Marcus explains that contrast by asserting that "Shakespeare ingeniously (albeit anachronistically) separates two levels of Roman influence in the play—that of the ancient Rome of Caesar Augustus, associated with the ideals of James I . . . and that of the Renaissance Rome of the degenerate Italians, associated rather with perversion, bawdry, and amorality."[64] I would only add that by play's end the latter Rome, in the person of Iachimo, has been reformed out of existence; his repentance is sincere, preceding even his revelation of wrongdoing at the end, and his status as commander of Roman troops unites him with "the ancient Rome of Caesar Augustus." The Rome we finally encounter is a uniformly positive one.

What *Cymbeline* overtly celebrates is the equality of Rome and Britain, made manifest in the aforementioned image of "A Roman, and a British ensign wav[ing] / Friendly together" (5.5.480–81).[65] However, the play also anticipates Romanization as eagerly as Camden endorses it. On the simplest level, this is implicit in the play's narrative, representing as it does the beginning of the period of Rome's successful invasion.[66] Less obviously, the play is invested in repudiating ancient British culture, represented in all its (imagined) patriotic provincialism by the Queen and Cloten, and embracing the civilizing influence of Rome.[67] The latter is hardly surprising given the significant role Rome played in the early modern cultural imagination,[68] as is made clear in Camden's account of Roman influence. However, I want us to think of Rome's influence on the landscape. In looking forward to Roman rule, *Cymbeline* also looks forward to the civilizing of both the culture and the landscape.

In celebrating the advent of Roman rule, *Cymbeline* also gestures toward a fantasy of national unification facilitated by road building. Roman roads were believed to link, physically and culturally, Wales and England (to speak anachronistically) through the creation of a shared landscape. Of course the Welsh landscape posed a problem to the Romans analogous to the one it posed to Norden, but Camden's conception of the Romans nevertheless attests to their perceived power as providers of a common civilization and a shared landscape. *Cymbeline* presents a very different picture; Milford Haven and Wales are alternately (or even concurrently) alien and unnavigable, sites of penetration, and screens across which the "[t]wo boys [and] an old man twice a boy" can both play out their desires and anxieties about the court and perform the actions that allow them to return to it. However, it is among other things the indeterminacy of this landscape that Rome hopes to civilize out of existence by subsuming Wales into its empire. In that regard, Rome is analogous to Lhuyd's England, engaged in cultural annexation in the name of unity.

It is worth noting that at the time of *Cymbeline*'s production the rhetoric of cultural unification was particularly resonant, suggesting as it did James's cherished scheme of unifying the kingdoms.[69] What has not been widely recognized is the significance of Wales to this scheme, a significance very clear to James himself. As James said to members of his first parliament, "Do you not gain from the union with Wales and is not Scotland greater than Wales?"[70] Thus Wales is both precursor to and model for a Scotland integrated into England. Moreover, as Jonathan Goldberg has shown, the example and analogue of Rome was crucial to both James's thinking about and his strategies of rule.[71] Given this, *Cymbeline*'s interest in a landscape and culture civilized by Rome inevitably echoes James's ambitions for a united kingdom (or, perhaps, a unified and homogenized landscape of sovereignty). However, while both James and *Cymbeline* may optimistically look forward to such a kingdom, Shakespeare's play also reveals the problematic nature of the enterprise. While on one level Wales exists only as that which is to be subsumed or civilized, its landscape and culture are alternately indistinguishable from and incompatible with those of England.[72] Roman roads offer the hope of a united (and conquered) Britain, but in the end the play only gives us the narrow path, the folkloric stature of which resists easy integration into the culture of the colonizers. In sum, Wales is arguably as unassimilable to Rome as it was to Norden's measurement.

I WANT TO CONCLUDE with a brief account of the fate of Roman roads in the early modern period. As is widely known, long before the sixteenth century most of these roads had degenerated, a fact that clearly and obviously marked the decay centuries earlier of Rome's imperial ambitions. Consider Camden's dispirited description of the fate of many of these roads: "But now adaies these of ours [i.e., Roman roads in Britain], being dismembred, as it were and cut one peece from another in some places, by reason that the countrey people digge out gravell from thence, are scarcely to be seene."[73] This is a vivid testament to the strategic and local uses of the raw materials (specifically gravel) previously employed for the expansion of the long-since fallen Roman empire. For Camden, the roads that once ran throughout the land have been "dismembred" by seventeenth-century Britons. Camden's dismay aside, this brief example provides a powerful metaphor for cultural appropriation, for the crafting of a postcolonial identity out of the raw materials of colonial authority. What I want to emphasize, though, is that what Camden sees as destructive is a crucial part of the construction of a landscape, one built out of, but radically different from, the Roman roads. While "the Roman roads may suggest in all their fabled straightness the "'geometrical' or 'geographical' space of visual, panoptic, or theoretical constructions," their dismemberment fifteen centuries later makes legible the power of "murky intertwining daily behaviors"—the power, that is, of practice and custom, and of the landscapes from which they are finally inseparable.

CHAPTER FIVE

Knowing One's Place

THE HIGHWAY, THE ESTATE,
AND 'A JOVIAL CREW'

From the cannibalization of Roman roads, I turn now to the relationship between estate and highway, a relationship connected in complex ways to early modern vagabondage. On the eve of the civil war, Richard Brome's *A Jovial Crew* presented audiences not only with a comic fantasy of vagabond life, but also an idealized image of estate management. Oldrents is "a great housekeeper" who is "pray'd for by all the poor in the country,"[1] and his steward, Springlove, equals him in charity. Indeed, Oldrents's estate functions as the primary source of hospitality in the play, and, at least in the beginning, it is also the model of an efficiently managed estate. Springlove's first appearance is marked by his presentation to his master of a written account of the condition of his estate:

> You may then be pleas'd
> To take here a survey of all your rents
> Receiv'd, and all such other payments as
> Came to my hands since my last audit, for
> Cattle, wool, corn, all fruits of husbandry.
> Then my receipts on bonds, and some new leases,
> With some old debts, and almost desperate ones,
> As well from country cavaliers as courtiers.
> Then here, sir, are my several disbursements
> In all particulars for yourself and daughters,
> In charge of housekeeping, buildings and repairs;

Journeys, apparel, coaches, gifts, and all
Expenses for your personal necessaries.
Here, servants' wages, liveries, and cures.
Here for supplies of horses, hawks and hounds.
And lastly, not the least to be remember'd,
Your large benevolences to the poor. (1.1.122–38)

Oldrents's charity is placed in the larger context of Springlove's exemplary management of the household and properties. Springlove's surveying pun is particularly intriguing in this light; "a survey of all your rents" involves not the remeasuring or revaluing of Oldrents's lands, but simply the landlord's scrutiny of the work performed and information collected by his steward. Just as John Norden's manorial landlord "sitting in his chayre, may see what he hath, where and how it lyeth, and in whose use and occupation euery particular is upon the suddaine view,"[2] Oldrents's "survey" of his steward's work provides him with all he needs to know about the management of his property. In this case, however, it is his steward's accounting of payments, debts, and expenses and not a written survey and map of his lands that provides Oldrents with that information. While in Norden the survey mediates between lord and land, in *A Jovial Crew* it is the steward Springlove who occupies that position.

Of course Springlove's status as "steward" marks him as hired manager of the affairs of Oldrents's estate; I will speak further of this kind of stewardship below. It will become clear, though, that the broader sense of the term, which suggests moral stewardship, is appropriate here. And yet, Springlove is also associated with surveyors and surveying. When Springlove leaves the estate to join the vagabonds, he tells Randall, who temporarily replaces him as steward, that he has gone on "a journey to survey and measure lands abroad about the countries" (2.2.57–58) with the aim of purchasing them for Oldrents.[3] Upon hearing this, Oldrents replies, "I know his measuring of land. He is gone his old way" (60). "His old way":

the phrase suggests not only old patterns of behavior, but a well-worn route, a way Springlove has traveled before. Oldrents knows that that "way" involves his "measuring" land not as a surveyor, but as a vagabond, one known as, in the words of one of Brome's beggars, a "stroll-all-the-land-over" (1.1.451–52)—intriguingly, the well-worn way, a single path, is associated with aimless wandering. Moreover, the surveyor's purposive measurement of the land should be contrasted with the directionless "strolling" of the vagabond. As Randall puts it, beggars "cannot give account from whence they came or whither they would; nor of any beginning they ever had, or any end they seek, but still to stroll and beg till their bellies be full, and then sleep till they be hungry" (282–86).

The wandering of the vagabond contrasts not only with the surveyor's purposive measuring of the land, but also with the aristocratic progress with its itinerary of pleasures. When Oldrents's daughters express their restlessness to their suitors, Vincent says, "Shall we project a journey for you? . . . [W]e would fain be abroad upon some progress with you. Shall we make a fling to London, and see how the spring appears there in the Spring Garden; and in Hyde Park, to see the races, horse and foot[?]" (2.1.69–75). Whereas spring inspires in Oldrents's steward the desire to stroll aimlessly, for Vincent it suggests a progress that includes a pleasure trip to Spring Garden. This plan is rejected by Rachel and Meriel in favor of a "begging progress" (158), about which I will say more later, but the crucial point is that Springlove's stroll is contrasted with the aristocratic journey. This opposition is articulated by Oldrents himself, who tries unsuccessfully to convince Springlove to turn his wandering into a version of Vincent's progress:

> . . . if to take
> Diversity of air be such a solace,
> Travel the kingdom over; and if this
> Yield not variety enough, try further,
> Provided your deportment be gentle.

> Take horse, and man, and money; you have all,
> Or I'll allow enough. (1.1.214–20)

Travel is acceptable, but only with "horse, and man, and money," the trappings of a gentleman on his "progress."

Oldrents's resistance to Springlove's vagabond desires also leads him to wonder about the difference between the lands Springlove manages and those across which he longs to roam:

> Does not the sun as comfortably shine
> Upon my gardens as the opener fields?
> Or on my fields, as others far remote?
> Are not my walks and greens as delectable
> As the highways and commons? Are the shades
> Of sycamore and bowers of eglantine
> Less pleasing than of bramble or thorn hedges?
> Or of my groves and thickets, than wild woods?
> Are not my fountain waters fresher than
> The troubled streams, where every beast does drink?
> Do not the birds sing here as sweet and lively
> As any other where? (189–200)

Oldrents contrasts gardens and open fields, greens and commons, sycamore and bramble, groves and wild woods: the manicured lands of his demesne with the common or unkempt land beyond it. In each of these cases, the first element in the comparison signifies exclusivity and order, while the second is a common space defined either by its uncultivated nature (bramble, wild woods) or its general accessibility (open fields, commons). Even his fresh fountain waters are compared with "troubled streams, where every beast does drink." Most important for my purposes, however, is the comparison between walks and highways, between Oldrents's paths and the main roads that link up estates (as well as towns and villages). Just as both surveying and aristocratic travel are set in opposition to beggarly wandering, paths are contrasted to highways, the spaces of the demesne to "opener fields" and commons. As Oldrents's commentary makes clear, these interlocking comparisons are not only descriptive—they do not simply classify spaces according to size or type—but also evaluative. These evaluations work to shore up notions of aristocratic identity that are entangled in conceptions of the land. Groves and gardens are the sites of aristocratic pleasure—it is to Spring Garden that Vincent hopes to lead his love—and they also suggest the exclusivity of land on the demesne. At the same time, aristocratic identity manifests itself also in modes of travel; if Springlove must leave the estate and its walks, Oldrents is willing to accept his journey "[p]rovided [his] deportment be gentle."

What precisely is meant by Springlove's passing from the paths of the estate to the highway? This chapter sets out to answer that question by elucidating the relationship between travel, land, and identity. Brome's play seems to suggest that while vagabond identity both dissolves in and is constituted by aimless wandering—vagabonds are those who "cannot give account from whence they came or whither they would; nor of any beginning they ever had, or any end they seek"—aristocratic identity emerges out of and is indissoluble from the land. However, the play imagines the dissolution of that identity, a dissolution understood in terms of travel. In order to show this, I must first talk of the highway in order to suggest the way in which it was set in opposition to the estate. I will then contrast the life of the vagabond, one who lives "on the road," to that of tenant or landlord. By doing so, I aim to show that traditional conceptions of identity predicated upon notions of estate as place and highway as placeless are both thrown into question and reaffirmed through Brome's theatrical exploration of life on the estate and on the road, an exploration that finally champions a landscape of stewardship. Through this analysis we will also catch a glimpse of the ideological struggles attendant upon the emergence in embryonic form of private property and the subjectivity it implies—of, that is, a landscape of absolute property.

It has been argued that in seventeenth-century England "place is identity." James Turner asserts that "'Land' and 'place' are equivalent to 'propriety'—meaning in seventeenth-century English both *property* and *knowing one's place*."⁴ The organic estate of the country-house poem, in which an idealized conception of social relations across all ranks is represented, functions as an emblem of this conception of propriety—one need only think of Jonson's "To Penshurst" to see the way in which identity seemingly emerges out of hierarchized social relations centered on the land. On the other hand, the highway registers in a completely different fashion. For the seventeenth century, the idea of the highway was overdetermined in a way that it is not for us today. The early modern period inherited and modified "[t]he ancient image that interprets man's life as a pilgrimage [in which] the road fork[s] in two ways, one being the straight and narrow path, the *via recta*, beset with hardships and obstacles but leading to the Heavenly City, and the other the broad highway of many temptations."⁵ (Perhaps Oldrents's opposition of paths and highways owes something to this distinction.) While this trope was sometimes directly deployed, as in Bunyan's *Pilgrim's Progress* (Pt. 1, 1678), it is also adapted in the sixteenth and seventeenth centuries. James McPeek has examined the way in which the highway, site of temptation, is transformed first in rogue literature and then in dramatic texts into a space populated by vagabonds and knaves. Thus, the highway is still associated with sin, but the nature of its sinfullness shifts. Of course this shift primarily reveals a different conceptual use for the highway—from an allegorical image dramatizing the temptations besetting a lone Christian, it becomes a social space populated with rogues and vagabonds—but the crucial point is that the negative associations registered in the ancient image still resonate in early modern portrayals of those who live on the road.

Roads "are assumed to be alien, violent places; people who inhabit them are thus doubly vile."⁶ Henry Tubbe scathingly refers to

Cromwellians as "Shifting Vagabonds, that make the Earth their Thorough-faire & their Home too."[7] Tubbe's attack only fully makes sense when we understand that he sees the use of the earth as both home and thoroughfare as profoundly unnatural; home and highway are opposites wrongfully collapsed into one another by Cromwellians. At the same time, Tubbe's comment suggests that "shifting vagabonds" upset the traditional distinction between home and highway. While one might say that on the estate place and identity are mutually constituting, the road is understood as both placeless and "home" to those who have no identity.

Beatrice and Sidney Webb intriguingly describe the early modern highway and its differences from its twentieth-century counterpart. I quote at length:

To the citizen of to-day, the "King's Highway" appears as an endless strip of land, with definite boundaries, permanently and exclusively appropriated to the purpose of passage, with a surface specially prepared for its peculiar function. To the citizen of the twelfth, the fifteenth, or even the eighteenth century, the King's Highway was a more abstract conception. It was not a strip of land, or any corporeal thing, but a legal and customary right—as the lawyers said, "a perpetual *right of passage* in the sovereign, for himself and his subjects, over another's land." . . . What existed, in fact, was not a road, but what we might almost term an easement—a right of way, enjoyed by the public at large from village to village, along a certain customary course, which, if much frequented, became a beaten track. But the judges held that it was "the good passage" that constituted the highway, and not only "the beaten track," so that if the beaten track became (as it inevitably did in wet weather) "foundrous" the king's subjects might diverge from it, in their right of passage, even to the extent of "going upon the corn." Of this liberty . . . the riders and pedestrians of the time made full use. . . . [E]ven fences were not respected. As late as 1610 we read . . . [in Thomas Proctor's *A Profitable Work to This Whole Kingdom Concerning the Mending of All the Highways*] of "great hurt and spoil of fences and grounds, with riding and going over the corn and such like, by shifting and seeking the best way diversely."[8]

Accounts of passage across property are in fact produced much later than 1610. Virginia LaMar reports a wet night's journey in 1667 in which "a guide . . . led the party through enclosed land, breaking down hedges as they went."[9] Similarly, in 1694 George Meriton states that "the highways . . . were grown so foundrous . . . that the owners and occupiers of land have been necessitated to suffer their fences to lie down and to permit people to travel over their enclosed grounds."[10] In these accounts, either bad weather or "shifting and seeking the best way" (if not both) can lead to the transformation of even enclosed property into road; the highway is less a determinate space than a right of passage.

Of course, as the Webbs suggest, certain "beaten paths" did take on the status of highways; occasionally they existed on the ruins of the once-splendid Roman roads, although the exigencies of trade and village growth often led to the formation of highways that branched off from or crossed the Roman roads in order to connect various communities.[11] Nevertheless, the crucial point is that the highway as physical space exists in a shifting relationship to the highway as right of passage; the latter can include even enclosed ground. At the same time, the physical space proved to be both exceedingly mutable and a site of contestation. We see this most clearly in the ongoing struggles over highway maintenance, struggles that reveal tensions in period conceptions of landed property.

It became clear during the Tudor period that the degeneration of the road system posed serious problems for the further development of internal trade. Consequently, in 1555 the first Highway Act was passed under Mary, and it is this act that establishes the terms for road maintenance until late into the seventeenth century.[12] Simply put, the Highway Act called for the following:

The Highway Act put the responsibility for maintaining the roads in reasonable condition on the parishes within whose boundaries they ran, and ordered the appointment of a highway surveyor for each parish, who must see that all the parishioners gave their share of work (as in the old manorial days) to the repair of the roads. . . . [E]ach parishioner was supposed to supply horses and carts, tools and materials free, and to give six days' work to road-mending in the year, or to send "one sufficient labourer in his stead."[13]

At the parish level this act was extremely unpopular, mainly because the six days' work was unremunerated. Joan Parkes tells us that "[t]he labourers—often poor men who could ill afford wageless days—would spend 'most of their time in standing still and prating', or asking for largesse of the passers-by . . . so that they became known as 'The King's Loiterers,' in derision of their earlier title, 'The King's Highwaymen.'"[14] Road workers, then, are at times hard to distinguish from roadside beggars.

While these laborers performed their tasks as a mandatory service to parish and country, the roads themselves became objects of struggle between parishes and property owners—struggle either for ownership or exemption from responsibility. On the one hand, parishes might deny that certain roads fall within their purview: "Sometimes two neighbouring parishes would both disavow responsibility for the upkeep of a highway. Then, until a ruling was made by the Justices [of the Peace], the road in question would lie neglected, perhaps for several years."[15] On the other, roads could also become the objects of acquisitive landowners. W. T. Jackman reports that in the 1630's

there were . . . proceedings against those who had actually injured the highways; for some had enclosed not only the greensward at the sides, but the whole road; some had blocked the highways by erecting various kinds of buildings on them and by piles of refuse; others stopped the water by not scouring out their ditches; and some encroached on the road allowance by planting their hedges out too far on it.[16]

Thus, while travelers could pursue their right of passage and claim enclosed lands as the highway, property owners often encroached upon "the beaten track," trying to integrate it into their productive land. "Where the soil was rich," Parkes tells us, "encroachments would be made by covetous landowners, rendering nugatory that excellent thirteenth-century statute [13 Edw I, Stat. Winchester (1285)] which enjoined the maintenance of an open space of two hundred feet on either side of the highway."[17]

These examples tell us of the vexed relationship between the highway and landed property. Highway as right of passage threatens to break down the fences and clear the hedges of enclosed property, while the physical space of the highway can be encroached upon by and subsumed into estate lands. The idea of the highway brings with it certain customary rights, but that those rights involved toppling fences and "going over the corn" led to local struggles over the nature and limits of such rights and the prerogatives of property. For instance, when the road became unpassable, a not uncommon event,[18] "[r]iders often deserted the road for higher ground, to the advantage, near the great highways, of canny landowners who sometimes made them pay for the privilege."[19] In this instance, the landowner asserted the absolute nature of his private property by demanding payment for the execution by travelers of what was supposedly a customary right.[20] A good example of conflict between traveler and landowner is to be found in Thomas Ellwood's (1639–1713) autobiography. Ellwood tells the story of how as a young man he and his father, traveling in a coach, meet resistance from a landholder for crossing his lands:

And when we came near the town, the coachman seeing a nearer and easier way (than the common road) through a corn-field, and that it was wide enough for the wheels to run, without endamaging the corn, turned down there: which being observed by an husbandman, who was at plow not far off, he ran to us, and stopping the coach, poured forth a mouthful of complaints, in none of the best language, for driving over the corn.

After evading the husbandman and coming to the town, Ellwood and his father discover that the way they had traveled "was a way often used, and without damage, being broad enough; but that it was not the common road, which yet lay not far from it, and was also good enough." Returning from town, they travel this time by the common road, where they are greeted by the husbandman and another who stop them and claim that still they tread upon the corn.[21] This episode is fascinating in its depiction of the relationship between the highway and property. Whether or not the husbandman is wrongfully accusing them of "driving over the corn" is less important than is the nature of his response, one perhaps fueled by previous experiences of this kind—he defies custom in the name of the sanctity of his property. Later, he ironically acts as if his property rights extend out into "the common road." His claim is an untenable one, but its significance is twofold: first, it recapitulates the encroachments of landowners onto the highway that we have seen above; second, it reveals considerable anger with those who use property as a right of passage—if you'll use my fields as if they were a highway, the husbandman seems to say, I'll use the highway as if it were part of my fields.

It is clear that "in Tudor times, land tenure was a complex structure of communal property right; in the centuries which followed the situation was transformed, there being a near total dominance of private property."[22] However, struggles over the meaning and nature of the highway render the early stages of this transformation visibly prominent. These examples show how the landholder or owner tries to place limits on custom in the name of the prerogatives of property understood in fundamental ways as private: a landscape of absolute property is formulated and defended in opposition to a landscape of custom. What all of this suggests is that the highway exists in a vexed relationship to property—as a physical space, the highway is encroached upon or maintained at the expense of surrounding lands;

as a right of passage, it allows the trampling of corn and the violation of property boundaries. In short, the highway is a site across which the nature, limits, and prerogatives of landed property are explored or contested.

IF THE HIGHWAY constitutes a threat to a landscape of absolute property, then such a landscape troubles "propriety" and the ideologies of place briefly mentioned above. As many critics have pointed out, even Jonson's formulation of the relationship between the estate and a conception of identity predicated upon neofeudal ideals of reciprocity in "To Penshust" is at best a nostalgic one; the conception of propriety articulated by Jonson undergoes a transformation in the late sixteenth and seventeenth centuries. Don Wayne expands upon and complicates Turner's argument as follows:

There is some linguistic evidence that in the sixteenth century, if not earlier, the self began to be thought of in territorial and possessive terms. A shift can be detected away from the idea of subjectivity as a quality shared by members of a community to a notion that located the subject *in* the individual. . . . The individual's 'person,' as C. B. Macpherson has persuasively argued, was identified with private property. And whereas the term 'property' (or 'propriety') had formerly signified a relationship, by the seventeenth century the relational concept was subordinated to the more reified notion of a thing.[23]

Thus, while conceptions of property may have once suggested the imbrication of land in a complex set of social relations manifested in the form of customs—a landscape of stewardship or custom—the term increasingly signifies individual ownership divorced from issues of social responsibility. This emergent conception of property is reflected in alterations in the social uses of the manors of country estates. Consider changes in the function of the great hall as articulated by G. R. Hibbard. Through much of the sixteenth century the great hall was the common meeting ground for members of the family and their servants and, very often, their tenants as well. It was in fact the heart of a self-contained community and, as such, it continued to dictate the design of the house so long as the relation of the lord to his dependants was that of the father to a family, and so long as the sixteenth-century custom of 'housekeeping' continued.[24]

However, by the end of the sixteenth century the great hall had been transformed from a site of paternalistic hospitality to an emblem of the owner's importance. At the same time,

The decline in 'housekeeping' which took place in the early seventeenth century meant that the great hall was no longer necessary as a communal dining-room. There was a marked tendency for the great man to make much more use of intermediary officials in his dealings with tenants and servants, and in this way to cut himself off from direct contact with the humbler day-to-day activities of his estate.

Hibbard's analysis suggests that the country house is understood less and less as the site of community relationships and more and more as what we think of as private property, as "an expression of individual pride."[25]

It is important to note, however, that while the country house was being reimagined—once a community site, now private property—it had always been primarily an emblem of the landowner's identity. The refiguring of the house and estate as private property doesn't change that fact, but what it does do is alter, often in both theory and practice, social relations on the estate; as I discuss in Chapter One, emergent ideologies of private property, instantiated in a landscape of absolute property, affect the landlord's conception of his role on the estate, and threaten to turn traditional, paternalistic social relations into more instrumental ones in which land and tenancy are understood only as exploitable resources. This transformation is forwarded by the rise of one who Hibbard refers to as an "intermediary official": the estate steward.

In his comprehensive account of the social role and function of the estate steward, D. R. Hainsworth asserts that "the full-blown estate steward discharging wide and varied responsibilities who was a conspicuous figure in every shire during the later Stuart period, had already emerged during the sixteenth century and was becoming more numerous before the Civil War."[26] Of course Springlove is such a steward—consider again Brome's representation of the fullness of his duties—but in *A Jovial Crew* there is an ironic reversal of what in the seventeenth century was usually the case. While Springlove abandons the estate to be a "stroll-all-the-land-over," the more common historical scenario involved the absence of the landlord. Hainsworth argues that the power and authority of the steward increased because of the landlord's absenteeism; in his master's absence the steward "was then a surrogate lord, feared, resented, courted, closely observed, a man who could influence the opinions of others merely by confiding his own." As we have already seen, this absence often attested to the attraction of the city, but the lure of the metropolis was not the only reason for the increased power of the estate steward. "Landowners continued to own and acquire estates widely scattered across different counties. ... Much ... absenteeism was probably due to residence on chief estates elsewhere rather than residence in London."[27] Thus, were Springlove actually journeying to survey and purchase land for Oldrents, he would also be working to increase the influence of an estate steward, if not himself. In short, Springlove abandons his responsibilities as steward while falsely claiming not only to act out of but also to extend such responsibilities.

The steward, then, rises in importance as the landowner disappears. Does this suggest that one representative of paternalistic authority, the landlord, has been replaced by another, Hainsworth's "surrogate lord," the steward? If so, then the deleterious effects of the emergence of ideologies of private property could be minimized through the actions of the steward. However, it would be wrong to assume that the steward replaces the landlord in such a way, at least in all instances. While the steward may on occasion function as benign patriarch, the salient point is that he is recognizably a surrogate who does not erase the fact of the landlord's absence, a phenomenon often greeted with moral opprobrium by everyone from period moralists to Crown officials. However, Brome presents us with an interesting case that contradicts this historical analysis. While Oldrents is, as I have suggested, a present landlord and "a great housekeeper," it is Springlove who is seen as central to the maintenance of estate and household, and whose absence precipitates a crisis in the management of the estate. In order to understand the cultural implications of both Springlove's departure and this crisis I must now delineate the complex ideological relationship between the road, vagabondage, and the estate.

IT IS SIGNIFICANT that Springlove describes himself as one who once "quarter'd with a ragged crew, / On the highway" (2.1.295–96), suggesting that his home was at one point the road. Add to this both Randall's description of vagabonds as those who "cannot give account from whence they came or whither they would; nor of any beginning they ever had, or any end they seek, but still to stroll and beg till their bellies be full, and then sleep till they be hungry" and the following one from a John Taylor poem putatively in praise of beggary:

> A begger lives here in this vale of sorrow,
> And travels here to day, and there to morrow.
> The next day being neither here, nor there:
> But almost no where, and yet every where.
> He never labours, yet he doth expresse
> Himselfe an enemie to Idlenesse.
> In Court, Campe, Citie, Countrey, in the Ocean
> A begger is a right perpetuall motion,
> His great devotion is in generall,
> He either prayes for all, or preyes on all.[28]

Taylor brilliantly manipulates the spatial and social unlocatability of the vagabond. The first line initially offers to locate the beggar, but we come no closer to him than a metaphoric vale of sorrow, and then we are told that he is neither here nor there, nowhere and everywhere. Of course he is in part suggesting that one cannot easily define "the beggar" because there are a multiplicity of beggars—from court beggars to country ones—but what is important is the beggar's "perpetuall motion," his spatial unfixability and thus, by extension, his social opacity. As we have seen, the highway, like the vagabond, is itself neither here nor there, nowhere and everywhere.

When Taylor suggests that the beggar never labors but is an enemy to idleness, he refers to his vagabondage, his life on the road. Wittingly or not, Taylor reminds us of the origins of the word "travel" in "travail"—to travel is by its very nature to suffer.[29] While the connection may not be clear to us today, it would be inescapable to an early modern audience; the act of traveling long distances was both a dangerous and a labor-intensive one. Ironically, if not surprisingly, that labor when performed by vagabonds is not understood as such; as in Taylor's poem, the vagabond, although not idle, "never labours." While this is true at the level of cultural representation, recent social-historical work has suggested that in many instances Taylor's description of the wanderer is an inaccurate one. Intriguingly, Springlove's seasonal migration, although not motivated by the search for work, parallels the migration patterns of many vagabonds: ". . . vagrants began to move in the spring, found agricultural work in the summer, and were then on the move again, looking for a berth for the winter, usually in a town. The rhythms of the agricultural year dictated seasonal employment and mobility."[30] Spring migration was also partly dictated by the roads—in winter many roads were unpassable, and it was only with the change of seasons that travel was readily possible. Moreover, far from aimlessly strolling all the land over, the vagrant often knew the roads of England like the back of his hand, and sometimes he had a regular itinerary between temporary bases. Edward Yovell, for example, a vagrant taken in Salisbury, had been born in London and begun wandering after ending an apprenticeship in Worcester. Twice in two years he took up casual work back in London, where he had friends, then helped with the harvest at his uncle's in Surrey, next worked at various inns in Chichester, and finally returned to Worcester via Salisbury, Bristol and Gloucester, where he might hope for casual work or charity.[31]

In addition, the distance covered by vagrants was often exaggerated. While many commentators thought that "the vagrant ranged from one end of the country to the other," travel was most often "a matter of stop and go, halting for a few days to work, beg or steal, then making 10 or 12 miles."[32] However, by the 1630's and until the second half of the seventeenth century, vagrants wandered farther and farther afield, their traveling amounting to as much as 1,000 miles a year.[33] Thus, Brome's play is written at a time when the number of vagrants has drastically increased and those vagrants are traveling farther than at any other time in the previous century. The vagrant is increasingly visible, while the fact that he is removed from the social networks that generate identity means that he is also anonymous.

The historical information adduced above reminds us that not all vagrants are ones who never labor. In fact, the vagrant population was often indistinguishable from a mobile labor force: "To the extent . . . that vagrants most commonly worked at the precarious and common jobs of labouring and cloth-making, it becomes hard to distinguish them from casual labourers, except that vagrants were homeless, on the move and subject to the rigours of the law."[34] This difficulty in distinguishing lies in part with the category of vagrant; Paul Slack has suggested that "vagrant and vagabond were emotive, elastic terms. Were vagrants, as statutory definitions often suggest, the useful or picturesque wandering pedlars and minstrels whom M.P.s on occasion wished to protect, or those able-bodied professional beggars of the criminal underworld . . . ?"[35]—that is, were vagrants those that were working, or those able to work who chose crime instead? Legal classification of the vagabond as criminal was based in this period on the distinction between the able-bodied and impotent poor—the latter were exempt from punishment, while the former were punished because while able to work they were instead on the road and, perhaps, begging. And yet the above example of Edward Yovell suggests that travel and occasional begging formed part of an ongoing search for work. With the uprooting of a once land-based labor force, lower-class mobility became an inevitable and visible reality. At the same time, as we have seen, traditional conceptions of identity were predicated upon relationship to place. In addition, place existed as an emblem of one's position in a larger social order: "The theory was that society was ordered in hierarchies that were unified by paternalism. *Every man had his place*, his function and his master in the scheme of things. There was no room here for the vagrant: he was 'masterless' and thus had broken away from the established order."[36] Thus, the mobile laborer, beggar, or vagrant (if one can hope to distinguish between these categories) exists outside of the structures which confer identity; he is guilty of "a physical wandering from the places (the parish, the social rank) where identity and relationship are constituted and fixed."[37] As Robert Jütte puts it, "The mobile beggar [or, I would suggest, the mobile laborer] . . . could not easily be integrated into the parish community and was therefore lacking special supervision and instruction in Christian virtues."[38] Attempts were made constantly to reintegrate wanderers into such communities; vagabonds who were arrested were often sent back either to their home parishes or to their last places of residence, most often carrying passports that sanctioned their travel "home."[39] Such efforts were usually ineffectual, driving as they did the vagrant back to a place that offered him no livelihood. At the same time, the nature of their ineffectuality is telling, suggesting the need to locate socially and spatially an unfixed population. Mobility, then, suggests an unmooring of identity with implications broader than those confronted only by the poor. The vagabond was a wandering testament to both the dissolution of a traditional, land-based social order and the burgeoning of a proto-capitalist wage-labor economy.

IN TRADITIONAL ideologies of landownership, what linked the vagabond to the estate was the idea and practice of hospitality, described by Daryl Palmer as "a profound nexus for English Renaissance thought."[40] Moreover, the traditional view had it that hospitality was crucial to the construction of aristocratic identity; it formed one of the ideological determinants of a nobility linked with but not identical to noble birth. In addition, hospitality was usually understood as being synonymous with housekeeping—generosity and household management went hand in hand.[41] As Palmer puts it elsewhere, "The essence of noble identity was supposed to hinge on housekeeping, that being the most conspicuous sign of a nobleman's worth. If hospitality was declining, then so was the state of England's gentry."[42] However, starting in the late sixteenth century, hospitality to the poor gave way before other methods of poor relief. According to Felicity Heal's definitive study of early modern hospitality, from the 1590's on we see

the direction of poor-relief legislation away from casual household alms and towards a disciplined and public approach to the problem of poverty. . . . The city fathers of Norwich and Warwick wholeheartedly subscribed to the belief that there were idle and vagrant poor who must be disciplined, and impotent poor who must be given consistent and well-structured relief. Moreover, such men had no close interest in the maintenance of the old world of domestic loyalties that were enshrined in the great house. . . . The endowment of almshouses and the establishment of funds for the assistance of the able-bodied poor who could be set to work satisfied their sense of personal duty, while the daily regulation of the supply of food, or of outdoor relief, was undertaken by actions that were merely an extension of the old urban traditions of collective action.[43]

In addition, while not completely eradicated, household giving found "its dominant place . . . taken by organized schemes of relief, based on the parish, the town, and on institutions such as the almshouse."[44] The increasingly thorough implementation of the poor laws led to the attenuation of hospitality to the poor, hospitality associated with "the old world of domestic loyalties that were enshrined in the great house." Moreover, the number of those with "no close interest" in this world is on the increase in the early seventeenth century. That is, there is a shift in the articulation of the relationship between hospitality and noble identity, a shift we have seen hinted at in Hibbard's account of the reimagining of the great hall as "private property." As Heal puts it,

By the later sixteenth century this image of an élite given in honour to open hospitality, but not excessively so, began to yield to alternative patterns, especially those produced by growing mobility and the growth of London. Both Court and City played an increasing role in the experience of the nobility and many of the gentry, and perceptions of a civil society encouraged new ideas of social separation. It became questionable if the honour code required even the semblance of hospitality, since no reputation was to be gained from the plaudits of the multitude.[45]

Thus, the noble identity that emerged out of both place and the housekeeping associated with it was threatened by mobility and the concomitant erosion of practices of hospitality. It is aristocratic and not vagabond mobility that here acts as a potential dissolvent of identity.

We must say a bit more about hospitality's workings and its significance, especially when both are so crucial to the logic of Brome's play. In most representations of the relationship between vagabonds and manorial landowners, the chosen point of contact between the highway and the estate is the gatehouse to the manor;

it is here that the landlord's hospitality to the poor is enacted. In her discussion of the idea of hospitality in the early modern period, Felicity Heal notes that the spatial location of acts of hospitality differs with rank:

it was usually acknowledged that degree would be maintained by the careful separation of the social location in which hospitality was offered: the great chamber for men of influence, the hall for those of lesser worship who had some specific claim on the head of the household, the gatehouse for the needy.[46]

Thus the poor exist outside the gate, outside the social world of the lord's household; they are not among those "who had some specific claim" on the landlord. And yet, as we saw above, their existence is crucial to a traditional conception of noble identity. In a shrewd representation of the relationship between shifting social practice and hospitality, John Taylor interrogates that conception. Taylor writes of

> [A] Noble Lord, [who] Ignobly did oppresse
> His Tenants, raising Rents to such excesse:
> That they their states not able to maintaine,
> They turn'd starke beggers in a year or twaine.
> Yet though this Lord were too too miserable,
> He in his House kept a well furnish'd Table:
> Great store of Beggers dayly at his Gate,
> Which he did feed, and much Compassionate.
> (For 'tis within the power of mighty men
> To make fiue hundred Beggers, and feed Ten.)[47]

For Taylor, hospitality to beggars is a sop offered to those onetime tenants who should have had some claim on the lord, but who were instead exploited by one who understands his lands and tenantry not in terms of paternalistic social relations but as objects of ignoble oppression. Shifting land-management practices represent a struggle between the prerogatives of landscapes of absolute property and stewardship, the latter suggested by late feudal customs that regulate relations between landowner and tenant. Beggars, then, exist as a peripatetic testament to the erosion of such customs, and, by extension, as evidence of the failure of the social order that strives to put everyone in his place; tenants are made beggars, and hospitality, putatively constitutive of gentlemanly identity, here indicates only the oblivious hypocrisy of the landlord who falls far short of the gentlemanly ideal. The traditional practice of housekeeping, which usually implies a landscape of stewardship, is read by Taylor as an ironic accommodation made to those dislodged by ignoble attitudes toward land and tenantry (suggestive of a landscape of absolute property). For Taylor, the lord's hospitality represents not the enactment of a social ideal but evidence of hospitality's attenuated and contradictory relationship to other aspects of estate management.

While Taylor's lord's offering of hospitality contradicts the principles of his ruthless management of his estate, Oldrents's hospitality is, as I suggested at the beginning of this chapter, part and parcel of his exemplary management of his estate; his generosity exemplifies his proper fulfillment of his responsibilities as beneficent landlord. Moreover, these responsibilities include his hospitality to the beggars, which Patrico acknowledges and praises as follows:

> Long may you live, and may your store
> Never decay nor balk the poor;
> And as you more in years do grow,
> May treasure to your coffers flow;
> And may your care no more thereon
> Be set, than ours are, that have none.
> But as your riches do increase,
> So may your heart's content and peace.
> And after many, many years,
> When the poor have quit their fears
> Of losing you, and that with Heaven

And all the world you have made even,
Then may your blest posterity,
Age after age successively
Until the world shall be untwin'd,
Inherit your estate and mind.
So shall the poor to the last day
For you, in your succession, pray. (2.2.210–27)

Patrico echoes Springlove in yoking hospitality to the poor with the strength of Oldrents's estate, even simultaneously hoping for both an increase in Oldrents's wealth and his continued willingness to share that wealth. Moreover, he prays for the perpetuation of that estate across generations, wishing Oldrents's daughters to continue their father's efforts to relieve the poor. This is a plea for the continuation of a paternalistic social order and the hospitality associated with it. And yet, the flight of Rachel and Meriel would seem to threaten the perpetuation of the estate, for it is their absence along with Springlove's that leads to a change in Oldrents and his conception of his estate. Moreover, like Springlove Oldrents's daughters are associated with housekeeping: it is "two daughters that knew well to order a house and give entertainment to gentlemen" (4.1.72–73) that have fled. Meriel at one point even suggests that it is the relentless execution of hospitality that has led to her flight; she compares favorably the beggars to "[us] . . . that are pent up and tied by the nose to the continual steam of hot hospitality here in our father's house . . ." (2.1.9–11). Patrico's prayer for continued hospitality from Oldrents's estate is threatened by his daughters' and his steward's pursuit of a vagabond's freedom.

Oldrents self-consciously abandons anxiety about Springlove's and his daughters' absence in favor of "jovial mirth," an abandonment that entails sadness being "banish'd" "from my furthest foot of land / While I have life" (2.2.105–9).[48] Land is constituted here in terms not of hospitality or estate management but of mirth and the abolishing of sadness. Moreover, there is a change in the business of the estate. Compare Springlove's extensive "survey" suggesting the precise control of Oldrents's assets with Oldrents's statement that "My house is for no business but the belly-business. . . . If you come to be merry with me, you are welcome. If you have any business, forget it; you forget where you are else" (4.1.288–94). There is the very real threat that this hospitality, which becomes more excessive over the course of the play, might lead to the erosion both of his estate through profligacy and, by extension, of his hospitality to the poor.[49] This threat has been visible from the beginning—Springlove's appearance to discuss estate matters occurs just as Oldrents and Hearty are about to "ride forth for air . . . and be merry" (1.1.97), which succinctly suggests the significance of Springlove's role as manager of estate business. Even Hearty, the parasite who thrives on Oldrents's generosity, "fear[s Oldrents's] overdoing" (2.2.141) once he begins in earnest his search for "jovial mirth."

Intriguingly, Oldrents's commitment to merriness not only includes the transformation of his house and lands into sites of merriness, but also involves his traversing of the countryside. His day consists of moving "Skice out this a-way, and skice out that a-way. (He's no snail, I assure you.) And tantivy all the country over, where hunting, hawking, or any sport is to be made, or good fellowship to be had" (4.1.900–93). Oldrents's travel and his reference to "jovial mirth" makes us think of the play's jovial crew, and arguably it is to the supposed carefree life of these beggars that Oldrents aspires. Oldrents at one point asks, "What is an estate / Of wealth and power, balanc'd with their freedom, / But a mere load of outward compliment, / When they enjoy the fruits of rich content?" (2.2.185–88). However, Oldrents's travel is clearly earmarked as the kind of aristocratic travel that he urged Springlove to pursue; it involves the passing from one landed household to another. Oldrents's commitment to good fellowship also suggests that travel never involves his removal from the social circuits that define his aristocratic identity—he travels in the way he desires Springlove to, with "horse, and man, and money." Joviality aside, Oldrents exists always within the milieu of the landed gentleman.

One of Oldrents's journeys is represented in the play. Eager to meet "this old odd-ceited [i.e., whimsical] Justice Clack," Oldrents travels to Clack's home both to pursue the question of Martin and Amie's supposed elopement and to test Clack's hospitality. In his pursuit of merriment, Oldrents shrugs off the length of the journey: "'Tis but crossing the country two days and a night's journey" (4.1.328–30). However, Justice Clack fails to live up to Oldrents's expectations. Clack's son, Oliver, reports to his father that "Master Oldrents, in that he enjoys not your company begins to doubt of his welcome" (5.1.91–92). Later, Randall, who accompanied Oldrents on his journey, grumbles about the deficiencies of Clack's board, accusing him of "fill[ing] my belly with thin drink to save his meat," while also commenting that "It's the manner in churls' houses" (186–88). So deficient is Clack that Randall tells him that "If you come not at once . . . [Oldrents will be] gone presently, before supper. He'll find an host at an inn worth a hundred o' you" (138–40). Churls' houses and inns—both are compared with Clack's household, so lax is he in administering hospitality.

This characterization of Clack and his dubious hospitality is surely in the service of creating a vivid contrast to Oldrents's exemplary household. And yet, as I have suggested above, there is something unsettling about Oldrents's eager pursuit of hospitality, just as there is about his nonchalance at making "two days and a night's journey." While Clack is shown up as failing to fulfill his requirements as host, Oldrents's newfound joviality has sent him on the road in pursuit of merriment in a way that seems to parody the peregrinations of the vagabond. Randall indirectly acknowledges the novelty of these proceedings when he says, "I was never twelve mile from [his birthplace, obviously in close proximity to Oldrents's house] i' my life before this journey" (156–57). This quotation attests to the traditional immobility of English rural life.

However, servants were among those who, with the shrinking of noble households, often became masterless men; this quotation evokes the newfound mobility of a rural labor force uprooted by changing land-management practice. And yet, the very presence of Randall as representative of Oldrents's household tells us that this journey is finally quite different from that made by a beggar— accompanied by both Oliver and his man, Oldrents's deportment remains gentle even while he is on the road. That journey does suggest, however, Oldrents's abdication of his responsibility. Brome takes pains first to show the significance of the steward to the running of the estate, and second to make clear that Randall will take Springlove's place when the latter goes on the road. With Springlove, Randall, Oldrents and his daughters all far from the estate, the question of who is managing it or how it is being managed is left unanswered. Similarly, we do not know who if anyone is relieving the poor. Oldrents's travels bespeak his identity as a gentleman, but they also gesture toward a definition of gentility divorced from responsible management of the estate and the poor. He threatens to become one of those men whose sense of nobility is divorced from "the old world of domestic loyalties."

While Oldrents's travels evoke the joviality and freedom of the play's vagabonds, they are to be distinguished from the travel of a vagabond population. There are gentlefolk in the play, though, who seem to embrace a vagabond's life on the road. Oldrents's daughters, Rachel and Meriel, and their suitors, Vincent and Hilliard, join the beggars because "They are the only people can boast the benefit of a free state, in the full enjoyment of liberty, mirth and ease, having all things in common and nothing wanting of nature's whole provision within the reach of their desires" (2.1.2–5). However, while they travel and beg with the jovial crew, in part to flee the onerous responsibilities of hospitality, one has the sense from the outset that they will not fully enter into this world. Instead, they go on something like "a short progress" (142). Vincent is not far off in describing the sisters' (and his) intentions when he says to Rachel, "Oh, I conceive your begging progress is to ramble out this summer among your father's tenants; and 'tis in request among gentlemen's daughters to devour their cheesecakes, apple pies, cream and custards, flapjacks, and pan-puddings" (158–62). While Oldrents passes from one manor house to another, his daughters are here accused of seeking a sanitized freedom through mobility that would never take them beyond their father's lands. They are less to beg than to collect tribute from their father's tenants. Of course Vincent's suggestion is met with scorn by Rachel and Meriel, but it is not long before the four lovers realize that the freedom they share with the vagabonds is far less appealing to them than would be Vincent's "begging progress," safely circumscribed as it is by both Oldrents's land and his authority.

THE LINE OF ARGUMENT that I have been pursuing suggests that while travel for vagabonds involves the eradication of their identities, their unfixing from a social order in which people are knowable only when they know their place, the peregrinations of the gentlefolk never take them beyond the spaces and constitutive structures of authority that shape a paternalistic, aristocratic identity. And yet, vagabonds suggest that those structures are increasingly brittle—we have seen the erosion of a paternalistic social order signified by both the absence of the landlord and the hollowness or hypocrisy of hospitality in the face of shifting land-management practices. One might argue that what this suggests is that in response to such changes the play offers up as a nostalgic fantasy a vision of a paternalistic social order based on the estate. (This nostalgia is not really very surprising if you consider that even his name associates Oldrents with a long-landed aristocracy that had been in crisis since at least the mid-sixteenth century.)[50] However, we have already discussed the problems inherent in Oldrents's hospitality. His beneficence is admirable, but when he offers to let "[his] tenants . . . sit rent-free for this twelvemonth; / And all my servants have their wages doubled" (2.2.110–11), one can see the threat of Oldrents's jovial mirth to the ordered estate represented in Springlove's survey at the beginning of the play. The problem in the play, then, lies in the profligacy of its owner. Thus, the play understands the crisis of the estate in terms not of shifting land-management processes but of the subjective tension within certain central characters between duty and a desire for freedom from that duty. It is this tension that structures the actions of these characters throughout the play, and that also bespeaks Brome's conception of a crisis of aristocratic identity, a crisis manifested in the renunciation of duties that are understood as constitutive.

As we have seen, the desire for freedom manifests itself as a desire for travel—Oldrents, his daughters, and Springlove all pursue jovial mirth at the expense of their duties as estate managers and/or sources of hospitality. The road seems to offer them the same opportunities for freedom that it does the play's vagabonds. However, this freedom is always circumscribed and finally curtailed: Oldrents's mirth is of a near-hysterical nature, his freedom of a kind that threatens to undermine his identity as "a great housekeeper," and it is presumably held in check with the return of Springlove; Rachel and Meriel desire to emulate the "liberty, mirth and ease" of the vagabonds, only to discover that they would have been better served by making "a begging progress" of their father's lands; and while Springlove eschews his duty, that which he is initially most strongly identified with,[51] by play's end he too has found the vagabond's wanderings to be "no course for gentlemen" (4.2.262). "No course": Springlove's repudiation of the vagabond's identity marks both an end to his wanderings and the acceptance of his status as gentleman, a status confirmed later by the revelation that he is Oldrents's son. The capable estate steward becomes a member of the family.[52] By the end of the play, each of these characters has replaced (dreams of) freedom with filiation—Springlove, Rachel, and Meriel marry, and Oldrents's disruptive jovial mirth is supplanted by a joy that "begins to be too great within me," a joy at acknowledging to Springlove, his daughters, and their husbands that "you all are mine" (5.1.443–45). Freedom, then, is finally less desirable than is a duty rendered filial. The integrity of the estate is reaffirmed, and both hospitality and identity are, it seems, resecured.

If the gentlefolk in the play wish to travel within the circuits of aristocratic authority, beggars are, as we have seen, those who wander aimlessly, who "stroll all the land over." When Springlove tells the four lovers and band of beggars that "we must quit this quarter," he specifies that they must do so by "leap[ing] hedge and ditch now; through the briers and mires, till we 'scape out of this liberty to our next rendezvous . . ." (3.1.419–21). In reporting to Justice Clack on his pursuit of beggars, Sentwell describes how "they in the instant vanish'd by more several ways than there were legs among 'em; how the cripples leap'd over pales and hedges; how the blind found their way through lakes and ditches; how a doxy flew with two children at her back, and two more, perhaps, in her belly" (5.1.82–86). The beggars ignore the strictures of property—pales, hedges, and ditches—in "vanish[ing] by more several ways." Moreover, the "vanishing" Sentwell describes is suggestive of the beggars' anonymity, their social opacity—they are those not represented in aristocratic households or among a landowner's tenants.

Thus we see that the freedom of the beggars is manifested in their mode of travel—not between estates or among family lands, but across hedges and pales. Moreover, in leaving the *road* the beggars are following the *highway*. Brome's vagabonds can be read as travelers pursuing their right of passage; they follow custom and unwittingly participate in an ongoing cultural contest over the meaning of property. What is intriguing, though, is that Brome associates the pursuit of customary rights with vagabondage—as we have seen, when not masquerading as beggars, the gentlefolk hardly leap over hedges or knock down fences. In fact, I have suggested that Brome's vision is wed to the sanctity of property and its privileged position within the social milieu of paternalistic, hospitable relations. What should be clear by now, though, is that what Brome means by "property" is very different from property as understood by Ellwood's disgruntled husbandman; it is the difference between a landscape of stewardship and one of absolute property. Moreover, it is this difference that allows us to see the sanctity of property and the violation of its boundaries as a part of the same cultural logic.

We can see this most clearly through returning to a topic discussed above—the pursuit of freedom. The freedom of the beggars is repeatedly valorized, while the attempts of members of the estate to attain such freedom are understood as a dereliction of duty. What this suggests is that the freedom of the vagabond is acceptable precisely because the vagabond is unmoored from the land, has no place. Brome inverts the cultural logic that sees the masterlessness of the vagabond as a social dissolvent.[53] For him, the problem lies not with those displaced from the land, but with those who deny the identity and duties that emerge from knowing (and maintaining) their places in a social order predicated upon the land. This includes the prodigal Oldrents and absent Springlove, but it also would include those, like either Ellwood's husbandman or Hibbard's "great man," who treat their property as private in the modern sense, as divorced from a paternalistic social order and a set of responsibilities. The passage of the vagabond across property is both in line with land's customary uses and an affront to those who, in the name of private property, deny the imbrication of the land in social custom. Like hospitality, the highway resists any conception of private property that divorces the land from the structures of customary obligation: from, that is, the intersecting landscapes of stewardship and custom.

We have seen that it is finally these structures that at the estate level are for Brome fundamentally constitutive. I suggest above that by play's end both hospitality and identity are resecured. However, this reading is complicated by the way in which the play's ending troubles as well as clarifies identity. Oldrents is himself again, but what self is that? The identity supplied by his name is undermined by the revelation that Patrico is "grandson to that unhappy Wrought-on, / Whom your grandfather craftily wrought out / Of his estate" (5.1.411–13). At least some of the landlord's rents are not so old after all. Similarly, what do we make of Springlove, the steward whose very name and frequent claims that nature compels him to roam belie his newfound commitment to no longer pursue courses not fit for the gentleman son of Oldrents? In these instances, the question of identity would seem to be less resolved than muddied further. However, while individual identity is confused, familial identity is consolidated—as noted above, we move from freedom to filiation. Moreover, I would also argue that for Brome identity emerges out of the relations of hospitality. Thus, the return of the Oldrents family to the estate and their duties is a return to an identity. While Don Wayne suggests that "whereas the term 'property' (or 'propriety') had formerly signified a relationship, by the seventeenth century the relational concept was subordinated to the more reified notion of a thing," Brome's play still understands property as a relationship. For Brome, duty inseparable from place is identity.

As we have seen, the vagabonds are emulated for their freedom from responsibilities and from identity. The vagabond is generally understood as being socially opaque, outside the structures of authority, unnameable. This both is and is not confirmed by the play. With the exception of Patrico, whose case, as we have seen, is peculiar, all of the full-time beggars are unnamed—they are labeled as 1 Beggar and so on. This is of course a not unusual theatrical practice when it comes to characters who function primarily as types, but these beggars are also given interesting genealogies—they are identified in terms of what they once were (poet, philosopher, courtier, and so on).[54] Intriguingly, each tells the other's story— that is, the beggar identified as onetime poet tells of the former philosopher, and on down the line. The effect of this is twofold. On the one hand, the world of beggars is one containing a range of people with different past occupations, occupations that they sometimes still take advantage of (the poet, for instance, writes a masque). On the other, identity is something that seems both de-ferred—no one speaks for himself—and largely in the past. In the present, these characters are nameless beggars, and with their namelessness comes the freedom that captivates both Brome and many of his characters.

However, even within the world of the play that freedom is cir-cumscribed. Critics have emphasized the utopian element to beg-gars' society in Brome's play while also noting the play's represen-tation of the stark realities of a beggar's life, realities that undercut that utopianism.[55] That is, the play tempers the utopian freedom of the beggars, freedom which extricates them from both duty and the place in the social order particular duties prescribe, with an aware-ness of the physical and social constraints placed upon them.[56] These constraints are read by Brome's beggars merely as a matter of course, however, as the price of their freedom—a price that is paid in the very form of their traveling. Consider the above examples of the beggars' leaping over hedges and ditches. In each case, the beg-gars pursue the customary rights of the highway because they are forced to, chased by either angry gentlemen or representatives of the justice of the peace. Similarly, the play ends with the jovial crew back on the road, but not exactly free. After they finish their per-formance for Justice Clack and his guests, Clack instructs his clerk to "give all the beggars my free pass, without all manner of correc-tion! That is to say, with a-hey, get 'em gone" (5.1.487–89). Clack considers himself generous for sparing the rod, but his "free pass" suggests that the beggars are to be sent via passport to their "homes." Thus, Clack aims to curtail the freedom of the vagabonds by sending them home, an act designed to erase their anonymity and reinstall them within what we have seen as "a classificatory grid within which the true identity of the subject may be 'read' by reference to the origin of the birthplace."[57] Moreover, the pass suggests the poor laws, laws that as we have seen were commonly understood as taking over the functions once performed by the hospitable landowner. Thus, the beggars are perched not only between freedom and constraint, anonymity and identity, but between hospitality and the poor laws that modify and replace it. Oldrents has earned Patrico's blessing for his kindness and generosity to the jovial crew. Clack, the inhospitable host whose disdain for charity to the poor is registered in the text,[58] stands in as an emblem of the new regime, one which is divorced from the principles of hospitality so dear to Brome.

We can now see why, while aristocratic travel, suggesting as it does the denial of hostly responsibilities, is read by the play as unacceptable, the peregrinations of the vagabond are valorized. Beggarly travel is finally understood in terms of and as an opportunity for hospitality, something that the poor laws suggest the erosion of. At the same time, it is worth remembering that the vagabond population is a mobile labor force of those displaced in part by shifting land-management practices; the "freedom" of the masterless entails the search for employment. This historical phenomenon, crucial to the development of the kind of wage-labor force necessary for the emergence of capitalism, is also understood by Brome in terms of hospitality. The social upheavals that lead to the visible emergence of a population of masterless men are here construed as the beggar's pursuit of freedom, a pursuit that leads him in search not of work but of alms. Thus, the visible and mobile labor force that suggests the death of a hierarchized, paternalistic social order is refigured in terms of housekeeping, of the threatened social order. By understanding vagabond mobility in such terms, the play is able to sidestep the position suggested by John Taylor in his description of the hypocritical lord—that hospitality is dead or, at best, an empty practice, a shadow of its former self. The ascendancy of the poor laws, which hollow out hospitality to the poor, are associated with a failed host, and lordly beneficence lives on in the Oldrents family, members of which will now hearken to Patrico's prayer that Oldrents's "blest posterity" emulate his actions.

And yet, as I have said, Clack has sent the beggars to their "homes"; their utopian freedom is to be curtailed in the name of forced reintegration into the "classificatory grid" of parochial control. However, the play stops short of their arrival; it ends with the beggars en route, somewhere between Clack's estate and the parish or town that will supposedly anchor their identities.[59] Is their journey one that will follow the itinerary tacitly prescribed by Clack's pass? This would involve the reinstallation of the masterless into the regimes of parochial authority. Or will they follow the "old way"? Just as the play as a whole balances utopian fantasy and what Martin Butler terms "contentious realism," Brome leaves his beggars somewhere between an idealized, nostalgic hospitality and the poor laws that have attenuated its authority. (It also leaves them on the highway, both place and placeless.) *A Jovial Crew* registers the decline of hospitality even as it champions it.

I BEGAN THIS CHAPTER with a reference to the civil war, and I would like to end with a very brief discussion of that conflict's relationship to some of the issues we have addressed here. Alan Everitt describes the impact of the war on the structures of manorial life as follows:

The reins of traditional authority were inevitably relaxed, the bonds of society weakened, and the gentry driven into harsh repressive measures to restore order. ... With rival armies plundering the countryside, and with thousands of estates under sequestration, many labourers could not tell to whom their rents, and their loyalty, were due. With many squires taking up arms for Charles I or Parliament, and leaving their home locality for years on end, the direct interest of many landlords in farming ceased, and absenteeism became, first a military necessity, then a social habit. As a consequence, an attitude of supercilious contempt for social inferiors developed, amongst both cavaliers and puritans ... In a word, the Civil War and the Interregnum dealt a death-blow to the age-old conception of society as a hierarchy of interdependent orders, and went far to replace it by the notion of society as a series of independent and necessarily antagonistic classes.[60]

For Everitt, the war marks, among other things, the end of housekeeping, and the road takes on new significance—it is necessary now not only for trade and travel, but for the passage of armies. It is important to note, though, that many of the changes Everitt describes—the absence of landlords, their loss of interest in their estates, the end of paternalistic interdependence—we have already seen under way in the period before the war. It is such changes that Brome's play so actively, if quixotically, denies and resists. At the same time, Brome is very aware of the conflict to come; in his prologue he "promise[s] mirth, which were a new / And forc'd thing in these sad and tragic days" (Prologue, 2–3).[61] It is of course mirth that Oldrents also seeks, an escape from the troubling events that have occurred in his family. As we have seen, the traveling nobles return to their estate, but only after mirth is transmuted into familial joy and the resumption of traditional housekeeping. This is very much the aim of Brome's play, to counteract the effect of "these sad and tragic days" by a return to hospitality.[62] That this attempt is of a piece with the utopianism of his play is suggested both by what came before and by what followed it—the beginning of the end of "the age-old conception of society as a hierarchy of interdependent orders." The death knell is sounded, however, less by the wanderings of the jovial crew than by the landlord who, for reasons whether of battle or of mirth, takes to the road and forgets the place that he knows.

London Under Fire
LANDSCAPE, SPACE, AND
THE REPRESENTATION
OF REVOLT

CHAPTER SIX

The Beleaguered City

GUILD CULTURE AND URBAN SPACE IN
HEYWOOD'S 'I EDWARD IV' AND
SHAKESPEARE'S '2 HENRY VI'

We have by now encountered a range of landscapes and charted their intersections with estate, road, and nation. While this chapter concerns itself with landscapes of custom and sovereignty, it emphasizes a category allied to but distinct from landscape, that of space. Michel Foucault has said of traditional social thought that it imagined "Space . . . as the dead, the fixed, the undialectical, the immobile. Time, on the contrary, was richness, fecundity, life, dialectic."[1] However, in the last twenty-five years or so social theorists such as Henri Lefebvre, Michel de Certeau, Edward Soja, and David Harvey have insisted on a dialectical conception of space that sees space as both determining history and historically determined. These "urban geographers" attend to, in Soja's terms, "the social construction of affective geographies, the concretization of social relations embedded in spatiality . . ."[2] At the same time, they show that spatiality not only gives concrete form to but also shapes social relations. "[O]bjective conceptions of time and space are necessarily created through material practices and processes which serve to reproduce social life,"[3] and these conceptions in turn participate in social reproduction. For both traditional historiography and the new historicism, these thinkers reconceptualize the role of spatial relations in social reproduction. The notion of history common to traditional historiography (and, as I shall show, to a Shakespearean history play) is that history is made by great men and women, and that spaces either reflect their greatness or, more frequently, provide a backdrop for its representation. The traditional historiographical privileging of time over space is accompanied by a concomitant privileging of political over social history, and of the Crown over the citizens—a privileging that is ironically replicated by much of the new historicism.[4] The work of the urban geographers suggests that history can be understood not merely as (the study of) actions unfolding in time and across space, but as (the examination of) the instantiation and production of sociospatial relations, the embeddedness of history in space and of space in history.

The points of contact between landscape and space are multiple: both emerge out of a historical engagement with built or "natural" topographies, both shape and are shaped by practice, and both represent potent alternatives to a historiography that sees topography as no more than the scene set for the unfolding of human action. Moreover, both offer a way of conceptualizing the subject's engagement with its environment, an engagement that suggests the subject's position in a broader sociotopographical (or sociospatial) matrix. However, I emphasize space here because of the particular utility of the term as it is anatomized by Henri Lefebvre, and because it offers a wider view than landscape can provide: landscape exists as but one form of spatiality. (At the same time, space as an inclusive term fails to offer us as detailed and nuanced a reading of subjective and social relationships to topography as landscape does.) More specifically, I turn to the category of space largely because the work of Lefebvre both furnishes a vocabulary that powerfully illuminates critical and dramatic conceptualizations of the city, and situates landscape in terms of broader concerns. This vocabulary, then, helps us to construct a landscape of early modern London and to see more precisely what is at issue in that construction.

WILLIAM SHAKESPEARE'S 2 *Henry VI* (1590) and Thomas Heywood's *1 Edward IV* (1599) depict rebellions that threaten the takeover of London.[5] What links these plays in my analysis is a trope with powerful implications for their conceptualizations of the city; each contains an uprising figured as an invasion in which forces from without jeopardize the city within the wall. As we shall see, it is through these invasions that specific civic cultures are defined; the sociospatial logic governing each play's representation of London comes into focus with the external threat posed to the city.[6]

The leader of the rebels in *1 Edward IV* is Falconbridge, a pretender to the throne who marshals a force largely composed of discontented rural laborers. The threat that the rebels pose to the city is a complicated one that combines pillaging with a struggle for control of those activities central to the functioning of a guild-based economy. Here is how Falconbridge sets forth their ambitions:

> We will be Masters of the Mint ourselues,
> And set our own stamp on the golden coin.
> We'll shoe our neighing coursers with no worse
> Than the purest siluer that is solde in Cheape.
> At *Leadenhall*, we'll sell pearles by the pecke,
> As now the mealmen vse to sell their meal.
> In *Westminster*, we'll keep a solemne court,
> And build it bigger to receiue our men.[7]

Falconbridge's desire to be master of the mint and to keep court in Westminster is a desire to usurp the functions of the monarchy, while the shoeing of his horses with silver suggests the extravagant exploitation of the city's resources. Most interesting for my purposes, however, is his aim of both regulating commerce and appropriating its spaces: they will sell pearls as if they were grain, and they will do so in Leadenhall, a guild commercial center.[8] Chub, one of the rebels, follows Falconbridge's lead in saying to one of his comrades, "No sooner in *London* will wee be, / But the bakers for you, the brewers for mee" (p. 11), and he proceeds to describe how various tradesmen will cater to their whims. As in Falconbridge's speech, the hedonistic appropriation of resources goes hand in hand with their economic control. When Chub refers to having "the brewers for mee," he means not merely that all beer will be his, but that he will control its production. Falconbridge's rebellion promises not only the plunder of London, but also the management of its productive spaces and practices.[9]

This scene offers a glimpse of a spatial logic that is crucial to this play. For Heywood, the spaces of the city are inextricably linked with a guild economy that had for centuries dominated the economic and social life of London. By the late sixteenth century, however, the hegemony of the guilds was troubled by the development of new labor practices concomitant with the city's rapid economic growth. *1 Edward IV* both represents and resists these developments by staging social change as a battle for the spaces of the city. By doing so, the play ensures that those spaces are always understood in terms of the very culture that is historically under siege. The practices and customs of guild culture are those that give shape to the city itself;[10] that is, Heywood's London is formed in accordance with the imperatives of a landscape of custom that emerges out of guild activity. More broadly, I will show that Heywood helps us to generate alternatives to two related conceptions of city space: the influential new-historicist one offered by Steven Mullaney in *The Place of the Stage* and the early modern dramatic one implicit in the attack on London in Shakespeare's *2 Henry VI*.

IN ITS EARLY PAGES, *The Place of the Stage* provides Steven Mullaney's reader with a richly nuanced discussion of London that, through its focus on the centrality of ritual, attests to the interpenetration of topography and practice, the extent to which the landscape of the city is historically both determined and determining. London is "a *ceremonial* city. It was shaped not by the dictates of urban planning and population control . . . but by the varied rites of initiation, celebration, and exclusion through which a ceremonial social order defined, maintained, and manifested itself, in time and in space."[11] Mullaney is persuasive in his discussion of the importance of ritual to early modern London, but his account goes too far, in that he sees little other than ritual or its traces in the spaces of the city. I quote:

[London,] in its unadorned streets and conduits, its everyday markets and common places, was a monumental record of the various ceremonies and rituals which had annually shaped and articulated it. The city was a symbolic artifact, a cultural emblem or device conceived in ceremony, ritual, and not always harmonious community, impressed with significance but difficult to read . . .[12]

To read London as a "monumental record" of ritual, to see even in its everyday spaces only vestiges of civic ceremony, is to create a city that is, paradoxically, univocal in its multiplicity, its array of "ceremonies and rituals." It is to neglect the determining (and determined) influence of other, nonritualistic forms of material practice on the landscape of the city. What, for instance, of the patterns of labor and their effect on the city's spatial organization, the patterns that we have already seen are so important to Heywood? Admittedly such patterns are alluded to in spectacles such as the Lord Mayor's show or Elizabeth's coronation procession, but in an incomplete and symbolic form; they cannot be reduced to their ritualistic representation. While, as Mullaney states, ceremony is a way in which the city defines itself,[13] it is not the only way, and we must understand that much of what the city contains—for example, foreign-born workers, nonguild industry, and a seasonally employed work force—is not registered within its rituals.[14]

The problem with Mullaney's analysis, then, is that it overemphasizes certain symbolic representations of London; his notions of civic space fail to accommodate the wide range of sociospatial practices that constitute a city. In order to see this, we must turn to Henri Lefebvre's *The Production of Space*, which offers a complex notion of social space that allows us to identify the limits of Mullaney's analysis. Lefebvre refers to a range of socially produced (and productive) spaces, three of which are important to us here: spatial practice, representations of space, and representational space. Spatial practice refers to various sociospatial networks—roads, trails, navigated waterways—and the social and economic practices they make possible and upon which they depend. Representations of space, on the other hand, are "conceptualized space, the space of scientists, planners, urbanists, technocratic subdividers and social engineers . . . all of whom identify what is lived and what is perceived with what is conceived."[15] This is the space of maps and charts, as well as being the pulverized and fungible space of private property: the lot or plot. In representations of space "ideology and knowledge are barely distinguishable," and the "objective" description of an "abstract" space works in the service of capitalist conceptions of ownership.[16] Finally, representational spaces are "space as directly *lived* through its associated images and symbols, and hence the space of 'inhabitants' and 'users' . . . This is the dominated—and hence passively experienced—space which the imagination seeks to change and appropriate. It overlays physical space, making symbolic use of its objects."[17] The term "representational space" encompasses both the symbolic significance accorded to a space, a significance often in conflict with either spatial practice or representations of space, and the space itself. The three terms, loosely described by Lefebvre as perceived, conceived, and lived space, should not be understood as existing either discretely or independently of one another, but as forms of space that come fully into being through their complex interrelationships. Moreover, transformations in one do not necessarily imply parallel transformations in the others; changes in spatial practice, for instance, are not transparently registered in representational spaces, and often particular spaces are sites of active contestation.

An example of these terms in action might be useful. Let us turn
to a by now familiar topic, taken up in terms not of landscape but
of space: the status of land in the sixteenth and seventeenth centuries. Developments in cartography made possible sophisticated *representations of space*, representations useful in the context of a society in which the role of land in *spatial practice* was changing radically: large landowners increasingly left their estates for the city,
managing their affairs from afar by the use of estate maps (representations of space), and thereby disrupted the tightly knit, spatially circumscribed set of exchanges upon which feudal conceptions of landownership were based; the national trade in land necessitated the gradual development of ideologies that saw land not
as site of responsibility, but as fungible lot or exploitable resource,
one to which the landlord was no longer closely linked by affective
ties or physical proximity. Whereas the lord's social and economic
centrality to feudal land arrangements was suggested by the physical centrality of both the manor and the lord within, changes in the
nature of his socioeconomic exchanges with his tenants—from fealty to rents, from father figure to landlord—went hand in hand
with his move from the manor to the city or the court. In short, the
sociospatial arrangements central to a land-based economy underwent a transformation; spatial practice changed. At the same time,
however, land as a *representational space* often still carried a symbolic significance that was feudal in origin—land as a social site
around which a series of paternalistic relationships formed—and
that continued to influence greatly cultural perceptions. New representations of space and emergent spatial practices did not immediately overturn a prevailing cultural sense of the land (land as representational space).

This example suggests the potency of space as a category broader
in its scope than is landscape. However, Lefebvre's taxonomy of
space also lacks the precision and specificity of landscape. As the
above example shows, "representational space" is the term that

comes closest to describing landscape, but when examined closely the term is unsatisfactory for the early modern period: representational space is "the dominated—and hence passively experienced—space which the imagination seeks to change and appropriate." This formulation cedes priority over the subjective to the spatial or topographical, rendering the complex dialectic between subjectivity and topography as the imaginative reaction to space's action. The reason for this is that Lefebvre focuses on modern and postmodern conceptions of spatiality—on a spatial order in which subjective relations to space are nearly completely dominated by the rationalized space of capitalism.[18] He assumes, that is, that space is fundamentally structured in accordance with representations of, or "conceived," space; imaginative appropriation is understood by Lefebvre as a second-order process that betrays the success of capitalist spatiality. Thus, Lefebvre's conception of space, like landscape and the landscape arts as they have usually been construed, assumes the triumph of a capitalist spatial order that, in the late sixteenth century, has not yet been installed. I want to suggest, then, that *we read representational space as landscape*—that we understand representational space not as a symbolic space dominated by a capitalist spatial order, but, as I defined landscape in the Introduction, as a construction and a way of seeing, the means by which social relations are negotiated across land, a way that topography is brought into discourse and into knowledge. (Specifically, I will focus on the representational space of the city within the wall as a customary landscape that gives shape to the privileges and imperatives of a guild economy.)[19] This retooling of Lefebvre's term acknowledges its potency in, and increases its relevance to, the early modern period, while also providing us with a compelling way of considering the place of landscape in a larger sociospatial order. In particular, we will see how a landscape (or representational space) of the city is threatened by shifting spatial practice.

In reading the city, with its "everyday markets and common

places," as a "monumental record of . . . ceremonies and rituals," Mullaney fails to distinguish between spatial practice and representational spaces—between the spaces of commerce, part of larger "routes and networks," and a landscape of monumentality. Of course one might argue that ritual encompasses both kinds of space, but to do so would be imprecise. The Lord Mayor's show, traversing "markets and common places," provides at best an idealized and ideological representation of the city,[20] and one that has, because of shifts in spatial practice, begun to ring increasingly hollow as we near the end of the sixteenth century.[21] The Lord Mayor's show is a guild production that in its form represents the primacy of the guilds to the city, but that primacy is threatened by the emergence of industries that lie outside the guild's influence, just as they often lie outside the city's wall.[22] It is to that wall that I will now turn. I do so in order to show that for both Mullaney and Heywood the wall is a representational space that offers illusory clarity of definition to a beleaguered city.

OF THE ROMAN WALL encircling what for lack of a better term we will call "London proper," Mullaney says the following:

The ultimate emblem of London's coherence and integrity, the most prominent of its figures of space, was the ancient Roman wall . . . It had long been useless for purposes of defense, and . . . [had] ceased to act in even the most residual capacity as an effective barrier against the outside world. In the sixteenth century it functioned solely as a means of symbolic definition, a monumental demarcation of the limits of community, an emblem of civic integrity that was annually 'refortified' by the ceremonial repertoire of the city.[23]

On the one hand, the wall emblematizes London's putative organic wholeness. On the other, it acts "solely as a means of symbolic definition" because it no longer functions as "an effective barrier." Mullaney moves from one interpretive register to another, suggesting that while the wall is an emblem of the city's "coherence and integrity," they are illusory, only symbolic and not indicative of the wall's status as "[in]effective barrier." In what *non*symbolic ways, then, can we define the city? This is a question Mullaney does not ask, but one answer is to be found in the way in which spatial practice contradicts a notion of the wall as representational space: the wall is no longer "an effective barrier against the outside world" because the socioeconomic expansion of the city means that outside cannot be easily separated from inside. In other words and as I shall show, while the wall continues to offer symbolic coherence to the city and its inhabitants—to suggest the form of a unified landscape—changing spatial practices render that coherence increasingly illusory.[24]

The wall in *1 Edward IV* signifies literally as a physical barrier. As a representational space it also draws distinctions between the citizens ("us") and the rebels ("them"); it symbolically demarcates a socioeconomic order defending itself against an alternative labor force.[25] That is, the battle for London can be read as a battle between two economies, two conceptions of labor, and two labor forces; it is a struggle for control not only of the spaces of London but also of their meaning. While Falconbridge justifies the assault through a spurious claim to the throne, those he leads have different motivations and are understood in very different terms. An apprentice, speaking from inside the city to the rebels without, calls them

> those desperate, idle, swaggering mates,
> That haunt the suburbes in the time of peace,
> And raise up ale-house brawls in the streete;
> And when the rumour of the warre begins,
> You hide your heads, and are not to be found.
> Thou term'st it better that we keep our shoppes.
> It's good indeede wee should haue such a care,
> But yet, for all our keeping now and then,

> Your pilfring fingers break into our locks,
> Until at *Tyburn* you acquit the fault. (p. 18)

The rebels are first characterized as idle rogues and rabble-rousers, but by the end of this short passage they are thieves who "break into our locks." The locks are those of the citizens' shops—that the apprentice refers to "our shoppes" suggests his investment in them and in the social order of which they are a part—but they can easily be conflated here with the "locks" of the city: the rebels have shortly before been "beat[ing] on the gates" of the city (p. 14), and we are told that "such places as were needfull" have been fortified to prevent their entrance (p. 17). The assault on the city is metaphorically aligned with an assault on citizens' shops.

Importantly, the rebel force is characterized as a suburban one, even though it is largely drawn from rural areas. This characterization probably attests to the fact that in the second half of the sixteenth century the suburbs were swelled by a rural population displaced by social upheavals such as enclosure. This population, often under- or unemployed, was read as criminal; as the historian A. L. Beier puts it, "In Tudor England unemployment was defined as a dangerous crime."[26] In addition, the suburbs functioned as symbols of disorder and license, and were commonly understood as the originary site for a whole range of "invasions." In describing the plague of 1603, Thomas Dekker talks of how "Death (like a Spanish Leagar, or rather like stalking *Tamberlaine*) hath pitcht his tents . . . in the sinfully-polluted Suburbes."[27] Plague is associated with the sinful suburbs, and its advance is metaphorized as a military invasion. An anonymous writer describes another type of invasion that reminds us of the one envisioned by Heywood's apprentice: he talks of how after "their Theeveries and Felonies committed within" London, many "Thieves and other misdoers" return to their homes, the suburban brothels of Southwark, "where they abide and watch their times, to return to do mischief."[28] This invasion is a recurring one, during each performance of which "Thieves and other misdoers" presumably "break into the locks" of the citizens' shops much as they slide through the gates of the city.

I mention these examples to suggest the way in which suburban spaces were regularly seen as posing a threat to the city proper.[29] That the suburbs were profoundly overdetermined for most Elizabethan Londoners is of course reflected in the apprentice's description: the suburbanites are accused of everything from idleness to theft to the evasion of military responsibilities.[30] Nevertheless, although he characterizes the rebel force in a sweeping way that preys upon Londoners' fears, Heywood also defines the rebels more narrowly. They are called "vagrant idle knaues" (p. 37), but they are not vagabonds. We are told the jobs of many of them: Smoke is a smith, Chub a chandler, and Spicing "the honestest lad that euer pound spice in a mortar" (p. 10).[31] Given this occupational specificity, it is significant that the suburbs were sites not only of anxiety, but also of industry. In a historical examination of the London underworld, John L. McMullan talks of the development of

new domestic industries of the city suburbs outside the regulations of the livery companies . . . Attracted by the tax benefits of escaping city jurisdiction, their industries—sugar refining, glassmaking, alum and dye works, copper and brass mills, clock making, weaving, printing, and the silk trade—made use of cheap labor without providing the benefits of apprenticeship.[32]

During the Elizabethan period the guilds attempted to regulate suburban industry, but with little success.[33] Moreover, the cheap labor McMullan refers to posed a threat not only to the guilds, but to the social composition of the city. The livery companies were traditionally responsible for those who became citizens and those who did not:

When a man finished his apprenticeship term [usually of seven years] he became a member of the company associated with his new craft or trade, swearing an oath of a Baker or a Weaver before the master and wardens, the company's governors, in a simple ceremony at the hall. In most cases a man was admitted at the rank of journeyman, though some men set up their own shops immediately after completing their training and thus never worked as wage labourers. On that same day or usually no more than a few days later, he and his late master and one of the wardens of his company walked to Guildhall where he was sworn as a citizen or "freeman" of London.[34]

This economic coming-of-age ritual through which an apprentice achieves his "freedom" ensures guild control over the citizenship of London and perpetuates a certain social order: the apprentice eventually becomes master, takes on apprentices, and reproduces the system. However, in the late sixteenth century there were an increasing number of complaints about the breakdown of this system; masters hired laborers they had no intention of promoting to journeymen status, and these workers, often suburban "cheap labor," would fill for a time the positions usually occupied by journeymen. In other words, apprenticeship was no longer definitely the first step toward a privileged position in a guild structure that provided economic security.[35] Moreover, historians such as Robert Tittler have suggested that the hegemony of the livery company was being threatened as early as the 1530's:

[F]aced with the sharpened competition for overseas trade, the expanding and more mobile labour force at home, and the burgeoning rate of inflation, it became difficult to reconcile the traditional patterns of regulation with the new demands for freedom of economic action. Such demands came from craftsmen and investors who found it unprofitable or inconvenient to function within the bounds of corporate jurisdiction, from labourers who were unwilling to observe conditions of apprenticeship, and from the forces of the market itself, where the pressures of competition sternly challenged traditional corporate jurisdiction.[36]

Suburban industries, existing largely outside the influence of city and guild regulations, competed with livery companies, offering a troubling alternative to guild hierarchies governing individual advancement. Of course such alternatives were also being explored within the city proper, but both suburban industry and the growing suburban labor force were figured as the sources of these unsettling social transformations (just as the suburbs were the "source" for plague and thievery); demands for suburban "economic freedom" conflicted with guild structures for doling out citizenship, called "freedom." The rebels in Heywood's play represent in part the guild's fear of the economy being wrested from its hands, the fear that those who regulate commerce in Leadenhall will not be liveried guild members who have risen through the ranks, but usurping smiths and chandlers from outside the city proper. The physical barriers of the city suggest a customary landscape: they are believed to mark the parameters of an economy, one that is imagined as being self-perpetuating, self-sufficient, and in an antagonistic relationship with the world beyond the wall. Just as it stages a struggle between guild and nonguild, Heywood's play imagines an urban economy freed of its dependence on and interdependence with commerce and production outside the city. Obviously such an economy had not existed in London for hundreds of years; the London economy was intertwined with both regional and international economies.[37] The play then not only denies emergent spatial practices, but also downplays traditional ones that trouble the integrity of the seamless representational space suggested by the city's walled perimeter.

While the rebels seek to wrest control of the city's economy from its citizens, the apprentices fight bravely to defend guild hierarchies and privileges. The attack on the city is understood by the citizens as an attack on their "property," described as "our goods, our children, and our wiues" (p. 14). For the (male) apprentices, this is an attack made on what they will one day own if they remain loyal to the livery companies. In fact, the advancement of apprentices is explicitly linked to their efforts against the rebels: if the apprentices "stick to [their] officers," the Lord Mayor, who is appointed yearly from among liveried guild members, tells them that they "may come to be as we are now" (p. 17). That is, the ideology of advancement usually deployed to ensure apprentices keep at their *work* is here adduced to keep them at their *posts*; it is both this ideology and the hierarchy it enables that are defended from those who would sell pearls in Leadenhall.

In their zeal to advance, the apprentices do more than merely stick to their officers. In a general "fierie assault," only the apprentices' exploits are alluded to: they "doe great seruice" (p. 20). The apprentices fight in the name of "the antient custom of [their] fathers" (p. 17), and in doing so collapse into one another paternity and guild structure, "custom" referring to those regulations which allow one member of a guild to practice the trade or craft of another.[38] Defense of the city is conflated with defense of a male-dominated household, and therein we see guild structures naturalized, made familial and patrilineal.[39] The play imagines the city's reproduction as an internal, paternalistic affair requiring the repulsion of those outside the walls. To do so, of course, is to resist the greatest fact of population growth in sixteenth-century London: both city and livery companies grew because of the immigration of "aliens and foreigners." Nonetheless, Heywood's London, demarcated by the wall that suggests its coherence and its separation from the suburbs, is a representational space "lived" as the embodiment of a social order. Defense of the city is the defense not only of guild buildings like Leadenhall, but of paternalistic ideologies that, for Heywood, are inseparable from the physical geography of London, a geography whose contours give shape to both guild fears and guild virtues: the wall does not merely reflect, but also lends coherence to, guild identity by suggesting the space of the guilds' prerogatives and resistances. At the same time, the symbolic meaning that "overlays [the] physical space" of the city, but cannot be abstracted from it, resists shifts in spatial practice that underlie the development of suburban industry and the erosion of livery-company influence. The battle for London that Heywood stages is a symbolic reworking of an economic struggle that the guilds had already begun to lose.[40] Moreover, it offers us a glimpse of a notion of social space as the complex interplay of spatial practice and representational space, and of a London that is something much more than a "ceremonial city."

ONE WAY OF THINKING of Falconbridge's rebellion is as a perceived assault on the "antient custom" of the city. Custom, I have suggested, refers narrowly to guild practices that enable members to participate in a number of different trades. In this context, custom works to ensure guild control of all urban economic activity, allowing the citizen to experience a certain amount of economic "freedom" while always acting under the auspices of the livery companies. At the same time, we have seen that this "antient custom" is linked to the paternalism governing the logic of advancement in the guilds. However, the word can be understood more broadly, for it encompasses not only guild activity but those sets of practices that give shape to the city's landscape. That is, custom can provide us with a way of defining more fully the distinctive nature of the spaces of the city.

Inextricably linked to the history and activity of a particular place, customs "taketh [their] force by degrees of time, and consent of a certaine people, or the better part therof . . ."[41] Moreover, customs are understood as offering a particular locality exemptions from laws that are designed for the country as a whole. As one anonymous writer puts it,

a Custome is applyed to the commoditie of some one prouince, circuite or citie, and grounded upon a speciall reason of conueniencie or comoditie, for those persons or place where it is obserued: whereas the Lawe hath a generall reason, extended to the whole Nation bound by the same, without priuate consideration of the due importances, of any peculiar place or people.[42]

Arguing for the "maintenance of the laudable customs of London," the same writer describes customs as

the principall ioyntes and uerie sinowes of all good corporations and fel-lowships, and being also the mainteiners of a sacred unitie and natural amitie betweene the husband and his wife, the parentes & their children, which (as *Aristotle* the wise Philosopher termeth it) is the beginning of a citie. For what is a citie but a manifold and ioynt societie consisting of many housholdes, and liuing under the same Lawes, freedomes and fran-chises?[43]

Corporations, households, and cities are inextricably linked by custom, the set of behaviors and practices that are understood here as being the joints and sinews upon which all social behavior is framed. In appealing to "antient customs," Heywood's apprentice gestures not only to long-standing guild practices, but to a notion of the city as a whole that accommodates both the spaces of commerce and those of the home.

Custom is what imbues the urban landscape of Heywood and the guilds with its meaning; it defines London's status as a repre-sentational space, and provides us with a spatialized history par-ticular to that city. The crucial point is that the threat to the guilds is understood in Heywood as also being a threat to the very social fabric of the city, to the customs that govern behavior at both the civic and the household level—indeed, at the level of the "sacred unitie and natural amitie between the husband and his wife." (This lends a certain significance to a phenomenon we will soon en-counter: the metaphoric conflation of city, shop, and female body.) Consider the use of the term in the following passage, in which the mayor decries the presence in London of "forreiners" and "stran-gers" who,

wholie intending their priuate profit, haue of late yeares deuised and prac-
tized by all sinister and subtil meanes, how to defraud and defeat the said
Charters, Liberties, Customs, good orders, and ordinances, and to that
end, do now inwardlie in priuie and secret places, usually and ordinarily,
shew, sel, & put to sale, their Wares, & Marchandizes, and use Arts,
Trades, Occupations, Misteries, and Handicraftes within the said Cittie
and Liberties . . . to the great detriment and hurt of the Freemen . . . [44]

The presence of foreigners and strangers—those who have not been
made citizens or freemen through participation in the guilds—
speaks to the existence of a thriving nonguild economy that inhab-
its "priuie and secret places." This document gestures toward a
shadow London, a secret city governed by "sinister and subtil
meanes" and devoted only to "priuate profit." This is not a London
made flesh out of the joints and sinews of custom, but rather one
thriving at custom's expense.[45]

THUS FAR I HAVE described the threat to the city as a shift in spatial practice: the development of an alternative economy demands
the reconfiguration of urban spaces in a number of ways, not the
least of which involves a change in the traditional relationship between center and periphery, a change that is symbolically resisted
through the staging of an external assault on a London read as an organic whole defined by the wall (as a particular representational
space). However, Heywood's play also records another threat to the
guild economy of London, one that undermines Heywood's own
stated conception of the history play and its impact. In his *Apology
for Actors*, Heywood asserts that history plays should work to

teach the subiects obedience to their King, to shew the people the
vntimely ends of such as haue moued tumults, commotions, and insurrec-
tions, to present [them] with the flourishing estate of such as liue in obedience, exhorting them to allegeance, dehorting them from trayterous and
fellonious stratagems.[46]

However, *1 Edward IV* raises questions about the abuse of royal prerogative, the limits of obedience, and the didacticism of drama.[47] Let us return for a moment to Falconbridge's speech:

> We will be Masters of the Mint ourselues,
> And set our own stamp on the golden coin.
> We'll shoe our neighing coursers with no worse
> Than the purest siluer that is solde in Cheape.
> At *Leadenhall,* we'll sell pearles by the pecke,
> As now the mealmen vse to sell their meal.
> In *Westminster,* we'll keep a solemne court,
> And build it bigger to receiue our men. (p. 10)

Falconbridge's multiple goals—his desire to control labor, to exploit urban resources, and to adopt kingly prerogatives—are of a piece, for Heywood is presenting us with his nightmare vision of a kingship in which the monarch exploits the city for his own ends. That the last two sentences are as syntactically similar as they are suggests that Falconbridge understands the city and the court to be intimately connected, to be part of the same prize.[48] What is intriguing about Heywood's play is that it considers, however briefly, the relationship between city and court as being deleterious to the citizens; it suggests that the customs of the city—"the mainteiners of a sacred unitie and natural amitie betweene the husband and his wife"—are threatened by the actions of the monarch. Falconbridge's plan to control not only the court but the city's commerce obviously tells the playgoer what s/he already knows, that "King" Falconbridge would abuse his authority in relationship to the city. However, in certain ways Falconbridge is similar to the rightful monarch, Edward IV; we see Falconbridge's invasion echoed in the king's forceful wooing of the wife of one of London's leading citizens, Jane Shore.

As noted above, the (male) citizens see the assault on the city as one aimed at their goods, children, and wives, and Falconbridge largely confirms their fears. Responding to the valorous speech of Matthew Shore, who is the play's central emblem of citizenly virtue, Falconbridge asserts before his attack on the city, "[T]hy wife is mine, thats flat. / This night, in thine own house, she sleeps with me" (p. 16). Again the assault on the walls of the city is conflated with the assault on a citizen's house, and Falconbridge plans to take over Shore's property, both his wife and his home. This threat is quashed by London's citizen army, but it is replaced by a subtler one described in similar ways. In response to King Edward's persistent wooing later in the play, Jane characterizes herself as a besieged fortress: "He, he it is, that with a violent siege / Labours to breake into my plighted faith" (p. 73). Later, after she has become the king's mistress, Jane admits to her husband that she "yeelded vp the fort, / Wherein lay all the riches of my joy; / But yet . . . before I yeelded it, / I did indure the longst and greatest siege / That euer batterd on poor chastity" (p. 84). Jane deploys a metaphor common to the early modern period, that of the female love object as a fort or town assaulted by an unwanted, forceful lover. This metaphor aligns female chastity with the impregnability of the fortress.[49] However, to say that this is a conventional topos is not to rob it of its specificity here. In the context of a play concerned early and at length with another assault, one in which not only "plighted faith[s]" but the city's walls and citizens' shops are to be broken into, Jane's metaphor forces us to imagine Edward as occupying a position in relationship to the city analogous to the one occupied by Falconbridge.[50] While Falconbridge hopes to sleep with Jane in Shore's "own house," Edward enters Shore's shop in the hopes of buying its "fairest jewel," Jane herself (p. 64). As Jane's metaphor tells us, this is to be less a purchase than a ransacking.[51]

In my discussion of *Arden of Faversham*'s representation of Alice, I emphasized that the play effaced (or perhaps demonized) the multiple contributions that women historically made to the maintenance of household and estate. *1 Edward IV*, on the other hand, represents Jane as an active contributor to the household economy. In the scene in which the king first appears in Shore's shop, stage directions say that Jane enters *"with her worke in her hand,"* and we later see her sewing; her first line in the scene tells us that she will "attend the shop [her]self" (p. 63). Heywood goes out of his way to represent Jane as both tending the shop and laboring for the good of the household. In pursuing the citizen's wife whom he reifies as a precious jewel, Edward not only recapitulates Falconbridge's actions but poses a specific threat to the livelihood of the Shore household, to which his "precious jewel" actively contributes. Certainly the logic of the play is primarily a masculinist one that figures women as property: at the moment that parallels this one, in which Falconbridge taunts Matthew by saying, "[T]hy wife is mine," it is clear that Jane functions largely as the vehicle by which a homosocial agon is extended, an agon defining relations between not only guild member and rebels but also the spaces inside and outside the wall. Nevertheless, Heywood presents us with a Jane Shore who signifies not simply as one man's wife and another man's mistress, but as a contributing member of an economy under attack. Moreover, while Matthew's giving up of his business after the loss of his wife is motivated primarily by grief, it also reminds us of the significance of the absent Jane to the running of that business.[52]

We have witnessed the metaphorical conflation of three spaces aligned by the logic of custom: the shops and houses of citizens; the city demarcated by the walls; and the (economically productive) female body. Each is figured as a space besieged first by Falconbridge and then in a subtler way by Edward. The latter siege complicates Heywood's notion of the history play as a form that teaches obedience. While the play again and again insists on the citizens' loyalty to their king, Jane and Matthew Shore, the affective centers of the play, are grievously wounded by that king: Jane is largely coerced into becoming Edward's mistress, and Matthew's despair drives him from the country. Even then Matthew asserts the primacy of the monarch; when Jane offers to go into exile with him, Matthew responds, "Oh God forbid / That I should be a traitor to my King!" (p. 84). And yet, the play troubles the appropriateness of such decisions. There is an underlying tension throughout between the citizens' interests and the monarch's, a tension that is obvious from the beginning, when the play stages a defense of the city from which the king is strikingly absent; he spends the night, admittedly that of his wedding, "in feast and iollity" with the intention of aiding the fight against Falconbridge the following day (p. 8). But the king arrives only after the battle has been won; as Lena Cowen Orlin puts it, "That Edward is finally proved unnecessary to the defense of London ... threatens not only to displace him but also to disable the kingship."[53] The king's absence may be partly explained by what Mowbray Velte has rightly referred to as the play's primary interest "in glorifying the deeds of [Heywood's] theatrical constituency, the prentices of the city" (although I would define that constituency more broadly as London's populace).[54] However, it is also that interest that leads the playgoer to sympathize with Jane and Matthew, and to question repeatedly the legitimacy of Edward's actions and perhaps of his rule. In the terms of his own definition of the history play, Heywood may attempt to "teach the subiects obedience," but, in the case of the Shores, that loyalty destroys rather than enhances "the flourishing estate of such as liue in obedience."

To read the play this way is to read it against the grain, for its intention is clearly if not to justify the ways of kings to men, then to inculcate in the citizen playgoer loyalty to the Crown. However, it would be a mistake to assume that *1 Edward IV* does not explore, however tentatively, the troubling possibility of the monarchy's abuse of power in its relationship to the city, an abuse figured here not as an assault on the representational space of the walled city but on its analogue in the play world, the chaste female body. As I have suggested, the integrity of the female body cannot be separated

from that of the shop, the wall, or the city itself. Edward slips in
secret across the river and into the city—"At *Lion quay* I landed in
... view [of the watermen], / Yet none of them took knowledge of
the King" (p. 64)—and besieges Shore's shop, attempting to take
from it its "fairest jewel"; his penetration of the city is aligned with
a metaphoric assault on both the exemplary citizen's shop and his
wife. While Falconbridge was repulsed attempting a similar act, the
king himself cannot be so easily expelled.[55] Edward talks of buying
that fairest jewel, but Jane insists that it is not for sale: "Whateuer
we possesse is all your highness; / Only mine honour, which I cannot grant" (p. 66). When she does become the king's mistress,
there is little doubt that she does so because she is forced to. Edward's rhetoric of economic exchange denies the unequal nature of
the relationship between citizen and king, and Edward's supposed
purchase is only made possible by his abuse of royal power; as king,
he knows that "he that offers fairer than [Edward] do[es], / Shall
hardly find a partner in his bargaine" (p. 65)—that is, the one who
can offer more than the king will have no equal with whom to
trade. And yet, Edward himself is hardly engaged in an equal
commercial exchange. Edward metaphorically intervenes in and
disrupts the commerce and custom of the city, transforming Jane
into a commodity and thereby buying that which is not for sale.

In short, as in the case of Falconbridge's attack, the threat to
Jane must be seen as intertwined with an economic threat. Also,
the interlocking metaphors discussed above suggest that Edward's
siege of Jane can be understood partly as the symbolic displacement
of anxiety regarding relations between the Crown and the city's
masculinized mercantile economy. This anxiety emerges out of the
relationship between the monarchy and the livery companies, a relationship that had deteriorated in the 1590's around an issue that,
like Edward's "violent siege" of Jane, centered on the nature and
limits of royal prerogative.[56] The issue was that of the Crown's
awarding of monopolies.

THE GRANTING OF royal charters of incorporation to what were
to become the livery companies dates from the late fourteenth
century; the Tailors received a charter as early as 1390, the Mercers
in 1394, the Saddlers in 1395. These charters "replaced the ecclesias-
tical sanction upon which the trade fraternities had rested by the
secular sanction of the State, whilst at the same time they preserved
for the livery companies a basis of voluntary association independent of the civic authority."[57] Charters granted the companies the
right to trade, but that right was not a monopolistic one:

Each fully developed livery company had its court in which trade disputes
were settled and by whose authority members could be fined and even
imprisoned . . . Similarly, each company based its existence on the possession of a royal charter, but this charter was not necessarily a grant of exclusive trading privileges . . . ; the essential point . . . was that it conferred
the immortal collective personality of a corporation.[58]

However, in the late Elizabethan period, new charters were increasingly monopolistic, as incorporation often went hand in hand
with the issuing of royal patents granting to the patentee exclusive
right to trade in a particular commodity: "the new companies
seeking incorporation were . . . in many cases the allies of the patentees."[59] New incorporation was resisted by the city, presumably
because of the negative impact on existing industry. Robert Ashton
tells us that "The history of the City fathers' attitude to new incorporation of craftsmen is the tale of bitter opposition to royal poli-
cies, defiance of royal commands and determined attempts to hold
out against them for as long as possible." This history "provides the
first of our major examples of a conflict of interest between the
crown and the City."[60] These patentees were often courtiers whom
Elizabeth owed money, received money from, or wanted to please;
we see the incursion of court politics into the spaces of city commerce.[61] Patents were not linked merely to the incorporation of
new companies, however. Instead, patents would often take ad-

vantage of the growing separation in existing livery companies between manufacturing and trading interests, a separation that would eventually aid in the total dissolution of the guilds and the emergence of capitalism.[62] I quote at length a relevant account related by George Unwin:

In 1592 Mr. Edward Darcy took up the cause of the glovers and other workers in leather, and proposed to protect them against the oppression of the leathersellers by establishing a place of inspection at Smithfield for all skins sold to them . . . in return for a fee . . . To this project the Leathersellers offered a stout opposition, in which they had the warm sympathy of the city. Darcy, who had spent £500 or £600 in procuring the patent . . . lost his temper and so far forgot himself as to strike an alderman in the Lord Mayor's presence during a discussion of the proposal. The insult was noised abroad, the city apprentices gathered, and Darcy would not have escaped with his life but for the protection afforded by the Lord Mayor. The patentee, however, with the support of the Government, persisted in his scheme, and as the Leathersellers were equally determined their four wardens were ultimately committed to prison. Their appeal to Burleigh . . . [reflected their] fervent loyalty to the Queen . . . blended with an even stronger attachment to the laws and liberties of their country. . . . They spoke boldly of the patents as being contrary to the laws of the land, and as a "great unnecessary taxing of all commons in the realm and especially of the poorest sort whose chief wearing leather is." . . . The wardens were released within a year and Darcy's patent withdrawn, but Elizabeth claimed £4000 from the city and the leathersellers in compensation.[63]

Fervent loyalty blended with an attachment to the laws and liberties of the land: the four imprisoned wardens rhetorically juggle the demands of obeisance to the monarch and the conflicting right of citizens to trade in ways traditionally allowed by livery companies; the skirmish between city and patentee becomes one between citizens and queen, and even the final rejection of Darcy's patented claim costs the city dearly.

The issue at stake here and in all struggles over the awarding of royal patents is not only the regulation of commerce. "During the last two parliaments of Elizabeth's reign," Ashton tells us, "holders of internal patents of monopoly, had been the object of bitter attacks, and . . . monopolies raised issues which transcended considerations of economics. For . . . the question of monopolies was intimately bound up with that of the royal prerogative."[64] What Unwin's example reveals to us is the way in which royal prerogative, strongly interrogated at the time of the production of Heywood's play, interfered with the traditional operation of city business. The apprentices gather to defeat not rural rebels but one of the queen's patentees; it is not only suburban industry, but also royally sponsored incursions into guild life that promise to steal the "fairest jewels" from the city. Royal prerogative lurks behind the actions of Edward IV and Edward Darcy, and in each case the rights of London's citizens, whether the assaulted alderman, the imprisoned wardens, or the brokenhearted Shore, prove secondary to the imperatives of monarchical desire and ambition.

We have noted Falconbridge's rhetorical yoking of the control of both commerce and the court—he plans to "build [the court] bigger" while also selling "pearles by the pecke" in Leadenhall. That the two phenomena are syntactically aligned may suggest Heywood's fear of the royal domination of London's economy through monopolies; presumably Falconbridge's courtiers, like Elizabeth's, will be those patentees governing trade in Leadenhall. What is overt in the case of Falconbridge is covertly explored by Heywood in his depiction of Edward. Heywood's play raises questions about the nature and limits of royal prerogative, questions also suggested by the fierce debates over the granting of monopolies that raged at the time of *1 Edward IV*'s production. While the play is unabashedly pro-monarchy, it, like the four wardens in the Darcy case, pledges allegiance to the queen while also subtly suggesting the problematic nature of certain of her actions. Moreover, in *1 Edward IV* royal prerogative is a spatial matter; the king sneaks into and through the city, symbolically violating the integrity of those besieged spaces, the wall, the shop, and the chaste woman. At the same time, the monarch is arguably sovereign over all of these spaces, or so the play wants to suggest, and the contradiction between sovereignty and violation is putatively resolved by the play in favor of the former. The conflict between the king's sovereignty and the city's autonomy is in part a jurisdictional one—who really is master of London?—and in *1 Edward IV* the tension between the two possible sources of authority is displaced onto the physical spaces of the city; the wall may seem to demarcate the boundaries of city and guild authority, but Edward's disguised presence attests to the troubling possibility that London, or at least its "fairest jewel," may be claimed by the monarch for his own. What we see, then, is the city alternately figured as a customary landscape and as one component of a larger landscape of sovereignty.[65]

WHAT HEYWOOD'S PLAY tries to work out is the relationship of the city and its customs to its own economic expansion, to its environs, and to a monarchy financially dependent upon it, yet often domineering.[66] In doing so, *1 Edward IV* insists on a citizen culture distinct from that of English culture as a whole and from the imperatives of the monarchy. Heywood's emphasis on the lives of London's citizens seems more appropriate to Jacobean city comedy than to Elizabethan history plays; his play offers an alternative to the dominant historiographical conventions identified by Phyllis Rackin as informing the production of Shakespeare's history plays. Both masculinist and aristocratic, "[Renaissance historiography's] heroic subject matter, its genealogical purpose, and its status as written text all served to exclude common men as well as women from the elite province its discourse constructed."[67] While Rackin's account may describe the biases of Shakespeare's drama, Renaissance historiography also foregrounded material that was ignored by Shakespeare but drawn upon by Heywood. Consider this selection from Edward Hall's 1548 account of the Cade rebellion:

The multitude of the rebelles drave the citezens from the stoulpes at the bridge foote, to the drawe bridge, and began to set fyre in divers houses. Alas what sorow it was to beholde that miserable chaunce: for some desyrynge to eschew the fyre, lept on his enemies weapon, and so died: fearfull women with chyldren in their armes, amased and appalled, lept into the river: other doubtinge how to save them self betwene fyre, water, and swourd, were in their houses suffocat and smoldered.[68]

Like those in Heywood's play, Hall's citizens attempt to defend their city and their houses from a rebellion that penetrates London. However, what Hall represents is largely absent from the Jack Cade scenes in *2 Henry VI*. Brents Stirling points to several important differences between *1 Edward IV* and *2 Henry VI*: while Heywood's London is defended by citizens, Shakespeare's is protected by a "muster of aristocrats";[69] a "humble miller" captures Falconbridge, but in Shakespeare it is "a gentleman [named Iden] . . . who is the nemesis of the rebels"; Heywood's citizens are shown as "a sober and intelligent force," while citizens are largely absent from Shakespeare's play, with the exception of "1 Citizen," who appears to tell Lord Scales, "The Lord Mayor craves aid of your honor from the Tower [of London] to defend the city from the rebels."[70] While Heywood shows us an embattled London with a distinct citizens' culture defined by the primacy of the guilds, Shakespeare's city, despite a degree of geographical specificity, is merely the stage for combat between aristocrats and rebels that functions primarily "as an ironic commentary on the main action," the aristocratic and monarchical struggle known as the Wars of the Roses.[71]

The difference between the London scenes in Heywood's play and in Shakespeare's may be put broadly as the difference between competing conceptions of space and history. In order to show this, I must make a short detour and turn to Richard Mulcaster's famous account of Elizabeth's coronation procession. This text represents a spatial logic followed by both Jack Cade and Shakespeare's play as a whole. The 1559 account informs us that "if a man should say well, he could not better tearme the citie of London that time, than a stage" upon which the queen greeted her subjects.[72] Elizabeth passed through streets decorated with elaborate tapestries, along which stood representatives of the city guilds "apparelled with many ryche furres and theyr livery whodes [hoods] upon theyr shoulders in comely and semely maner . . ." At one point the queen came "to the upper ende of Cheape," where the Master Recorder, as spokesperson for "the Lord maior, hys brethren, and comminaltie of the citie," presented her with "a purse of crimosin [crimson] satin richly wrought with gold, wherin the citie gave unto [Elizabeth] a thousand markes in gold . . . to declare their gladnes and good wille towardes the Quene's majestie . . . *desyering her grace to continue their good and gracious Quene*, and not to esteme the value of the gift, but the mynd of the gevers."[73] The presentation of the gift represents the obeisance of the city to the Crown; the city fathers pay tribute to the new queen. At the same time, what is striking about this description is the opulence and splendor of the city and of representatives of city industry. Guild leaders and civic officials, the latter elected from within guilds, parade their wealth before the queen in a display that simultaneously shows their loyalty and their power, for as sources of wealth for an impoverished monarchy these city fathers wield more than influence.[74] With that in mind, one might see in the gift of the satin purse not only a tribute but an assertion of authority, and perhaps a not so hollow demand that Elizabeth continue to be their "good and gracious Quene."[75]

We might understand this text in terms of a conflict between two spatial conceptions of the city, a conflict displayed in the form of the coronation account itself. To put it schematically, the city of this monarchical spectacle, traversed from the Tower to "the upper ende of Cheape," is on the one hand a space to be passed through;

we cross it with the monarch, and the distinctive social spaces of London are read as the site for a series of scripted exchanges (interactions upon a stage). This is the city as part of a landscape of sovereignty. On the other hand, the city offered to us by these urban fathers suggests a customary landscape, for it is the instantiation of a set of social and material practices: the guild masters in their livery hoods embody a socioeconomic structure that encompasses masters, journeymen, and apprentices; the bedecking of Cheap, the principal commercial area of London, speaks to the centrality of mercantile activity, its privileged position in the city's self-definition, and the aforementioned interconnection of city government and the guilds. We see in Elizabeth's exchange with the civic and guild officials the negotiation at the symbolic level of urban and monarchical imperatives through this clash of particular spaces. The difference is not the difference between a true and false representation of the city, but between two landscapes, two potentially conflicting conceptions of urban space inherent in one larger ritualized, symbolic conception.[76]

For Shakespeare's Jack Cade, monarchical ritual involves the enactment of only one of these two conflicting conceptions. Cade parodies Henry VI's royal entry into London when he says, "I charge and command that, of the city's cost, the pissing-conduit run nothing but claret wine this first year of our reign" (4.6.2–4).[77] In civic ceremonies, conduits were where pageant devices were often located; pageantry becomes for Cade the magician's trick of turning pissing-conduit water into wine. Moreover, while the city fathers, in an equivocal act of obeisance, greet Elizabeth's ascension with a tribute of gold, that gift here becomes money extorted from London: at Cade's command the wine flows "of the city's cost."[78] A projected royal procession becomes an act of violence done to the city; it is to be put on by the city against its will and with its money. We see elsewhere civic spaces ritualistically inscribed by Cade's authority. In a parody of the struggle between Henry and

York that is the focus of the play, Cade promises to execute those who refuse loyalty to him: "The proudest peer in the realm shall not wear a head on his shoulders unless he pay me tribute" (4.7.119–21). After making good on this promise, Cade orders that soldiers pass through the city and make the decapitated heads of Lord Say and Sir James Cromer "kiss" "at every corner" (4.7.136). In this projected perversion of monarchical pageantry, the city's spaces are to be transformed into a landscape of sovereignty in accordance with Cade's authority. Of course Cade, whose character emerges out of the traditions of the Land of Cockaigne and of festive misrule, has no legitimate claim to the throne. But his plans for the appropriation and abuse of the city mirror the play's broader insistence on the idea of the city as one of the stages upon which a national struggle for royal power is enacted. The fate of London is subsumed in the fate of the nation and the monarchy: "Thus stands *my* state," King Henry says, "'twixt Cade and York distressed" (4.9.31, emphasis mine). In Heywood's play we are constantly reminded that the defense of the city, enacted without aid from king or nobles, is a defense of the nation; the citizens act in the name of "our soueraign and our countries peace" (p. 15). At the same time, we never lose a sense of the city as a distinctive social space with its own logic and imperatives. But in *2 Henry VI*, Shakespeare's nameless citizen appeals to aristocrats for protection. London is read not in terms of its citizenry but as the site of a contest between "the commons" misled by Jack Cade and those nobles loyal to the king. Yet Cade has been commissioned by York to "make commotion . . . Under the title of John Mortimer" (3.1.358–59). The king and his state *actually* stand distressed between York and York's representative, a fact that underscores the sociospatial homogeneity of Shakespeare's notion of history.

The historiographical logic of Shakespeare's *2 Henry VI* necessitates an urban space like the stage passed over by England's monarch. That is, while civic spaces are particularized in terms of places and streets, London landmarks are stripped of the broader social context from which they emerged. Hall's gruesome battle between citizens and rebels for the control of London Bridge is reduced in Shakespeare to two discrete moments: first, a messenger's report that "Jack Cade hath gotten London Bridge; / The citizens fly and forsake their houses" (4.4.49–50); second, Cade's unfulfilled command to "set London Bridge on fire, and, if you can, burn down the Tower too" (4.6.14–15). Shakespeare's city reads largely like a congeries of dead monuments abandoned by its citizens to the battle between aristocrats and rebels, rebels who are led by a figure who both entertains mad monarchical ambitions and acts in the service of York.[79] Heywood, on the other hand, understands the architectural spaces of the city not as backdrop, but as the embodiment of a social order, that of the guild. For Shakespeare, history is performed on and across the blank stage of the city; for Heywood, the city's history is inseparable from its social spaces, the spaces that it simultaneously emerges out of and constructs.[80] Thus, Shakespeare offers us a landscape of the city much like that assumed by Heywood's Edward during his "invasions," a landscape of sovereignty in which the imperatives of the city and its culture are effaced through, as I have defined it, "the conceptual annexation of distinct cultural spaces in the name of [the] monarch," or, more precisely, monarchical history.

The distinctions I have drawn between the two plays are of course not absolute ones; the suburbs in Shakespeare's play, for instance, are recognizably figured as a staging ground for rebellion,[81] and the rebels include laborers: Dick the Butcher, Smith the Weaver, and so on. And yet, these rebels find no opposition from loyal guildsmen of London. If we want to locate even the faintest trace of guild culture in this play, we must turn to a moment earlier on, where we encounter division, not solidarity, between master and apprentice. I am referring to the fight between Horner and Peter, an armorer and his man. In this parody of a duel of honor,

Peter defeats his master, who finally confesses that he has treacher-ously asserted that York is the rightful king. This might seem a tri-umph of right over rank, but Peter is represented as a coward, and Horner loses because he is too drunk to fight. Each is surrounded by his supporters: the neighbors, presumably householders, who ply Horner with liquor, and the apprentices, who encourage Peter to "Fight for credit of the prentices" (2.3.71) while bolstering his spirits with beer. What we witness, then, is both a parody of the aristocratic duels that proliferate in Shakespearean history plays[82] and a debased and self-divided version of the kind of world cele-brated by Heywood. Moreover, Shakespeare's comic denigration of these characters is in the service of what Richard Helgerson has identified as the playwright's larger effort "to efface, alienate, even demonize all signs of commoner participation in the political na-tion."[83] Helgerson shows that over the course of 2 *Henry VI* we witness the gradual exclusion of all but the aristocratic few from the political nation, an exclusion that culminates in the demonizing of the commons in Cade's rebellion. Helgerson's account of this play is persuasive, but I would add that Shakespeare's representation of the spaces of London suggests the extent to which he successfully has, in Helgerson's term, "staged exclusion." It is Heywood who offers us a theatricalized glimpse of a landscape unified by guild practice, and of a history that places citizen culture at center stage.

Retrieving Lost Landscapes

A landscape unified by guild practice, and a history that places citizen culture at center stage: this description attests not only to the difference between Heywood and Shakespeare, but to the difference between texts produced by a writer located outside an established literary tradition and one who is planted squarely inside it. Traditions are, of course, always under construction, and the recent resurgence of interest in plays like *A Jovial Crew* and *1 Edward IV* may mark the beginning of the reconstitution of a dramatic tradition. However, the success of such a reconstitution should be measured not in terms of the simple inclusion of once-ignored texts, but in terms of the excavation of lost epistemologies. This is what Heywood's play offers us, a new (and of course old) way of seeing, a mode of landscape distinct both from Shakespeare and from the landscape arts. This way of seeing is not a perspective—not, that is, the ego-centered form that landscape takes under the regime of private property. It instead takes shape as a landscape inseparable from a guild-centered set of social relations, a landscape that comes into being through, in de Certeau's phrase, "the murky intertwining daily behaviors" of everyday practice. The existence of such landscapes has not been widely recognized, but not because of accident or omission. In much the same way that the early modern survey could be corrosive of the customary, the landscape arts and the conception of landscape they enact have effaced everyday practice and the landscapes it implies.

The aim of this book has been to retrieve lost landscapes. In doing so, it has often illuminated the cultural and conceptual struggles attendant upon the slow and fitful reconceptualization of land as private (or absolute) property. We have seen the theater play a crucial and socially conservative part in these struggles and this reconceptualization. What plays such as *Arden of Faversham*, *Woodstock*, and *A Jovial Crew* do is both foreground the costs of absolute property and champion a landscape of stewardship. That the fate of the estate is intertwined with that of the nation is made clear in *Woodstock* and *Richard II*: a nation or estate read as absolute property necessitates the decay of a land-centered social order. My aim has been to suggest that while the landscapes of absolute property have come to be seen as the only landscapes, the social costs of this phenomenon, so clearly recorded and imagined in the plays I have discussed here, have been largely ignored. This is no accident or simple act of forgetting, for forgetting in this case has been produced by the triumph of absolute property: to modify Walter Benjamin's famous formulation, the landscape of absolute property is a landscape of barbarism, institutionalized at the expense of other conceptions of land and dependent upon their erasure. It is these other conceptions that are both central to and embattled in early modern drama, as embattled as Heywood's guild culture is. And if these conceptions are finally those of the losing side, the mere recounting of the story of their loss constitutes a victory against forgetting.

Reference Matter

Notes

INTRODUCTION

1. Denis E. Cosgrove, *Social Formation and Symbolic Landscape* (London: Croom Helm, 1984), 9. For more of Cosgrove's crucial work on landscape, see, among many articles, "Landscapes and Myths, Gods and Humans," in *Landscape: Politics and Perspectives*, ed. Barbara Bender (Providence and Oxford: Berg, 1993), 281–305; "An Elemental Division: Water Control and Engineered Landscape" and "Platonism and Practicality: Hydrology, Engineering and Landscape in Sixteenth-Century Venice," in *Water, Engineering and Landscape*, ed. Cosgrove and Geoff Petts (London: Belhaven Press, 1990), 1–11, 35–53; "The Geometry of Landscape: Practical and Speculative Arts in Sixteenth-Century Venetian Land Territories" and, with Stephen Daniels, "Introduction: Iconography and Landscape," in *The Iconography of Landscape*, ed. Cosgrove and Daniels (Cambridge: Cambridge University Press, 1988), 254–76, 1–10. I am also grateful to Dan Beaver for sharing with me at an early stage in this project a provocative essay concerned with the category of landscape. That essay is now the first chapter in Beaver's book *Symbol and Boundary: Parish Communities and Religious Conflict in the Vale of Gloucester, 1590–1690* (Cambridge, Mass.: Harvard University Press, 1998).

2. D. W. Meinig ("Introduction," in *The Interpretation of Ordinary Landscapes*, ed. Meinig [New York and Oxford: Oxford University Press, 1979]) says

> [T]he idea of landscape runs counter to recognition of any simple binary relationship between man and nature. Rather, it begins with a naive acceptance of the intricate intimate intermingling of physical, biological, and cultural features which any glance around us displays. Landscape is, first of all, the unity we see, the impressions of our senses rather than the logic of our sciences. (2)

One should add that "the impressions of our senses" are hardly unmediated. Instead, they are formed in accordance with the ideological and perceptual categories structuring apprehension. Thus, such impressions do not simply precede landscape, but they simultaneously give shape to and are shaped by it.

3. Cosgrove, *Social Formation*, 13.

4. "[L]andscape represents an historically specific way of experiencing the world developed by, and meaningful to, certain social groups. Landscape . . . is an ideological concept" (Cosgrove, *Social Formation*, 15). See also Alan R. H. Baker, "Introduction: On Ideology and Landscape," in *Ideology and Landscape in Historical Perspective*, ed. Baker and Gideon Biger (Cambridge: Cambridge University Press, 1992), 1–14.

5. Raymond Williams, *The Country and the City* (Oxford: Oxford University Press, 1973); James Turner, *The Politics of Landscape: Rural Scenery and Society in English Poetry, 1630–1660* (Oxford: Basil Blackwell, 1979); Don E. Wayne, *Penshurst: The Semiotics of Place and the Poetics of History* (Madison: University of Wisconsin Press, 1984).

6. Chris Fitter, *Poetry, Space, Landscape: Toward a New Theory* (Cambridge: Cambridge University Press, 1995), 5, 10.

7. Ibid., 10, 12.

8. Baker, "Introduction: On Ideology and Landscape," 7.

9. Barbara Bender, "Introduction: Landscape—Meaning and Action," in *Landscape: Politics and Perspectives*, 1–2.

10. On "sartorial extravagance," see Karen Newman, "Dressing Up: Sartorial Extravagance in Early Modern London," in *Fashioning Femininity and English Renaissance Drama* (Chicago: University of Chicago Press, 1991), 111–27.

11. From John Williams, "Sermon on Apparel," 1620. Quoted in Peter J. Smith, *Social Shakespeare: Aspects of Renaissance Dramaturgy and Contemporary Society* (New York: St. Martin's, 1995), 28.

12. Of course I overstate the twentieth-century conception of land, which remains for many not only an important source of livelihood but a cornerstone of personal or familial identity. The crucial point, however, is that a subjective sense of one's relationship to the land is subordinated to the logic of capitalism, which defines land in terms of commodity relations.

13. Ben Jonson, *Every Man Out of His Humour*, in *The Complete Plays of Ben Jonson*, 4 vols., ed. G. A. Wilkes (Oxford: Clarendon Press, 1981), 1:1.2.33–39.

14. Ben Jonson, *Epicoene*, ed. L. A. Beaurline (Lincoln: University of Nebraska Press, 1966), 2.2.86–106.

15. Igor Kopytoff, "The Cultural Biography of Things: Commoditization as Process," in *The Social Life of Things: Commodities in Cultural Perspective*, ed. Arjun Appadurai (Cambridge: Cambridge University Press, 1986), 64. Kopytoff's analysis should be supplemented by Chandra Mukerji's insightful for-

mulation of the problems attendant upon the expansion of commodification: a "level of social strain and conceptual discomfort ... accompanied changes in the meanings of goods. ... [T]he proliferation of goods and their exchange in the early modern period was an important source of cultural confusion and innovation" (*From Graven Images: Patterns of Modern Materialism* [New York: Columbia University Press, 1983], 13).

16. Lawrence Stone, *The Crisis of the Aristocracy, 1558–1641,* abridged edition (Oxford: Oxford University Press, 1967), 22. Consider the above argument in relation to L. C. Knights's description of the impact (and origin) of the growth of the land market: "When Henry VIII ... redistributed the great monastic estates, much of the land, in large or small quantities, came into the hands of those who wanted it as a permanent possession for their families— members of the new aristocracy, citizens wishing to become 'gentlemen', prosperous yeomen building up small farms. But a very large proportion indeed was secured by land-jobbers who bought to sell again as a business speculation" (*Drama & Society in the Age of Jonson* [London: Chatto & Windus, 1937], 101). Land that becomes a permanent possession for families has its commodity status effaced, whereas that which becomes the object of business speculation is (re-)marked as a commodity. In addition, the development and prominence of the land market meant that, as far as land went, this kind of effacement became increasingly difficult to perform.

17. Jonson, *Epicoene,* 1.4.56–62.

18. Valentyne Leigh, *The Moste Profitable and Commendable Science, of Surveying* (London: Miles Jennings, 1577), F3r.

19. In the final chapter of this book, the landscape of custom that I identify in Heywood's *1 Edward IV* emerges out of urban guild practice; in that case, those who appeal to custom are not economically disadvantaged, but they do perceive themselves as advocates of traditional practices that are under siege. Obviously custom is a category that is relevant in arenas other than that of the estate, but for now I am focusing on the estate.

20. Andrew McRae, *God Speed the Plough* (Cambridge: Cambridge University Press, 1996), 172.

21. Ibid., 280. Or, as McRae puts it elsewhere, "As the individualist farmer was metamorphosed from a covetous canker on the body politic into a godly man of thrift and industry, the meaning of agrarian England shifted accordingly from a site of manorial community and moral economy toward a modern landscape of capitalist enterprise" (7). This shift took place in part in the name of economic freedom and at the expense of custom: "For the improver, ideals of manorial order had given way to the desire for 'profit'; the hon-

est ploughman had been displaced by the thrifty freeholder; and cries for economic freedom and rationalism were driving an assault upon the authority of custom" (168).

22. C. B. Macpherson, "Capitalism and the Changing Concept of Property," in *Feudalism, Capitalism and Beyond*, ed. Eugene Kamenka and R. S. Neale (Canberra: Australian National University Press, 1975), 111. As David H. Fletcher puts it, "in Tudor times, land tenure was a complex structure of communal property right; in the centuries which followed the situation was transformed, there being a near total dominance of private property" (*The Emergence of Estate Maps: Christ Church, Oxford, 1600 to 1840* [Oxford: Clarendon Press, 1995], 61).

23. For more on the subject of "progressive estate management," see Chapter Two.

24. Alastair Fowler, *The Country House Poem* (Edinburgh: Edinburgh University Press, 1994), 18.

25. Certainly gardens were prevalent in the sixteenth and seventeenth centuries, but they have suffered from a twofold erasure: first, the failure of garden historians to devote much attention to Renaissance formal gardens, a failure that Roy Strong gives as his reason for producing his authoritative book on the subject (*The Renaissance Garden in England* [London: Thames and Hudson, 1979], 7); and second, the destruction of such gardens by eighteenth-century landscape architects such as Capability Brown. The occlusion of the Renaissance garden from garden history is reflected in texts such as Laurence Fleming and Alan Gore's *The English Garden* (London: Michael Joseph, 1979), which devotes only one of seven chapters to the period up to 1660. This occlusion is arguably the result of the fact that the Renaissance garden is for the most part a formal one; it is only in the early seventeenth century with the importation of the Continental discovery of perspective that the garden even begins to be organized in terms of landscape as the term is usually understood—that is, in terms of a point of view.

26. "Prospect paintings were large, usually no less than six feet by four, sometimes larger still. They were displayed prominently in private houses, not just in the ones they depicted but also in other properties of their owners, perhaps a London mansion. They were not for the gaze of their owners alone. No less than heroic portraits of ancestors they were meant to impress visitors. And the main impression they made was of landed property" (Stephen Daniels, "Goodly Prospects: English Estate Portraiture, 1670–1730," in *Mapping the Landscape: Essays on Art and Cartography*, ed. Nicholas Alfrey and Stephen Daniels [Nottingham: University Art Gallery and Castle Museum, 1990], 9).

27. William A. McClung asserts that "'Upon Appleton House' is a product

of topographical poetry and the enthusiasm for solitude and gardens as much as it is a continuation of the country-house genre. . . . The genre asserts itself most fully in this poem as a vehicle for praise of a virtuous person (or persons), rather than as a statement about the social function of country houses" (*The Country House in English Renaissance Poetry* [Berkeley: University of California Press, 1977], 154). This emphasis on the landlord and the estate as solitary retreat places Marvell's poem in stark contrast to Jonson's, which champions the "virtues of economics and human relationships touching upon all the classes of society embraced within the poems, from King James down to the tenants, and even to the animals and the fruits of the garden" (104–5). Or, as Christopher Kendrick puts it in comparing Marvell's poem with Jonson's, "the manor of Appleton House has been decisively removed from the village, [and] the communal ethos of Jonson's house has been subverted and replaced by what is in effect an individual ethic." Moreover, "*Upon Appleton House* amounts to a surreptitious celebration of absolute property, premised as its praise is on his manor's independence of customary ties and obligations, whether to monarch or village" ("Agons of the Manor: 'Upon Appleton House' and Agrarian Capitalism," in *The Production of English Renaissance Culture*, ed. David Lee Miller, Sharon O'Dair, and Harold Weber [Ithaca: Cornell University Press, 1994], 25, 50).

28. Kenneth Robert Olwig, "Sexual Cosmology: Nation and Landscape at the Conceptual Interstices of Nature and Culture; or, What Does Landscape Really Mean?" in *Landscape: Politics and Perspectives*, 331–32.

29. Olwig's account of gradual changes in the meaning of the word "landscape" reinforces this point. Here he first summarizes the history of the word from the Renaissance on, then discusses an original meaning effaced by that history:

> There is thus a transition from a term referring to a painting, to a way of painting, to the material subject matter of the painting. Thus, as in the case of [the word] nature, the meaning of the word landscape is reified. Its meaning is transferred from an artistic symbol, to the concrete world depicted in that symbol. One consequence of this process is that the original Germanic meaning of landscape, as an enclosed area identifiable with a people, is replaced by a meaning in which landscape becomes a scene, projecting into infinity, defined by a given individual viewpoint. ("Sexual Cosmology," 318)

This etymological history reveals the triumph of landscapes of absolute property over those of custom: the land is finally identified not with inhabitants, as in its original definition, but with the perspective of the landlord naturalized as it emerges out of and is imposed upon topography.

30. What Julian Thomas ("The Politics of Vision and the Archaeologies of Landscape," in *Landscape: Politics and Perspectives*) says about perspective art also largely obtains for the estate map:

> Perspective art represents a form of visual control, which freezes time and presents things as they empirically appear to be. At the same time, perspective establishes not merely a set of spatial relations on the canvas, but a fixed relationship between object and subject, locating the viewer outside of the picture, and outside of the relationships being depicted. The viewer is thereby rendered transcendental, outside of history. Landscape painting is thus a representation of place which alienates land, such that it can be appropriated by a gaze which looks in from outside. (21–22)

In the case of the map, this "form of visual control" can go hand in hand with exploitative relations between the landlord and a tenantry rendered as object to the landlord's subject.

31. Stephen Greenblatt, *Shakespearean Negotiations: The Circulation of Social Energy in Renaissance England* (Berkeley: University of California Press, 1988).

32. Raymond Williams's discussion of landscape is typical in this regard:

> A working country is hardly ever a landscape. The very idea of landscape implies separation and observation. It is possible and useful to trace the internal histories of landscape painting, landscape writing, landscape gardening and landscape architecture, but in any final analysis we must relate these histories to the common history of a land and its society. (*Country and City*, 120)

Williams passes from the idea of landscape, which "implies separation and observation," to specific activites demarcated as what I have called the "landscape arts." This formulation sees the idea as instantiated in and inseparable from the arts, while also demanding that the history of landscape be integrated into a "common history of the land and its society." My notion of landscape obviously sees separation and observation as representing one mode of landscape (in fact, Williams's terms evoke nicely de Certeau's discussion of panorama, taken up in Chapter Five). However, I suggest that the common history Williams refers to is also a mode of landscape, and thus it offers not a true relationship to the land but a different and equally ideological one.

33. For the connections between prospect paintings and maps, see Daniels, 9–12.

34. The term "imagined community" comes from Benedict Anderson's now famous work on nation-formation (*Imagined Communities*, rev. ed. [Lon-

don: Verso, 1991]). His conceptual framework is tremendously enabling, but I have two problems with his argument. First, he sees the nation as coming into being only in the nineteenth century, whereas recent scholarship on the early modern period has made clear that it is an emergent, variegated, but crucial category for the sixteenth and seventeenth centuries. Second, Anderson seems to suggest that other, older forms of community, such as that of the estate, are not "imagined." While there are important differences in kind between the forms of affiliation that obtain at the levels of village and of nation, to assume a kind of unmediated transparency of relations within the former is a mistake. My definition of landscape insists upon the ideological and thus in a sense "imagined" nature of relations at all social levels.

35. A powerfully useful book for thinking of the effects of the beginning of this transition on literary production is Richard Halpern's *The Poetics of Primitive Accumulation* (Ithaca: Cornell University Press, 1991).

36. It is worth noting that this tradition accords more respect to early modern plays than they were granted in the period of their production. For an account of the social status of play and playwright, see G. E. Bentley's useful and richly suggestive *The Profession of Dramatist and Player in Shakespeare's Time, 1590–1642* (Princeton: Princeton University Press, 1986), an edition that combines his two important works on playwrights and actors.

37. Svetlana Alpers, *The Art of Describing: Dutch Art in the Seventeenth Century* (Chicago: University of Chicago Press, 1983).

CHAPTER 1: SURVEYING, LAND, AND 'ARDEN'

1. J. R. Hale, *Renaissance Europe: Individual and Society, 1480–1520* (New York: Harper & Row, 1972), 52.

2. Anonymous, *Arden of Faversham*, ed. Martin White (London: Ernest Benn, 1982), Epilogue, 1. Subsequent quotations from the play will be cited in the text.

3. Quoted in Lawrence Stone, *The Crisis of the Aristocracy, 1558–1641,* abridged edition (Oxford: Oxford University Press, 1967), 144.

4. Quoted in R. H. Tawney, *Religion and the Rise of Capitalism* (Gloucester: Peter Smith, 1962), 150.

5. Keith Wrightson, *English Society, 1580–1680* (New Brunswick: Rutgers University Press, 1982), 60.

6. Ibid., 63.

7. Stone, *Crisis*, 155.

8. White, "Introduction," in *Arden*, xx–xxi.

9. Stone, *Crisis*, 129.

10. Elizabeth I, "Ordering Coast Dwellers to Their Country Places," in

Tudor Royal Proclamations, ed. P. L. Hughes and J. F. Larkin, 3 vols. (New Haven: Yale University Press, 1969), 2:541–42.

11. Elizabeth I, "Enforcing Orders Against Dearth; Ordering Hospitality Kept in Country, and Defenses Maintained," in Hughes and Larkin, *Tudor Royal Proclamations*, 3:171–72.

12. James I, "A Proclamation Enjoyning All Lieutenants, and Justices of Peace, to Repaire into Their Countreys, and All Idle Persons to Depart the Court," in *Stuart Royal Proclamations*, ed. James F. Larkin and Paul L. Hughes, 2 vols. (Oxford: Clarendon Press, 1973), 1:44.

13. Richard Helgerson, *Forms of Nationhood: The Elizabethan Writing of England* (Chicago: University of Chicago Press, 1992), 112.

14. Ibid.

15. Ibid., 114.

16. For a few illustrative examples of this critical tendency, see Louis Adrian Montrose, "'Eliza, Queene of Shepheardes,' and the Pastoral of Power," in *Renaissance Historicism*, ed. Arthur F. Kinney and Dan S. Collins (Amherst: University of Massachusetts Press, 1987), 34–63; Stephen Greenblatt, *Renaissance Self-Fashioning* (Chicago: University of Chicago Press, 1980), esp. chapters on Wyatt and More; Jonathan Goldberg, *James I and the Politics of Literature* (Stanford: Stanford University Press, 1989).

17. Helgerson says that in the sixteenth and seventeenth centuries, "chorography" could refer to "mapbook, prose discourse, or poem . . ." (*Forms*, 131). While this may be so, I would argue that one must attend to the significant differences between these three forms; they are not identically produced, circulated, or consumed textual products. For more on the distinction between cartography and chorography, see Howard Marchitello, "Political Maps: The Production of Cartography and Chorography in Early Modern England," in *Cultural Artifacts and the Production of Meaning*, ed. Margaret J. M. Ezell and Katherine O'Brien O'Keeffe (Ann Arbor: University of Michigan Press, 1994), 13–40.

18. Peter Eden, "Three Elizabethan Estate Surveyors: Peter Kempe, Thomas Clerke and Thomas Langdon," in *English Map-Making, 1500–1650*, ed. Sarah Tyacke (London: The British Library, 1983), 68.

19. P. D. A. Harvey, *Medieval Maps* (Toronto: University of Toronto Press, 1991), 8. See also R. A. Skelton and P. D. A. Harvey, "Introduction," in *Local Maps and Plans from Medieval England*, ed. Skelton and Harvey (Oxford: Clarendon Press, 1986), 16.

20. Skelton and Harvey, *Local Maps*, 17.

21. Eden, "Three Elizabethan Estate Surveyors," 68–69.

22. Ibid., 76.

23. I talk of surveying in the narrow sense of land measurement, but the term has broader connotations. F. M. L. Thompson explains:

> In the course of the sixteenth century some form of estate map became a desirable tool for efficient overlooking of agricultural property, and hence the development of land surveying. Subordinate to the prime purpose of estate management, and later on subordinate to military needs, land surveying developed into a specialized occupation. . . . But the overlooking of property was and is the central function of surveyors. (*Chartered Surveyors: The Growth of a Profession* [London: Routledge and Kegan Paul, 1968], 2–3)

We see an example of the surveyor as estate manager in Shakespeare and Fletcher's *Henry VIII*, in which Buckingham's onetime surveyor claims that Buckingham made treasonous utterances to him (see *Henry VIII*, ed. R. A. Foakes [London: Routledge, 1991], 1.2). Intriguingly, Katherine imputes the surveyor's false accusations to the fact that he had "lost [his] office/On the complaint o' th' tenants" (1.2.172–73), an account that suggests the surveyor's corruption and Buckingham's status as a landlord responsive to his tenantry.

24. J. A. Bennett, *The Divided Circle: A History of Instruments for Astronomy, Navigation and Surveying* (Oxford: Phaidon-Christie's, 1987), 38. Bennett says elsewhere that "Medieval survey was largely a matter of direct measurement with poles and ropes, perhaps supplemented by primitive instruments" (39).

25. A. W. Richeson, *English Land Measuring to 1800: Instruments and Practices* (Cambridge, Mass.: Society for the History of Technology and the MIT Press, 1966), 45.

26. Ibid.

27. These two quotations are drawn from Bennett, *Divided Circle*, 46, 47.

28. Aaron Rathborne, *The Surveyor* (London: W. Stansby for W. Burre, 1616), Preface. For information on the precise problems with plane-table measurements, see 125.

29. Maurice Beresford, *History on the Ground* (London: Lutterworth, 1957), 66.

30. John Norden, *The Surueyors Dialogue* (London: Hugh Astley, 1607), 2–3.

31. J. B. Harley, "Maps, Knowledge, and Power," in *The Iconography of Landscape*, ed. Denis Cosgrove and Stephen Daniels (Cambridge: Cambridge University Press, 1988), 285.

32. Michel Foucault, *Discipline and Punish*, trans. Alan Sheridan (New York: Vintage, 1979). This process might also be described as denigrating one form of knowledge—that of custom—in favor of another—that produced by the surveyor. In this light it is worth considering William Folkingham's dis-

cussion of the rightness of the measurements produced by a surveyor in comparison with the knowledge circulated by "private intelligencers":

> Take away Number, Weight, Measure, you exile Iustice, and reduce and haile-vp from Hell the olde and odious Chaos of Confusion. Priuate Intelligencers, intimating (by their roaued Aymes at Quantities and Qualities) vnder-hand and sinister informations, abuse the Lessor & wrong the Lessee, where the iust and iudicious Feudigrapher . . . duly and discreetly obseruing all particulars incident to the Plot, certifies a true Relation. (*Feudigraphia: The Synopsis of or Epitome of Surveying Methodized* [London: Richard Moore, 1610], A3r)

The surveyor (or feudigrapher) produces a "true" account of the estate, and in doing so dismisses "vnder-hand and sinister informations." It is not hard to imagine that these "informations" might represent the grievances of those who appeal to customs abridged by the surveyor, who, as we have seen, is first and foremost a landlord's man. If so, then what we see here is not simply the production of a "true Relation," but the conquest of custom by the truth of measurement, a truth obviously suited to a landscape of absolute property. For more on measurement, custom, and landscape, see Chapter Four.

33. Norden, *Surueyors Dialogue*, 94–95.

34. Ibid., 16.

35. J. B. Harley, "Meaning and Ambiguity in Tudor Cartography," in Tyacke, *English Map-Making*, 27.

36. Stone, *Crisis*, 159.

37. Andrew McRae, *God Speed the Plough* (Cambridge: Cambridge University Press, 1996), 178.

38. The OED tells us of two definitions of "plot" that are of interest here. One meaning (OED 2)—"An area or piece (of small or moderate size) of ground"—is first registered in a text from around 1100, while the other—"A ground-plan of a building, city, field, farm, or any area or part of the earth's surface; a map" (OED 3)—hails from 1551. Thus, there is a certain rhetorical slippage to be noticed in the lord of the manor's scrutiny of the "plot rightly drawne," the plot (map) that stands in for an aggregation of plots (parcels of land).

39. Sarah Bendall, *Maps, Land and Society* (Cambridge: Cambridge University Press, 1992), 78.

40. In a discussion of the discourses of agrarian improvement, Andrew McRae makes a similar point:

> The discourse of improvement not only challenged the orthodoxies of moral economics, but itself erected a powerful new set of values, which would

underpin the consolidation of capitalism in both country and city. 'Improvement' overturns traditional constructions of individual endeavour, agrarian production and rural change; indeed, its association from the early sixteenth century with enclosure strikes at the very foundation of moral economics, confronting the doctrine of manorial stewardship with the logic of absolute property. (*God Speed*, 18)

Moreover, the surveyor is a crucial figure here, for "The surveyor's strictly legalistic appreciation of tenures and new geometric methods of land measurement effectively strip away moral concerns, and establish instead a representation of the land as a field open to the improving intents of its owner" (18–19). Or, as McRae puts it in his exhaustive discussion of surveying manuals, surveyors "promote a rational definition of social and economic relationships, in preference to the network of duties and responsibilities which constitutes the conservative ideal" (172).

41. Raymond Williams, *The Country and the City* (New York: Oxford University Press, 1973), 9–12.

42. R. B. Smith (*Land and Politics in the England of Henry VIII: The West Riding of Yorkshire, 1530–1546* [Oxford: Clarendon Press, 1970]) sees the reformulation of traditional conceptions of land beginning during the reign of Henry VIII:

> In the disposal of monastic property we see land not as a sacred trust but as the object of multifarious transactions whose ultimate object was to gain more wealth . . .The whole sequence of events which followed the suppressions must be seen as a factor of the greatest importance in the transformation of men's attitude to land and wealth. (259)

The era Smith discusses is that of the historical Arden, who received lands from the king in 1540 and was murdered in 1551. M. L. Wine ("Introduction," in *Arden of Faversham*, ed. Wine [London: Methuen, 1973]) rightly points out that

> The play takes into account . . . the widespread dislocation resulting from the dispersal of church property, from the enclosures of small farms by large land-owners, and, above all, from the slow disintegration of a rural economy and its values before the new agrarianism of middle-class entrepreneurs intent on amassing property while disregarding the social obligations that ownership of property entails. (lxii)

43. Norden, *Surueyors Dialogue*, 1. Ostensibly, the survey existed less to supplant custom than to formalize it. For instance, Valentyne Leigh suggests that the surveyor keep records of customary practices performed on the estate.

However, the fruits of this record keeping fall mainly to the landlord, as Leigh makes clear in registering custom as that to which tenants will appeal in order to cheat the landlord. For Leigh, the efficacy of these records is to be found in the fact that "the Tenauntes maie at no time claime any more, or other customes then they ought to haue, ne the Lorde bee preiudiced by any newe custome, by his Tenauntes claimed" (*The Moste Profitable and Commendable Science, of Surveying* [London: Miles Jennings, 1577], G2v).

44. Beresford, *History on the Ground*, 30.

45. Ibid., 30.

46. Ibid., 28–29.

47. Norden, *Surueyors Dialogue*, 24.

48. Edwin Davenport discusses in detail Rogationtide ceremonies in this period ("Elizabethan England's Other Reformation of Manners," *ELH* 63 [1996], 255–78). While Davenport analyzes these ceremonies in relation to customary practice, he also shows that under Elizabeth "Rogation Week reveals a reorganization of custom [that] the official reformation tried to cull from an aspect of shared life" (261). This reminds us that the landscape of custom does not represent a pure, demotic relationship to the land, but bears the traces of influences other than the local or popular, in this case the government's appropriation and reshaping of traditional practice.

49. David Harvey, *The Condition of Postmodernity* (Oxford: Basil Blackwell, 1990), 254.

50. Of course land can *always* be situated in terms of a set of social practices. When I argue that capitalist conceptions of space "efface the social," I am also suggesting that these conceptions are disingenuous ones in that they downplay the inevitable interconnectedness of land and social relations of one sort or another. The point that I make in the Introduction is relevant here: property under capitalism comes to be seen not as a relation to an object (and through the object to others), but as the object itself.

51. White, *Arden*, xix. In the early pages of this chapter I use a number of terms—"lord," "landed gentleman," "aristocrat"—interchangeably, and allude to the social responsibilities aligned with the office of property owner. That Arden is neither aristocratic nor a member of the gentry but is instead one whose "personal mobility and status . . . [are] defined from the beginning in terms of his acquisition of the Abbey lands" (David Attwell, "Property, Status, and the Subject in a Middle-Class Tragedy: *Arden of Faversham*," *English Literary Renaissance* 21 [1991], 336–37) does not in the logic of the play exempt him from such responsibilities. Instead, Arden's ambition and status mark him as one ill-equipped to appreciate the fact that, in the words of R. H. Tawney, "Property is

not a mere aggregate of economic privileges, but a responsible office" (*Religion and the Rise of Capitalism*, 149).

52. White, *Arden*, xxvii. It is worth noting that *Arden* has commonly been read as a "domestic tragedy," defined by H. H. Adams as "a tragedy of the common people, ordinarily set in the domestic scene, dealing with personal and family relationships rather than with large affairs of state, presented in a realistic fashion, and ending in a tragic or otherwise serious manner" (*English Domestic Or, Homiletic Tragedy, 1575 to 1642* [New York: Columbia University Press, 1943], 1–2). Adams quietly gestures toward timeless conceptions of family, domesticity, and realism, conceptions which in the case of *Arden* prove to be quite misleading.

53. Catherine Belsey, *The Subject of Tragedy* (London: Routledge, 1993), 130.

54. Belsey, *Subject*, 193.

55. Ibid., 129.

56. Ibid., 132.

57. Lena Cowen Orlin, *Private Matters and Public Culture in Post-Reformation England* (Ithaca: Cornell University Press, 1994), 73.

58. For accounts that address the historical construction of this binary, see Nancy Armstrong, *Desire and Domestic Fiction* (New York: Oxford University Press, 1987); Jürgen Habermas, *The Structural Transformation of the Public Sphere*, trans. Thomas Burger and Frederick Lawrence (Cambridge, Mass.: MIT Press, 1989); Joan B. Landes, *Women and the Public Sphere in the Age of the French Revolution* (Ithaca: Cornell University Press, 1988).

59. Orlin's book also provides an exhaustive description and acute discussion of the life of Thomas Ardern. Other recent readings of the play, some of which appeared after I first composed this chapter, also raise questions about the relationship between public and private. In addition to *Private Matters and Public Culture in Post-Reformation England*, see Orlin's "Man's House as His Castle in *Arden of Feversham*," *Medieval & Renaissance Drama in England* 2 (1985), 57–89. Julie R. Schutzman compellingly shows that, in relation to an analysis of the mechanisms of social control in sixteenth-century small towns and villages, "both the play's content and its context . . . defy the limits of a public/private binary" ("Alice Arden's Freedom and the Suspended Moment of *Arden of Faversham*," *SEL* 36 [1996], 296). In a fine analysis of the play, Frances E. Dolan mentions the fact that Arden "[a]bsent[s] himself from . . . his roles as husband, master, and landowning gentleman," overlapping roles that make clear the permeability of the public and private. Moreover, like Orlin she rightly detects the play's sense of Arden's culpability in his lack of con-

trol over his household: "[Arden], like the husbands who became targets of cuckold jokes and popular shaming rituals, is presented as responsible for his disordered household and his own humiliation" (*Dangerous Familiars* [Ithaca: Cornell University Press, 1994], 75).

60. Alice T. Friedman, *House and Household in Elizabethan England* (Chicago: University of Chicago Press, 1989), 47.

61. Ibid., 48.

62. Ibid.

63. Sir Walter Raleigh, "Instructions to His Son and to Posterity," in *Advice to a Son*, ed. Louis B. Wright (Ithaca: Cornell University Press, 1962), 21–22.

64. *The Lisle Letters*, ed. Muriel St. Clare Byrne, selected and arranged by Bridget Boland, abridged edition (Chicago: University of Chicago Press, 1983), 72, 150, 131–32.

65. Susan Amussen, *An Ordered Society: Gender and Class in Early Modern England* (Oxford: Blackwell, 1988), 41.

66. Mosby also compares his relationship with Alice to "sleeping in a serpent's bed" (8.42), an image that deepens the language of estate or domestic economy by offering a glimpse of the land read in terms of the Fall. Of course, in religious discourse the expulsion from Eden marked the birth of the need for agricultural labor, and estate practices talked of in this chapter are necessary in a postlapsarian world. As I will suggest, Mosby's solipsism marks a fall from even the conscientious pursuit of these practices.

67. Martin Holmes, *Elizabethan London* (London: Cassell, 1969), 86.

68. Orlin, *Private Matters*, 91. Orlin argues that the play "is focused strictly on its protagonist's sovereign domestic role and locates its claim to tragedy in his disastrous domestic misrule" (97). I largely agree, but I would expand the "domestic," which always threatens to collapse back into an anachronistic conception of the private, to accommodate the business of estate management.

69. Frank Whigham, *Seizures of the Will in Early Modern English Drama* (Cambridge: Cambridge University Press, 1996), 118. Whigham's excellent discussion of *Arden* provides a nuanced account of kinship and rank relations in the play. On "petty treason," see Dolan, *Dangerous Familiars*.

70. Attwell, "Property, Status, and the Subject," 332.

71. Ibid., 333.

CHAPTER 2: STRANGE METAMORPHOSES

1. Anonymous, *Woodstock: A Moral History*, ed. A. P. Rossiter (London: Chatto and Windus, 1946), 5.3.106. Henceforth cited in the body of the text.

2. In discussing Shakespeare's *Richard II*, Donna Hamilton argues that the

reference to Richard as landlord suggests that "The profit of the ruler, not that of the people, is being advanced. For Richard to act like a landlord is . . . [for him] to act as though the royal prerogative allows a king to do anything he wishes" (Donna B. Hamilton, "The State of Law in *Richard II*," *Shakespeare Quarterly* 34 [1983], 7). While Hamilton understands the term merely as a pejorative one suggesting the king's selfishness, we must think further about the phrase, for *Woodstock*, like *Arden of Faversham*, is deeply concerned with both estate and nation management, and with the distinction between good and bad landlords.

3. While Richard is a medieval king and *Woodstock* takes up events ascribed by Holinshed to his reign—for instance, the farming out of the kingdom—it is my contention that the play is very much of its era, and that the historical phenomena central to it owe that centrality to their timeliness. More specifically, it will become clear that Richard's abuses of authority have their Elizabethan analogues, and the play's emphasis on the survey clearly places *Woodstock* in the context of late-sixteenth-century surveying innovations.

4. "Preface" to *Woodstock: A Moral History*, 47–53. Not everyone thinks that *Woodstock* precedes *Richard II*, however. See for instance D. J. Lake, "Three Seventeenth-Century Revisions: *Thomas of Woodstock*, *The Jew of Malta*, and *Faustus B*," *Notes and Queries* 228 (1983), 133–43. I find Rossiter convincing, and while my argument about Shakespeare's play does not depend upon one text's preceding the other, it is reinforced by the notion that *Richard II* assumes a social and cartographic context fully articulated in *Woodstock*.

5. *Strangers and Pilgrims* (Chicago: University of Chicago Press, 1983), 80.

6. Schell, *Strangers and Pilgrims*, 98. Schell reads *Woodstock* in terms of the history play's relation to the morality tradition. For more on this topic, see also A. P. Rossiter, "Preface," 1–76; Irving Ribner, *The English History Play in the Age of Shakespeare* (Princeton: Princeton University Press, 1957).

7. John Norden, *The Surueyor's Dialogue* (London: Hugh Astley, 1607), 4. It is worth remembering here that the construction of the survey did not necessitate the production of a map. However, as we shall see, in *Woodstock* the survey is used in association with a map.

8. Lena Cowen Orlin ("Man's House as His Castle in *Arden of Feversham*," *Medieval & Renaissance Drama in England* 2 [1985]) succinctly describes the development of the Tudor land market as follows: "The sale of the old monastic estates did not engender the land market; it was the land market that had already sprung up by the early sixteenth century that made such distribution of monastic property practical and, indeed, conceivable. But the flooding of that market with enormous amounts of property—property available on such a scale for the first time in English history—certainly stimulated

the revolution in landownership. By the last two decades of the sixteenth century, a brisk land market had grown into a booming one" (60).

9. Richard Hoyle, "Introduction: Aspects of the Crown's Estate, c. 1558–1640," in *The Estates of the English Crown, 1558–1640*, ed. R. W. Hoyle (Cambridge: Cambridge University Press, 1992), 1. Hoyle refutes the historical argument that understands "the Crown lands . . . [as] asset[s] awaiting liquidation in times of emergency" (3).

10. Madeleine Gray, "Exchequer Officials and the Market in Crown Property, 1558–1640," in *The Estates of the English Crown, 1558–1640*, 116.

11. Orlin, "Man's House," 59. It is worth noting that the expansion of the land market is also the primary reason for the growth of the profession of surveying. See Edward Lynam, *British Maps and Map-Makers* (London: Collins, 1947), 14.

12. David Thomas, "The Elizabethan Crown Lands: Their Purposes and Problems," in *The Estates of the English Crown, 1558–1640*, 64–69.

13. F. M. L. Thompson, *Chartered Surveyors: The Growth of a Profession* (London: Routledge and Kegan Paul, 1968), 16.

14. Herbert Hope Lockwood, "Those Greedy Hunters After Concealed Lands," in *An Essex Tribute: Essays Presented to Frederick G. Emmison*, ed. Kenneth Neale (London: Leopard's Head Press, 1987), 153–54.

15. D. Thomas, "Elizabethan Crown Lands," 69.

16. Joan Thirsk, "The Crown as Projector on Its Own Estates, from Elizabeth I to Charles I," in *The Estates of the English Crown, 1558–1640*, 322.

17. D. Thomas, "Elizabethan Crown Lands," 69.

18. Thirsk, "The Crown as Projector," 301–3.

19. Hoyle, "Introduction," 5.

20. Richard Hoyle, "Disafforestation and Drainage: The Crown as Entrepreneur?" in *The Estates of the English Crown, 1558–1640*, 354. For a discussion of communities inhabiting forests before and during the civil war, see Christopher Hill, *The World Turned Upside Down* (Harmondsworth: Penguin, 1991), 50–56.

21. Thirsk, "The Crown as Projector," 301; Hill, *The World Turned Upside Down*, 52.

22. Thirsk, "The Crown as Projector," 308.

23. D. Thomas, "Elizabethan Crown Lands," 70.

24. Lockwood, "Those Greedy Hunters," 158.

25. Thomas Clay, *Briefe, Easie, and Necessary Tables, of Interest and Rents Forborne . . . Together with a Chorologicall Discourse of the Well Ordering, Disposing, and Gouerning of an Honorable Estate or Reuennue* (London: G. Eld and M. Flesher, 1624), 62–63. In his catalogue of the duties of the surveyor,

Aaron Rathborne mentions determining "what lands, tenements, rents, se-ruices, or other profits, are concealed or detayned from his Maiestie, how long since, by whom, and what the yeerely value therof is" (*The Surveyor* [London: W. Stansby for W. Burre, 1616], 202).

26. Lockwood, "Those Greedy Hunters," 164.

27. Thirsk, "The Crown as Projector," 322; for other, related methods of payment, see Lockwood, "Those Greedy Hunters," 155.

28. Lockwood, "Those Greedy Hunters," 155.

29. R. A. Skelton, *Saxton's Survey of England and Wales* (Amsterdam: Nico Israel, 1974), 1.

30. Ifor M. Evans and Heather Lawrence, *Christopher Saxton: Elizabethan Map-Maker* (Wakefield: Wakefield Historical Publications and the Holland Press, 1979), 9, 40–44.

31. Sarah Tyacke and John Huddy, *Christopher Saxton and Tudor Map-Making* (London: The British Library, 1980), 25; Skelton, *Saxton's Survey*, 8. I talk in greater detail of Saxton's maps in Chapter Three.

32. Quoted in Tyacke and Huddy, *Christopher Saxton and Tudor Map-Making*, 32. For a compelling if somewhat conjectural account of the method by which Saxton performed his survey, see Gordon Manley, "Saxton's Survey of Northern England," *Geographical Journal* 83 (1934), 308–16; see also Evans and Lawrence, *Christopher Saxton: Elizabethan Map-Maker*, 40–44.

33. Alan Everitt, "The Marketing of Agricultural Produce," in *The Agrarian History of England and Wales*, 7 vols., gen. ed. H. P. R. Finberg, vol. 4: *1500–1640*, ed. Joan Thirsk (Cambridge: Cambridge University Press, 1967), 467.

34. Ibid., 488–89.

35. David Cressy, "Levels of Illiteracy in England, 1530–1730," in *Literacy and Social Development in the West: A Reader*, ed. Harvey J. Graff (Cambridge: Cambridge University Press, 1981), 109. Cressy points out that sixteenth-century children learned how to read before they learned to write, so these court records cannot accurately convey ability to read. See also David Cressy, *Literacy and the Social Order: Reading and Writing in Tudor and Stuart England* (Cambridge: Cambridge University Press, 1980). For a critique of literacy statistics based upon evidence of the ability to write, see Keith Thomas, "The Meaning of Literacy in Early Modern England," in *The Written Word: Literacy in Transition*, ed. Gerd Baumann (Oxford: Clarendon Press, 1986), 97–131.

36. Keith Thomas, "The Meaning of Literacy," 113.

37. Roger Chartier, *The Cultural Uses of Print in Early Modern France*, trans. Lydia Cochrane (Princeton: Princeton University Press, 1987), 5. For a fascinating discussion of the rise of privatized reading and of the study as site

of the same, see Roger Chartier, "The Practical Impact of Writing," in *A History of Private Life*, gen. ed. Philippe Aries and Georges Duby, vol. 3: *Passions of the Renaissance*, ed. Roger Chartier, trans. Arthur Goldhammer (Cambridge, Mass.: Harvard University Press, 1989), 111–59.

38. Tessa Watt, *Cheap Print and Popular Piety, 1550–1640* (Cambridge: Cambridge University Press, 1991), 7–8. For more on the intersection of oral and written traditions, see Natascha Würzbach, *The Rise of the English Street Ballad, 1550–1650*, trans. Gayna Walls (Cambridge: Cambridge University Press, 1990), 14–15; Margaret Spufford, *Small Books and Pleasant Histories: Popular Fiction and Its Readership in Seventeenth-Century England* (London: Methuen, 1981), 2.

39. P. M. Handover, *Printing in London from 1476 to Modern Times* (Cambridge, Mass.: Harvard University Press, 1960), 102.

40. Watt, *Cheap Print*, 5.

41. Peter Burke, *Popular Culture in Early Modern Europe* (London: Temple Smith, 1978), 253.

42. Watt, *Cheap Print*, 5.

43. For a discussion of whispering in this play, see Alan C. Dessen, *Elizabethan Drama and the Viewer's Eye* (Chapel Hill: University of North Carolina Press, 1977), 88–91. Dessen intriguingly argues that in performance it would be clear that the "actual whispering . . . is performed by the men who manipulate the king, betray Woodstock, and rape the country" (91).

44. These references to Shakespeare are all drawn from *The Complete Works*, ed. Alfred Harbage (New York: Viking Penguin, 1969).

45. For a historical analysis that elegantly illustrates this point, see Carlo Ginzburg, *The Cheese and the Worms: The Cosmos of a Sixteenth-Century Miller*, trans. John and Anne Tedeschi (Baltimore: Johns Hopkins University Press, 1992).

46. It would be more precise to insist upon varieties of knowledge—I do not want to collapse different forms into one all-inclusive category and imply that equivalent knowledges are created in radically divergent social situations. The point is that certain forms and practices, especially text-based ones, are understood as knowledge when others are not; the category is often less descriptive than evaluative and exclusionary, predicated upon classificatory distinctions that expel certain practices from the domain of Knowledge with a capital K—think of the eventual fate of alchemy under empiricism.

47. See Roger Chartier, "Culture as Appropriation: Popular Cultural Uses in Early Modern France," *Understanding Popular Culture: Europe from the Middle Ages to the Nineteenth Century*, ed. Stephen L. Kaplan (Berlin: Mouton, 1984), 229–53.

48. Norden, *The Surueyor's Dialogue*, 16.

49. Sir Thomas Elyot, *The Boke Named the Gouernour*, 2 vols. (New York: Burt Franklin, 1967), 1:77–78.

50. This range of texts confirms Chartier's argument, echoed by Watt, that "it is pointless to try to identify popular [or elite] culture by some supposedly specific distribution of cultural objects. Their distribution is always more complex than it might seem at first glance, as are their appropriations by groups and individuals" (Chartier, "Culture as Appropriation," 233).

51. F. J. Levy, "How Information Spread Among the Gentry, 1550–1640," *The Journal of British Studies* 21 (1982), 25–26.

52. I do not intend to create an opposition between the public and private worlds, between the individual in his closet and the social collective beyond the walls of the study. Moreover, I don't want to suggest that map reading in a study isn't also a process by which certain forms of knowledge are produced. Instead, I would suggest that different texts and different sites of consumption lend themselves to the production of certain forms of knowledge without absolutely precluding others. Recent work has shown that the closet, a site often associated with the emergence of the bourgeois subject, was actually a transactional space. Alan Stewart puts it this way: "[T]he male closet is not designed to function as a place of individual withdrawal, but as a secret nonpublic transactive space between two men behind a locked door" ("The Early Modern Closet Discovered," *Representations* 50 [Spring 1995], 83).

53. I should point out that the fact of a shared culture does not mean that all who are members of that culture are equally involved in it or in the consumption or production of knowledge. The play reads the good knight as both a member of this culture and as a central figure in it. We should not understand the butcher simply as a mouthpiece for the ideas of his landlord, but at the same time we must realize that because of the land-based paternalism of rural society the good knight's contributions to a shared culture weigh more heavily than those of butcher, farmer, and grazier. While representing the workings of the rural community at a variety of social levels, this is decidedly not a populist play; its final rebellion, motivated in part by the Crown's gradual impoverishment of its subjects, is still a struggle generated by aristocrats shut out of the political life of the nation. At the same time, as A. P. Rossiter has pointed out, the Dunstable scenes show the playwright's sympathy toward those Shakespeare usually classifies as an unruly mob (Rossiter, "Preface," in *Woodstock*, 31–32).

54. Quoted in François Laroque, *Shakespeare's Festive World*, trans. Janet Lloyd (Cambridge: Cambridge University Press, 1991), 24, 41.

55. R. H. Tawney, *Religion and the Rise of Capitalism* (New York: Harcourt, Brace and Co., 1926), 149.

56. Susan Amussen, *An Ordered Society: Gender and Class in Early Modern England* (Oxford: Blackwell, 1988), 134.

57. For an argument that works to differentiate between father-child and king-subject relations as articulated through this analogy, see Debora Kuller Shuger, *Habits of Thought in the English Renaissance* (Berkeley: University of California Press, 1990), 218–49.

58. See Keith Wrightson, *English Society, 1580–1680* (New Brunswick: Rutgers University Press, 1982), esp. 24–27.

59. William Shakespeare, *King Lear*, ed. Kenneth Muir (London: Routledge, 1991), 1.1.85. I take up this scene in greater detail in the next chapter.

60. Richard Helgerson, *Forms of Nationhood: The Elizabethan Writing of England* (Chicago: University of Chicago Press, 1992), 105–47.

61. Richard's mocking term is a gendered one that associates management of the household with the housewife. However, as we shall see, Woodstock represents domestic economy in a positive way that is set in opposition to Richard's conspicuous consumption. Moreover, we have seen in Chapter One that at the level of the estate the management of domestic affairs is not an activity specific to either gender.

62. Greene here refers not only to Woodstock but to all of Richard's "frosty beards"(1.3.191), his old advisers. However, Woodstock both is spokesperson for them and stands in for them here and on many occasions, and I take the comment to be most pointedly about him.

63. I appeal to the OED not to provide a point of origin for these meanings, but rather to suggest the approximate time of their emergence. Thus, I take it that meanings that the OED indicates may have arisen a few decades after *Woodstock* were very likely current at the time of the play.

64. The term can also suggest in this period a rustic or clown (OED B2, 1590). While this may be implicit in Richard's pejorative use of the term, Woodstock's positive homespunness clearly has a different valence.

65. S. T. Bindoff, *Tudor England* (London: Penguin, 1950), 123–24. Bindoff goes on to discuss the midcentury rise of the master clothier, a protocapitalist who owned the cloth and parceled out the labor to various artisans who would work for a wage (124–27).

66. Quoted in Joan Thirsk, *Economic Policy and Projects* (Oxford: Clarendon Press, 1978), 15–16.

67. In making this argument, I follow Karen Newman's important chapter, "Dressing Up: Sartorial Extravagance in Early Modern London," in *Fashioning Femininity and English Renaissance Drama* (Chicago: University of Chicago Press, 1991), 111–27. Newman asserts that "In early modern London, the relation between fashion and the failure of domestic economy was a common-

place," and writes of "[t]he relation of sartorial extravagance to the early English economy—political, linguistic, domestic" (111).

68. Similarly Woodstock says elsewhere, "You've heard of the fantastic suits they wear?/Never was *English* king so habited" (3.2.37–38, my emphasis).

69. On sumptuary legislation, see Frances Elizabeth Baldwin, "Sumptuary Legislation and Personal Regulation in England," in *Johns Hopkins University Studies in Historical and Political Science* 44 (Baltimore: Johns Hopkins University Press, 1923), 9–282; Wilfrid Hooper, "The Tudor Sumptuary Laws," *English Historical Review* 30 (1915), 433–49.

70. It is worth pointing out, though, that sumptuary statutes also had "a protectionist . . . purpose. They protected the native cloth industry by barring widespread use of imported dyes and fabrics" (Jean E. Howard, *The Stage and Social Struggle in Early Modern England* [London: Routledge, 1994], 33; also see Hooper, "The Tudor Sumptuary Laws").

71. William Harrison, *The Description of England*, ed. Georges Edelen (Washington and New York: The Folger Shakespeare Library and Dover Publications, 1994), 148. It is important to note that Harrison is not entirely dismissive of expensive clothing. Instead, he contrasts gaudy imports with "black velvet or other comely silk, without such cuts and garish colors as are worn in these days *and never brought in but by the consent of the French*" (148, my emphasis).

72. Felicity Heal, *Hospitality in Early Modern England* (Oxford: Clarendon Press, 1990), 6.

73. Daryl W. Palmer, *Hospitable Performances: Dramatic Genre and Cultural Practices in Early Modern England* (West Lafayette: Purdue University Press, 1992), 27.

74. For more on the masque in *Woodstock*, see Janet C. Stavropoulos, "'A Masque Is Treason's License': The Design of *Woodstock*," *South Central Review* 5 (1988), 1–14.

75. Lawrence Stone, *The Crisis of the Aristocracy, 1558–1641*, abridged edition (Oxford: Oxford University Press, 1967), 159.

76. This is not intended to be an exhaustive list of historical phenomena relevant to the play's depiction of estate and nation management. Another topic particularly worthy of consideration in relation to *Woodstock* is wardship, a phenomena involving the control not only of marriage but of landed property. While many landowners attempted to hide the facts of their tenure from the Court of Wards so as to enable their heirs to escape wardship, the Crown worked via concealment hunters to establish tenancies in order to increase the revenues available from wardship. The play's anxiety about the blank charters cum survey, then, could have much to do with fear of the extension of the

Court of Ward's knowledge. The definitive work on wardship in this period is Joel Hurstfield, *The Queen's Wards: Wardship and Marriage Under Elizabeth I* (London: Longmans, Green and Co., 1958).

77. David Bevington astutely identifies the play as "old-fashioned in its social values and unorthodox regarding Tudor monarchism" (*Tudor Drama and Politics: A Critical Approach to Topical Meaning* [Cambridge, Mass.: Harvard University Press, 1968], 253).

CHAPTER 3: READING SHAKESPEARE'S MAPS

1. Benedict Anderson, *Imagined Communities*, rev. ed. (London: Verso, 1991). On the role of the map in the construction of imagined communities, see 170–78.

2. Brian S. Osborne, "Interpreting a Nations' Identity: Artists as Creators of National Consciousness," in *Ideology and Landscape in Historical Perspective*, ed. Alan R. H. Baker and Gideon Biger (Cambridge: Cambridge University Press, 1992), 230–31.

3. William Shakespeare, *The First Part of King Henry IV*, ed. A. R. Humphreys (London: Routledge, 1988), 3.1.66–67. Line references henceforth given in the text.

4. Hotspur seems motivated not only by the desire to increase the value of his property, but also by the need to impose a kind of cartographic symmetry on the land. The river is to run "[i]n a new channel fair and evenly"; after Worcester remarks that under Hotspur's plan the river will "[run] straight and even," Hotspur replies, "I'll have it so" (3.1.110–11).

5. John Gillies (*Shakespeare and the Geography of Difference* [Cambridge: Cambridge University Press, 1994]) reads the scene similarly to the way that I do, arguing that Hotspur desires to change the course of the river because of his "blatantly (and subversively) literal interpretation of cartographic convention. If the river is a border, and he diverts the river, then he can claim to have solemnly abided by the letter of the cartographically expressed agreement" (46–47). The crucial point is that both of us agree that "the cartographically expressed agreement" for Hotspur takes precedence over the land itself.

6. Richard Helgerson, *Forms of Nationhood: The Elizabethan Writing of England* (Chicago: University of Chicago Press, 1992), 105–47.

7. Sir Thomas Elyot, *The Boke Named The Gouernour*, 2 vols. (New York: Burt Franklin, 1967), 1:77–78.

8. The OED suggests that this meaning has by the late sixteenth century given way to the sense of the term most common today—beholding as looking. I argue that this passage suggests that certain kinds of looking involve the older sense of the word.

9. Note also that "In 16th-century London the bookseller was the engraver's principal employer. The majority of maps executed by English engravers appeared as book-illustrations" (R. A. Skelton, *County Atlases of the British Isles, 1579–1850* [London: Carta Press, 1970], 232).

10. Thomas Nashe, *The Works of Thomas Nashe*, 5 vols., ed. R. B. McKerrow (Oxford: Oxford University Press, 1958), 2:299. An extremely rich topic that I will not be able to consider fully here is the relationship between maps, travel, and the shaping of the subjectivity of a gentleman. The education of a gentleman usually included as a prerequisite an obligatory tour of the Continent. However, such tours were unsettling in many ways, for travel both helped shape and threatened an English gentleman's identity. Bacon's essay "On Travel" recommends the tour, but warns travelers not to learn too much—that is, not to allow one's experiences to shape one, to *over*educate one in an inappropriate fashion. Books to some extent but maps even more were understood as giving one experience of a place, but in a way that never threatened the foundations of one's identity as an English gentleman. For a discussion of the role of travel in the making of a gentleman, see Ruth Kelso, *The Doctrine of the English Gentleman in the Sixteenth Century* (Gloucester: Peter Smith, 1964), 142–46.

11. For a fascinating discussion of the different cartographic forms that existed in this period, see Victor Morgan, "The Cartographic Image of the 'Country' in Early Modern England," *Transactions of the Royal Historical Society*, 5th ser. 29 (1979), 129–54.

12. John Dee, "Preface," *The Elements of Geometrie of the Most Auncient Philosopher Euclide of Megara*, trans. H. Billingsley (London: John Daye, 1570), A4r.

13. James R. Akerman and David Buisseret, *Monarchs, Ministers & Maps: A Cartographic Exhibit at the Newberry Library* (Chicago: The Newberry Library, 1985), 1.

14. See Kelso, *Doctrine of the English Gentleman*, 140. These writers also stress the beauty of maps and their role in the imaginative reconstruction of historical events.

15. Morgan, "The Cartographic Image," 138.

16. Quoted in William Ravenhill, "Projections for the Large General Maps of Britain, 1583–1700," *Imago Mundi* 33 (1981), 25.

17. J. B. Harley, "Meaning and Ambiguity in Tudor Cartography," in *English Map-Making, 1500–1650*, ed. Sarah Tyacke (London: British Library, 1983), 27.

18. Patricia Parker, "Fantasies of 'Race' and 'Gender': Africa, *Othello*, and Bringing to Light," in *Women, "Race," and Writing in the Early Modern Period*,

ed. Margo Hendricks and Patricia Parker (London: Routledge, 1994), 87. As her language might suggest, Parker's emphasis is on the connections between the acquisition of knowledge and an appetitive voyeurism that informs the writing and reading of travel narratives, but she is also aware of the power of maps in this period; see her discussion of a particular map on page 88.

19. Francis Bacon, "The Plan of the Work" to *The Great Instauration*, in *The Complete Essays of Francis Bacon*, ed. Henry LeRoy Finch (New York: Washington Square Press, 1963), 177.

20. Timothy Reiss, *The Discourse of Modernism* (Ithaca: Cornell University Press, 1982).

21. Elizabeth Hanson, "Torture and Truth in Renaissance England," *Representations* 34 (Spring 1991), 54.

22. For a discussion of the enabling nature in Bacon's work of contradictions such as this one, see Ronald Levao, "Francis Bacon and the Mobility of Science," *Representations* 40 (Fall 1992), 1–32.

23. Denis Cosgrove, "Mapping New Worlds: Culture and Cartography in Sixteenth-Century Venice," *Imago Mundi* 44 (1992), 66.

24. For a discussion of the traditional / Ptolemaic relationship of geography to cosmography, see Cosgrove, "Mapping New Worlds," 66.

25. Graham Huggan, *Territorial Disputes: Maps and Mapping Strategies in Contemporary Canadian and Australian Fictions* (Toronto: University of Toronto Press, 1994), 4.

26. Ravenhill, "Projections," 21.

27. For a compelling discussion of the old and new geographies in England in this period, a discussion that suggests the continued hegemony of the old, see Gillies, *Shakespeare and the Geography of Difference*. However, Gillies downplays the innovations in English cartography and surveying that occurred in Shakespeare's time. For instance, Gillies mentions Saxton only once, and then in passing, whereas most cartographic historians agree with Ravenhill in asserting the tremendous influence and importance of Saxton's achievement.

28. Quoted in Phyllis Rackin, *Stages of History* (Ithaca: Cornell University Press, 1990), 143.

29. Morgan, "The Cartographic Image," 138.

30. William Shakespeare, *King Lear*, ed. Kenneth Muir (London: Routledge, 1991), 1.1.36–37. Further citations will appear in the body of the text.

31. Francis Barker, *The Culture of Violence* (Chicago: University of Chicago Press, 1993), 3–4. For a discussion of Lear's map in relationship to the unification of the kingdom and cultural anxiety surrounding James's ascension to the throne, see Terence Hawkes, *Meaning by Shakespeare* (London: Routledge, 1992), esp. 121–38. Gillies talks briefly of Lear's map (*Shakespeare and the Geog-*

raphy of Difference, 46); he argues that its "imagery is entirely consistent with the rich pictorial ornamentation of Saxton's maps of England and English Counties." As he puts it, "The very movement of Lear's thought from direct cartographic reference to a rich (almost iconic) imagination of the cartographic content, suggests a national map of monumental or iconic force" (46).

32. R. A. Skelton, *Saxton's Survey of England and Wales* (Amsterdam: Nico Israel, 1974), 11.

33. One might also discuss the iconography of the map, which includes illustrations of sea monsters, church steeples, manor houses, and representative topographical features such as hills and trees. In this study, however, I have deliberately deemphasized iconographic readings of maps of this period. This is in part because that topic has been provocatively addressed by Helgerson and Gillies, but mostly because I am concerned with the epistemological implications of period cartographic reading practice. I read maps not in terms of the iconographic features that proliferate on them, but in terms of the relationship between maps and both material practices and shifting epistemologies. I do this in part because I believe that while maps may present us with iconographic representations of the social—the aforementioned steeples and manor houses—those representations do not seriously undermine the maps' tendency to create, in Barker's words, "an ideal emptiness." Instead, the iconography of maps reduces the social to interchangeable, indistinguishable icons.

34. Skelton, *Saxton's Survey*, 8.

35. Quoted from Victor Morgan, "Lasting Image of the Elizabethan Era," *The Geographical Magazine* 52 (1980), 404.

36. Helgerson, *Forms of Nationhood*, 114.

37. I am grateful to Arthur F. Kinney for suggesting to me this reading of Lear's division.

38. See Hawkes, *Meaning by Shakespeare*, 121–38.

39. Michael Neill, "Broken English and Broken Irish: Nation, Language, and the Optic of Power in Shakespeare's Histories," *Shakespeare Quarterly* 45 (1994), 15.

40. For these metaphors, see William Shakespeare, *Richard II*, ed. Peter Ure (London: Routledge, 1991), 2.1.40–68. Citations will henceforth appear in the body of the text.

41. I do not merely want to suggest that Gaunt's representation of England is a confused one, and that the proliferation of metaphors attests to no more than an old man's ramblings. One can never forget the real poetic power of his depiction even as one explores its inconsistencies, and that power gestures toward what is at stake in Gaunt's speech: the conceptual status of the nation.

This attempt to imagine a nation speaks to the potent incoherence of certain conceptions of nationhood in this period. It also speaks to the implications of cartographic texts, which, as we will see, represent England in a way crucial to understanding Richard's inability to recognize the metaphorical and geographical limits of his power.

42. Gillian Beer, "The Island and the Aeroplane: The Case of Virginia Woolf," in *Nation and Narration*, ed. Homi K. Bhabha (London: Routledge, 1990), 269.

43. Rackin, *Stages of History*, 122–23.

44. Alexander Leggatt, *Shakespeare's Political Drama* (London: Routledge, 1988), 62.

45. Wales was administratively unified with England under Henry VIII; the Treaty of Berwick in 1586 forged an offensive and defensive alliance between England and Scotland, but the two countries were often on tense terms, especially as Elizabeth grew older and the succession remained unclear. On England's relations with Wales see Chapter Four.

46. Alan G. R. Smith, *The Emergence of a Nation State* (London: Longman, 1984), 246.

47. The most fervent of Bolingbroke's early admirers, the Lord Marshal delineates the geographical limits of the kingdom by pledging to accompany the banished Bolingbroke "As far as land will let me by your side" (1.3.252).

48. Neill, "Broken English," 3.

49. Ibid., 13.

50. Ann R. Jones and Peter Stallybrass, "Dismantling Irena: The Sexualizing of Ireland in Early Modern England," in *Nationalisms and Sexualities*, ed. Andrew Parker et al. (New York: Routledge, 1992), 157–71.

51. The first statement is Richard's, the second John of Gaunt's.

52. One might also consider here the role of surveys and maps in enabling the kinds of land-management practices, and social dislocations, associated with enclosure. See Chapter One for more on this topic.

53. I take the reference to Rogationtide ceremonies and their social aspects, their communal definition of the land, to suggest popular support for Bolingbroke. However, this is not a construction of nation or land that the play finally endorses, and Henry's support has started to erode by Act Four.

54. These different effects are played out in terms of different kinds of maps: the national wall map and county maps. Saxton's survey of England made possible both kinds of texts, first the county maps and then the wall map. This chapter concerns itself mostly with the wall map, but on several occasions I conflate different kinds of cartographic products. I do so not because differences between them are unimportant, but because all circulate and are

consumed within the same social world (with the possible exception of the playing cards).

55. A partial exception to this may be found in Lear's "poor naked wretches" speech, a moment in the play at which Lear arguably recognizes the social costs of his previous indifference to the plight of his subjects—an indifference manifested in his map-enabled partitioning of the kingdom.

CHAPTER 4: CIVILIZING WALES

1. William Shakespeare, *Cymbeline*, ed. J. M. Nosworthy (London: Methuen, 1986), 3.2.51–53. Henceforth cited in the text.

2. In this light, consider Gower's description of travel in another Shakespearean romance, *Pericles*: "Thus time we waste and long leagues make short; / Sail seas in cockles, have and wish but for't; / Making, to take our imagination, / From bourn to bourn, region to region" (from William Shakespeare, *The Complete Works*, ed. Alfred Harbage [New York: Viking Penguin, 1969], 4.4.1–4).

3. John Norden, *England: An Intended Gvyde for English Travailers* (London: Edward All-De, 1625), "To All Kinde Gentlemen and Others, Who Have Occasion to Make Use of These Tables or Any of Them," n.p.

4. Norden, *England*, Table for Wales, n.p.

5. Norden, *England*, Table showing distances between cities and shire towns in England, n.p.

6. R. D. Connor, *The Weights and Measures of England* (London: Her Majesty's Stationery Office, 1987), 70. This statute should be understood as one part of Elizabeth's larger effort to standardize measurements of all kinds. Between 1582 and 1602, Elizabeth created standards for troy and avoirdupois weights, as well as capacity-measure standards (see Ronald Edward Zupko, *British Weights and Measures: A History from Antiquity to the Seventeenth Century* [Madison: University of Wisconsin Press, 1977], 86–93). Moreover, one of the achievements of which Elizabeth was most proud—it is recorded in Latin on her tomb at Westminster—was her stabilizing of English currency (James O'Donald Mays, *The Splendid Shilling* [Burley, Ringwood, Hampshire: New Forest Leaves, 1982], 37). For more on Elizabeth's restoration of "right value," see C. E. Challis, *The Tudor Coinage* (Manchester: Manchester University Press, 1978).

7. J. B. Harley, "Introduction," in John Ogilby, *Britannia*, facsimile edition (Amsterdam: Theatrum Orbis Terrarum, 1970), xxii.

8. Katherine S. Van Eerde, *John Ogilby and the Taste of His Times* (Folkestone, Kent: Dawson, 1976), 95.

9. Ibid., 127. For more on Ogilby and *Britannia*, see also Harley, "Intro-

duction," v–xxiii; Sir Herbert George Fordham, "John Ogilby: His *Britannia, and the British Itineraries of the Eighteenth Century," The Library*, 4th ser. 6 (1926), 157–78.

10. The category of utility is adduced advisedly here, since it is an anachronistic one that favors narrow conceptions of the "uses" of a text. What P. D. A. Harvey says of estate maps also applies, with obvious modifications and slight qualification, to productions such as Ogilby's: "Nor need [their ornamental beauty] be seen as a less practical, less functional purpose than the[ir] use . . . in the detailed work of running the estate. They were meant to be looked at and to impress, to excite the beholder's admiration and to satisfy the owner's pride of possession without even the trouble of travelling to the spot" (P. D. A. Harvey, "English Estate Maps: Their Early History and Their Use as Historical Evidence," in *Rural Images: Estate Maps in the Old and New Worlds*, ed. David Buisseret [Chicago: University of Chicago Press, 1996], 46). While Ogilby's atlas obviously does not attest to estate ownership, part of *Britannia*'s "utility" would lie in its opulent form, in the cultural capital that accrues to its owner (because it is a fine and expensive book), and in its status as an emblem and accouterment of gentlemanly identity. See the next note.

11. This is reinforced by the fact that Ogilby's atlases were produced in a form that makes them anything but convenient traveler's companions. *Britannia*, like the others, is an "[i]mperial-sized foli[o made with] fine paper, clear type, large margins, handsome and numerous illustrations, drawn and engraved by the best illustrators he could find" (Van Eerde, *John Ogilby*, 122). Obviously *Britannia* was both expensive and unwieldy, suited more for a gentleman's study than the open road.

12. Norden, *England*, "To All Kinde Gentlemen," n.p.

13. A topic that I don't take up here is the problem of time, obviously important to the answering of Imogen's question. In fact, *Cymbeline* is quite interested in the relationship between time, distance, and disparate locations, as evidenced by 3.2.79–83, most of which is discussed below, or Imogen's wish that she and Posthumus had arranged to pray at the same hour, the shared time of their "orisons" uniting them despite the distance between them (1.4.30–33). Given that it took the national extension of the railroads and the concomitant necessity of railroad timetables to synchronize Britain's watches, regional temporal variations were undoubtedly significant in the early modern period, and must have played a powerful role in the customary practices of particular areas.

14. The imprecision obviously lies in the fact that a view of the land is an experience of it, but I draw this distinction in order to emphasize different kinds of relationships to the land.

15. Michel de Certeau, *The Practice of Everyday Life*, trans. Steven Rendall (Berkeley: University of California Press, 1988), 93.

16. For more on this topic in relation to maps, see Chapter Three.

17. Custom and practice are obviously not identical, but they are allied. While I at times use them as if they are practically synonymous terms, I mean to suggest not their status as equivalences, but the complex interpenetration and mutual constitution of the two in the early modern period. Also, I do not mean to oppose to the statute mile an "authentic" customary mile; I want only to consider the implications of the imposition of the London mile on the rest of the country, an imposition made at the expense of the customary. For more on roads in relation to custom and landscape, see the next chapter.

18. De Certeau, 93.

19. For more on the survey and its "bringing the land into knowledge," see Chapter Two.

20. Emrys Jones, "Stuart Cymbeline," *Essays in Criticism* 11 (1961), 84–99. See also Frances A. Yates, *Majesty and Magic in Shakespeare's Last Plays* (Boulder: Shambala, 1978), esp. 26–29; Leah Marcus, *Puzzling Shakespeare* (Berkeley: University of California Press, 1988), 131; D. E. Landry, "Dreams as History: The Strange Unity of *Cymbeline*," *Shakespeare Quarterly* 33 (1982), 71–73.

21. John Selden's note to a section in Drayton's poem that focuses on Milford Haven reads: "At *Milford* hauen arriued *Henry* Earle of *Richmont*, aided with some forces and summes of money by the *French Charles* VIII. but so entertained and strengthened by diuers of his friends, groaning under the tyrannicall yoake of *Rich.* III. that, beyond expectation, at *Bosworth* in *Leicester*, the day and Crown was soone his. Euery Chronicle tels you more largely" (Michael Drayton, *Poly-Olbion* [London: M. Lownes, I. Browne, I. Helme, I. Busbie, 1612], 83).

22. John Speed, *The Theatre of the Empire of Great Britaine* (London: Thomas Bassett and Richard Chiswell, 1676), n.p.

23. William Camden, *Britain, or A Chorographicall Description of the Most Flourishing Kingdomes, England, Scotland, and Ireland*, trans. Philémon Holland (London: George Bishop & John Norton, 1610), 651.

24. Quoted in B. G. Charles, *George Owen of Henllys: A Welsh Elizabethan* (Aberystwyth: National Library of Wales Press, 1973), 154.

25. Anonymous, "A Plain Disquisition on the Indispensable Necessity of Fortifying and Improving Milford-Haven" (London: P. Davey and B. Law, 1759), 15.

26. Glanmor Williams, *Recovery, Reorientation and Reformation: Wales c. 1415–1642* (Oxford: Clarendon Press, 1987), 366–67; Eric N. Simons, *The Devil of the Vault: A Life of Guy Fawkes* (London: Frederick Muller, 1963), 37–40.

27. G. Dyfnallt Owen, *Wales in the Reign of James I* (Suffolk: Boydell Press for the Royal Historical Society, 1988), 70.

28. George Owen, "Milford Tracts," in *The Description of Penbrokshire* (London: Chas. J. Clark, 1892), 564.

29. Ibid., 565.

30. Ibid., 565

31. Imogen is not the only one who gets lost on the way to Milford Haven. Despite the fact that "th' place where [Imogen and Posthumus] should meet" has been "mapp'd"—it is not clear whether the term suggests verbal or visual description—for him by Pisanio (4.1.1–2), Cloten too gets lost. Arguably Pisanio gave Cloten bad directions; if so, this opens up the scene to a comic reading predicated on Cloten's being duped, but that comedy nevertheless reinforces our sense of the Welsh landscape as being as difficult to navigate as Milford Haven is to locate.

However, the problem of location becomes more complex. Cloten has read in a letter held by Pisanio that Posthumus has arranged to "Meet [Imogen] at Milford-Haven" (3.5.131), and he even echoes Imogen's earlier questioning of Pisanio when he asks, "How long is't since she went to Milford-Haven?" (150). At the end of the play, though, Pisanio reports that Cloten has read a "feigned letter" that "directed him/To seek her on the mountains near to Milford" (5.5.279–81). This change probably represents a rewriting of the contents of the letter through the lens of the scenes involving those "rustic mountaineer[s]" (4.2.100)—Cloten's term—Belarius, Guiderius, and Arviragus. However, it is also more broadly suggestive, accommodating as it does the two spaces invoked in the Wales scenes: Milford Haven and an unnamed, stereotypically mountainous Welsh landscape.

32. This contention is confirmed by a pair of lines from the play in which Cymbeline conflates Milford Haven and Wales: Lucius desires of Cymbeline "A conduct over land, to Milford-Haven" (3.5.8); Cymbeline agrees, but the order he then gives specifies that Lucius only be accompanied "Till he have cross'd the Severn," the river that marks the Welsh border (17). I should note that Lucius's request could also suggest the difficulty of navigating this landscape. However, unlike Imogen or Cloten, the Roman ambassador traveling by land uneventfully reaches Milford Haven and meets up with the invading legions that disembark at Milford Haven. This points toward a topic that I will take up at the end of the chapter—the play's hope that the Roman presence will unify the landscapes of England and Wales, making the way to Milford Haven as accessible as Imogen once imagined it to be.

33. Marcus, *Puzzling Shakespeare*, 134–35.

34. See, for example, Glanmor Williams's catalogue of the period's defin-

ing Welsh stereotypes (*Recovery*, 465), a catalogue that makes palpable the perceived difference that lies at the heart of the kingdom's administrative sameness.

35. I am indebted to an essay by Philip Jenkins ("Seventeenth Century Wales: Definition and Identity," in *British Identity and British Consciousness*, ed. Brendan Bradshaw and P. R. Roberts [Cambridge: Cambridge University Press, 1998]) for an insightful account of this phenomenon in relation to the critical and historical construction of the nation.

36. Glanmor Williams, *Religion, Language and Nationality in Wales* (Cardiff: University of Wales Press, 1979), 171.

37. Humfrey Lhuyd, *The Breviary of Britayne*, trans. Thomas Twyne (London: R. Johnes, 1573), 60r. Different spellings of Lhuyd's name are registered in the Notes, not in the body of the text.

38. J. Gwynfor Jones, *Wales and the Tudor State* (Cardiff: University of Wales Press, 1989), 78. The historian A. H. Dodd has said that "the Welsh gentry, educated by the Tudors into a sense of active British (as distinctive from exclusively Welsh) citizenship, entered into the broader fields of politics thus opened to them with a vigour, independence and understanding not to be recaptured till ... the [19th] century" ("The Pattern of Politics in Stuart Wales," *The Transactions of the Honourable Society of the Cymmrodorion* [London: Honourable Society of the Cymmrodorion, 1949], 9).

39. Lhuyd, *Breviary*, 60r.

40. Quoted from G. Williams, *Religion*, 132.

41. Arguably the spatial logic of *Cymbeline* owes a great deal to the influence of classical oppositions between city and wilderness, with garden as a middle category absent here. Moreover, these categories can be and have been mapped onto narratives of British nationhood. Denis Cosgrove has shown how the classical paradigm shapes to this day the way in which London (the metropolis characterized both by civility and corruption), the cultivated English countryside (a middle landscape of garden lands that represents a harmonized relationship between nature and civilization), and the "hinterlands" (the untamed and "historic" wilderness of Scotland, Ireland, and Wales) have been conceptualized ("Landscapes and Myths, Gods and Humans," in *Landscape: Politics and Perspectives*, ed. Barbara Bender [Providence and Oxford: Berg, 1993], 281–305). According to Cosgrove, Wales has been seen both as uncultivated territory and the originary site of a primitive British nationalism, both an uncivilized land distinct from the English urbanity associated with London and assimilable to an Anglocentric notion of Britishness.

42. Marcus situates this scene in terms of the play's larger concern with riddles: "Even out in remote Wales, far from the world of the court, there are

emblematic 'texts' to be interpreted, natural lessons in morality imprinted upon the landscape. . . . [A] hill signifies dangerous eminence like that won and lost in the courts of princes; the low mouth of their cave teaches the virtue of humble devotion" (*Puzzling Shakespeare*, 120). However, of all of the riddling allegories that she analyzes, these are the only ones that emerge out of, or are projected on, a landscape. Of course this kind of allegorical reading of the landscape is not unusual in this period, but it is worth noticing that only in Wales does the landscape appear as a text to be read in this way; no other landscape is allegorical. Also, here allegory, like panorama, involves the evacuating of "murky intertwining daily behaviors" from the landscape.

43. Lhuyd, *Breviary*, 56v. For the same etymology, see also Richard Carew, *The Survey of Cornwall* (London: John Jaggard, 1602), B1r–B1v.

44. This paradox differentially obtains in Shakespearean portrayals of Welsh characters. This is clearest in *1* and *2 Henry IV* and *Henry V*, where we encounter a range of Welsh characters: the eccentric mystic Owen Glendower (or Owain Glyn Dwr); Glendower's unnamed daughter, the wife of Mortimer, whose potentially emasculating alienness, registered in the foreignness of her speech, is admirably explicated by Phyllis Rackin (*Stages of History* [Ithaca: Cornell University Press, 1990], 146–200); "Davy Gam, esquire," or Dafydd ap Llewellyn ap Hywel, who is included in the list of those "of name" who died at Agincourt (*Henry V*, ed. J. H. Walter [London: Routledge, 1990], 4.8.106–7); and most notably Fluellen, who is on the one hand respected for his fierce defense of Britain and on the other rendered a comic butt because of the strangeness of his language. Henry also refers to his own Welsh origin—to Fluellen he says, "For I am Welsh, you know, good countryman" (*Henry V*, 4.7.109)—a historical fact which as we have seen enabled the smooth political integration of Wales into England.

45. Williams, *Recovery*, 464.

46. See Ann R. Jones and Peter Stallybrass, "Dismantling Irena: The Sexualizing of Ireland in Early Modern England," in *Nationalisms and Sexualities*, ed. Andrew Parker et al. (New York: Routledge, 1992), 157–71; Michael Neill, "Broken English and Broken Irish: Nation, Language, and the Optic of Power in Shakespeare's Histories," *Shakespeare Quarterly* 45 (1994), 1–32; see also Chapter Three.

47. Raphaell Holinshed, "The Description of Britaine," in *The First Volume of the Chronicles of England, Scotlande, and Irelande* (London: John Harrison, 1577), 120r.

48. It is not unusual at all for Wales to be collapsed into England in either chronicle histories or descriptions of the nation (two genres which in practice cannot be easily distinguished from one another, as geographical accounts,

usually chorographical in nature, provide readers with much historical material, while chronicles include geographical information): see, for example, William Smith, *The Particular Description of England, 1588* (Hertford: Stephen Austin and Sons, 1879). However, this strategy was not always embraced by the Welsh. For a discussion of the ways in which Wales and the ancient British are either omitted from or maligned in chronicle histories, see David Powel's letter "To the Reader" in Caradoc of Llancarian, *The Historie of Cambria, Now Called Wales*, trans. Humphrey Lhoyd (London: R. Newberie at H. Denham, 1584).

49. "The Masculine Romance of Roman Britain: *Cymbeline* and Early Modern English Nationalism," *Shakespeare Quarterly* 46 (1995), 301–22.

50. It is important to note that the play simultaneously endorses patriotism that manifests itself as heroic behavior: consider the martial activities of Belarius, Guiderius, Arviragus, and Posthumus against the Romans. However, their actions do not finally interfere with their acceptance of Roman authority at play's end.

51. G. Wilson Knight articulates this paradox nicely. On the one hand, "the wicked Queen and her normally repellant son are, at this moment, primarily Britons and their reaction to the Roman threat [reveals] the measure of British toughness and the islanded integrity of their land." On the other, "The Queen and Cloten, though British and the upholders of Britain's integrity, are nevertheless conceived as types which Cymbeline, that is, Britain, must finally reject" (*The Crown of Life* [London: Oxford University Press, 1947], 136–37).

52. Camden, *Britain*, 63.

53. Not all chroniclers share Camden's sanguine view. Holinshed, for instance, states that the Britons were civilized by the Romans, but is more ambivalent about the benefits of civilization (see "The Historie of Englande," in *The First Volume*, 69).

54. Camden, *Britain*, 63.

55. Ibid., 63–64.

56. John J. Brigg, *The King's Highway in Craven* (Cross Hills: Dixon & Stell, 1927), 6.

57. Sheppard Frere, *Britannia: A History of Roman Britain*, 3rd. ed. (London: Pimlico, 1991), 3.

58. David E. Johnston, *An Illustrated History of Roman Roads in Britain* (Buckinghamshire: Spurbooks, 1979), 49.

59. Frere, *Britannia*, 86; Johnston, *Roman Roads*, 53.

60. One example among many is Sir Walter Whorehound's Welsh ex-mistress, who masquerades as a gentlewoman who is "heir to some nineteen mountains" (Thomas Middleton, *A Chaste Maid in Cheapside*, ed. Alan Bris-

senden [London: A&C Black, 1994], 1.1.131–32). In reference to *Cymbeline*, Knight points out that "The setting is a cave in a 'mountainous country', among the Welsh mountains. Nowhere else in Shakespeare do mountains . . . receive a primary emphasis. The setting is rugged; we face nature in its primal grandeur" (*The Crown of Life*, 157). This critical move is both different from and typical of accounts of the play's Welsh setting. Unusually, Knight focuses on the Welshness of the setting, pointing out the uniqueness of mountains in the Shakespeare canon, but then he subsumes the specificity of the setting into an account of "primal grandeur." Most critics have read the Welsh landscape in a similarly symbolic fashion. Maurice Hunt, for example, reads Wales as backdrop for and agent in Imogen's development: "experience expands the understanding in Wales. . . . In Wales, Imogen is instructed in faithful love" ("Shakespeare's Empirical Romance: *Cymbeline* and Modern Knowledge," *Texas Studies in Literature and Language* 22 [1980], 331). William Barry Thorne's account is also typical in that it sees Wales's meaning as emerging out of its opposition to the court. In addition, Wales is defined in terms of its "naturalness": "In general, the nature scenes . . . are designed as a sharp philosophical contrast to the action of the court, and the conceptual structure is thus based on the simple dichotomy of court-country" ("*Cymbeline*: 'Lopp'd Branches' and the Concept of Regeneration," *Shakespeare Quarterly* 20 [1969], 152).

61. This kind of martial homosociality, which binds noble rivals together even as it sets them against one another, finds its fullest Shakespearean articulation in *Coriolanus*. For more on this topic, see Bruce R. Smith, *Homosexual Desire in Shakespeare's England* (Chicago: University of Chicago Press, 1994), 31–77. See also Coppélia Kahn's discussion of emulation in *Roman Shakespeare: Warriors, Wounds, and Women* (London: Routledge, 1997).

62. Linda Woodbridge notes the similarities between Milford Haven and this lane: "When the Romans invade, they press into Britain at an inlet, Milford Haven, and try to penetrate through a lane whose narrowness is repeatedly emphasized. . . . Here, the attempted invasion of a country is paralleled by the attempted invasion of a woman's body" (*The Scythe of Saturn* [Urbana: University of Illinois Press, 1994], 55). These similarities suggest that both lane and Milford Haven function as national loci of vulnerability, and the imagined wholeness of a Britain figured as a woman's body dovetails intriguingly with my assertion that Wales is assimilated into a unified British landscape that is actually an English one.

63. Consider in light of this Philip Edwards's observation that "With curious forgetfulness, Shakespeare makes Posthumus's father (who was supposed to have died with grief at the death of his sons) go on to fight in the Roman

army. (Philario in Rome says, '[H]is father and I were soldiers together' [1.5.26].)" (*Threshold of a Nation: A Study in English and Irish Drama* [Cambridge: Cambridge University Press, 1979], 89).

64. Marcus, *Puzzling Shakespeare*, 126. On ideal versus degenerate Romans, see also Knight, *The Crown of Life*, 150.

65. See also 5.5.475–6, which mentions how "Th' imperial Caesar, should again unite/His favour with the radiant Cymbeline."

66. This is made clear in the queen's references to Julius Caesar's two preceding invasions (3.1.23–27), which did not result in the establishment of colonies. It was the next invasion, that of Augustus Caesar, that would do so, and the Roman presence in Britain clearly suggests this eventuality.

67. Robert S. Miola ("*Cymbeline*: Shakespeare's Valediction to Rome," *Roman Images*, ed. Annabel Patterson [Baltimore: Johns Hopkins University Press, 1984], 51–62) and William Barry Thorne read the play's embracing of the Roman influence as suggesting either the salutary fusion of Rome and Britain (Miola, 60) or the transformation of the kingdom through "regeneration and reconciliation" (Thorne, 159). While these two critics shrewdly identify the dynamic of the ending, with its promise of revitalization, I differ from them in insisting that that revitalization is possible only through the Romanization of the Britons.

68. On *Cymbeline* and Rome, see J. Leeds Barroll, "Shakespeare and Roman History," *Modern Language Review* 53 (1958), 327–43; David M. Bergeron, "*Cymbeline*: Shakespeare's Last Roman Play," *Shakespeare Quarterly* 31 (1980), 31–41; Miola, "*Cymbeline*: Shakespeare's Valediction"; and Mikalachki, "Masculine Romance." For information on period attitudes toward Augustus, see especially Barroll.

69. For readings of *Cymbeline* in relation to this scheme, see Marcus, *Puzzling Shakespeare*, 118–48; Howard Felperin, *Shakespearean Romance* (Princeton: Princeton University Press, 1972), 188–95; E. Jones, "Stuart Cymbeline."

70. Quoted in G. Williams, *Recovery*, 474.

71. Jonathan Goldberg, *James I and the Politics of Literature* (Stanford: Stanford University Press, 1989).

72. As Claire McEachern (*The Poetics of English Nationhood, 1590–1612* [Cambridge: Cambridge University Press, 1996]) has shown, James "rationalized the union by citing the integrity of British geography, 'so indivisible that almost those that were Borderers themselves on the late [Scottish] border, cannot distinguish, nor know or discerne their owne limits. These two countries being separated neither by sea, nor great river, mountain, nor other strength of nature, but only by little small brookes, or demolished little walls, so as rather they were divided in apprehension, then in effect'" (143; the inter-

polated quotation is from James I's 1603 Entry Speech). On the other hand, writing during Elizabeth's reign, William Harrison (*The Description of England*, ed. Georges Edelen [Washington and New York: The Folger Shakespeare Library and Dover Publications, Inc., 1994]) asserted the distinctive nature of the topographies of England, Scotland, and Wales:

> It hath been commonly reported that the ground of Wales is neither so fruitful as that of England, neither the soil of Scotland so bountiful as that of Wales, which is true for corn and for the most part; otherwise, there is so good ground in some parts of Wales as in England, albeit the best of Scotland be scarcely comparable to the mean of either of both. Howbeit, as the bounty of the Scottish doth fail in some respect, so doth it surmount in other, God and Nature having not appointed all countries to yield forth like commodities. (430)

73. Camden, *Britain*, 64.

CHAPTER 5: KNOWING ONE'S PLACE

1. Richard Brome, *A Jovial Crew*, ed. Ann Haaker (Lincoln: University of Nebraska Press, 1968), 4.1.64–65. Further citations will appear in the body of the text.

2. John Norden, *The Surueyors Dialogue* (London: Hugh Astley, 1607), 16.

3. In the beggars' masque at the end of the play, Randall is to play what he is throughout—a "steward for the beggars in Master Steward's [i.e., Springlove's] absence"—and tell the Oldrents character that Springlove has "gone to measure land for him to purchase" (5.1.396–98).

4. James Turner, *The Politics of Landscape: Rural Scenery and Society in English Poetry, 1630–1660* (Oxford: Basil Blackwell, 1979), 6, 5.

5. James A. S. McPeek, *The Black Book of Knaves and Unthrifts* (Storrs: University of Connecticut Publications, 1969), 54.

6. Turner, *Politics*, 166.

7. Henry Tubbe, "On the Dominical Nose of O[liver] C[romwell]," in G. C. Moore Smith, *Henry Tubbe, Oxford Historical and Literary Studies*, vol. 5 (Oxford: Clarendon Press, 1915), 91.

8. Sidney and Beatrice Webb, *The Story of the King's Highway, English Local Government*, vol. 5 (Hamden: Archon Books, 1963), 5–6. My focus in the following few paragraphs will be on highway maintenance, which was the responsibility of the parish. Maintenance of smaller roads such as by-ways was usually the responsibility of individual landowners.

9. Virginia A. LaMar, *Travel and Roads in England* (Washington: Folger Books, 1960), 7.

10. Quoted in LaMar, *Travel and Roads*, 14.

11. Ibid., 18.

12. In 1662 an act was passed that "revived, extended, and modified" the system of statute labor first developed under Mary. Complaints of unpassable roads persisted, however; 1691 saw the passage of yet another act designed to address this problem, while starting in 1663 Turnpike Acts were passed to raise funds for the maintenance of major arteries through the nation. See W. T. Jackman, *The Development of Transportation in Modern England*, 2 vols. (Cambridge: Cambridge University Press, 1916), 1:58–59, 61–64.

13. Jane Oliver, *The Ancient Roads of England* (London: Cassell, 1936), 124–25.

14. Joan Parkes, *Travel in England in the Seventeenth Century* (Oxford: Clarendon Press, 1968), 9.

15. Ibid., 10.

16. Jackman, *The Development of Transportation*, 57–58.

17. Parkes, *Travel in England*, 11. In his famous *Survey of London* (1598), John Stow mentions as an "enormit[y] . . . meet to be reformed" the encroachment of property owners into "highways, lanes, and common grounds, in and about this city" (*A Survey of London*, ed. Henry Morley [Dover: Alan Sutton, 1994], 109).

18. Charles Henry Wilson tells us that "[English roads] were everywhere deplorable and getting steadily worse. In many places they were little more than grassy tracks tracing a wayward and fitful passage through open fields, and liable to disappear under flood water which retreated to leave only a sea of mud behind it" (*England's Apprenticeship, 1603–1763* [New York: St. Martin's Press, 1965], 43). "Wayward and fitful": as described by Wilson, the roads themselves are like the vagabonds commonly associated with them.

19. Parkes, *Travel in England*, 13.

20. See the first chapter in Dan Beaver's *Symbol and Boundary: Parish Communities and Religious Conflict in the Vale of Gloucester, 1590–1690* (Cambridge, Mass.: Harvard University Press, 1998).

21. Thomas Ellwood, *The History of the Life*, 4th ed. (London: James Phillips, 1791), 30–31.

22. David H. Fletcher, *The Emergence of Estate Maps: Christ Church, Oxford, 1600 to 1840* (Oxford: Clarendon Press, 1995), 61. Fletcher also articulates what I argue in Chapter One, that "[t]he growth in the importance of private property is inextricably linked with the increasing significance of cartography as a mode of representation" (61). See also Ben Baack, "The Development of Exclusive Property Rights to Land in England: An Exploratory Essay," *Economy and History* 22 (1979), 63–74. As Baack puts it, "Enclosure meant the

elimination of the existing non-exclusive property rights by the establishment of exclusive ownership" (63). The custom of the highway, on the other hand, allows one to ignore the boundaries that demarcate exclusive ownership.

23. Don E. Wayne, *Penshurst: The Semiotics of Place and the Poetics of History* (Madison: University of Wisconsin Press, 1984), 23.

24. G. R. Hibbard, "The Country House Poem of the Seventeenth Century," *Journal of the Warburg and Courtauld Institutes* 19 (1956), 160.

25. Ibid., 161, 163. While clearly referring to the general shift in conceptions of the country house, the phrase actually emerges from Hibbard's discussion of "To Penshurst."

26. D. R. Hainsworth, *Stewards, Lords and People: The Estate Steward and His World in Later Stuart England* (Cambridge: Cambridge University Press, 1992), 7–8.

27. Ibid., 13, 15.

28. John Taylor, *The Praise, Antiquity, and Commodity, of Beggery, Beggers, and Begging* (London: E. A. for Henry Gosson, 1621), C4r.

29. "Travel by land from one point to another still retained the meaning of its biblical origin—travail. It was dangerous, difficult and exhausting" (Stella Margetson, *Journey by Stages* [London: Cassell, 1967], 2).

30. Paul Slack, *Poverty and Policy in Tudor and Stuart England* (London: Longman, 1988), 95.

31. Slack, *Poverty*, 94–95.

32. A. L. Beier, *Masterless Men: The Vagrancy Problem in England, 1560–1640* (London: Methuen, 1985), 70.

33. Beier, *Masterless*, 70–71, 83; Slack, *Poverty*, 44–45.

34. A. L. Beier, "Vagrants and the Social Order in Elizabethan England," *Past and Present* 64 (1974), 13. See Peter Clark, "The Migrant in Kentish Towns 1580–1640," in *Crisis and Order in English Towns, 1500–1700*, ed. Peter Clark and Paul Slack (London: Routledge and Kegan Paul, 1972), 117–63, for a discussion of subsistence migration and betterment migration that suggests the range of experience and variety of backgrounds of vagrants.

35. Paul A. Slack, "Vagrants and Vagrancy in England, 1598–1664," *The Economic History Review*, 2nd ser. 27 (1970), 362.

36. Beier, "Vagrants," 27 (my emphasis).

37. Barry Taylor, *Vagrant Writing: Social and Semiotic Disorders in the English Renaissance* (London: Harvester Wheatsheaf, 1991), 9. Taylor writes of both the vagrant and the actor, each of whom he sees as existing outside traditional structures conferring identity. Taylor reads "the geography of hundred and parish [as] a topography of supervision, a classificatory grid within which the true

identity of the subject may be 'read' by reference to the origin of the birthplace" (9).

38. Robert Jütte, *Poverty and Deviance in Early Modern Europe* (Cambridge: Cambridge University Press, 1994), 143.

39. "The certificate or passport is a piece of writing which stands in for the 'natural' relation between subject and place of birth which the vagrant has broken, an artificial means of resealing the relation of person to origin" (B. Taylor, *Vagrant Writing*, 10).

40. Daryl W. Palmer, "Jacobean Muscovites: Winter, Tyranny, and Knowledge in *The Winter's Tale*," *Shakespeare Quarterly* 46 (1995), 334. See also Daryl W. Palmer, *Hospitable Performances: Dramatic Genre and Cultural Practices in Early Modern England* (West Lafayette: Purdue University Press, 1992), 1–49; and Felicity Heal, *Hospitality in Early Modern England* (Oxford: Clarendon Press, 1990).

41. Heal, *Hospitality*, 6.

42. Palmer, *Hospitable Performances*, 27.

43. Heal, *Hospitality*, 133.

44. Ibid., 393.

45. Ibid., 391–92.

46. Felicity Heal, "The Idea of Hospitality in Early Modern England," *Past and Present* 102 (1984), 78. Heal also discusses conflicting social imperatives to aid all of the poor and to avoid supporting an "idle" population of vagabonds and rogues (77).

47. J. Taylor, *Beggery, Beggers, and Begging*, C2r.

48. The immediate catalyst for this declaration is the discovery of his daughters' departure, but I would argue that the loss of Springlove contributes to his strained pursuit of mirth. This is made clear by the fact discussed below, that Oldrents treats Springlove as what he turns out to be at play's end—a son.

49. Martin Butler also writes of Oldrents's renunciation of his duties (Martin Butler, *Theatre and Crisis, 1632–1642* [Cambridge: Cambridge University Press, 1984], 276–77). Felicity Heal quotes an Elizabethan writer who speaks of the dangers of excessive hospitality: "According to thy abilitie mainteyne Hospitalitie: for that is the harbourer of two hopes, prayes and prayers: yet let Liberalitie be the Linke to light thee, lest Covetousnes might corrupt, or *Prodigalitie procure penurie*" (I. M., in *A Health to the Gentlemanly Profession of Servingman* [1598], quoted in Heal, "Idea," 74; my emphasis). Patrico offers up in his speech I. M.'s "prayes and prayers."

50. Lawrence Stone, *The Crisis of the Aristocracy, 1558–1641*, abridged edition (Oxford: Oxford University Press, 1967).

51. Springlove's first words in the play, uttered in relation to his putting before Oldrents the "survey" that interrupts the latter's merry riding forth (see above, 1.1.97), are, "Sir, 'tis duty" (1.1.107).

52. Oldrents also "estate[s Springlove with] a thousand pound a year to entertain his wife, and to their heirs forever" (5.1.473–75).

53. It is important to note that at the level of literary representation this kind of inversion increasingly took place in the decades before the civil war. Mark Koch describes how "The beggars' brotherhood, so often depicted as a diabolical conspiracy by earlier writers, begins to take on the shadings of a carefree, idyllic society" ("The Desanctification of the Beggar in Rogue Pamphlets of the English Renaissance," in *The Work of Dissimilitude: Essays from the Sixth Citadel Conference on Medieval and Renaissance Literature*, ed. David G. Allen and Robert A. White [Newark: University of Delaware Press, 1992], 101). One of Koch's examples of this shift is *A Jovial Crew*.

54. This process of identification is reminiscent of what is found in scenes such as those in *The Duchess of Malfi* in which madmen, all former scholars and professionals, are paraded before the imprisoned duchess. Those characters do not tell their own or each other's tales, however; they are identified by a servant and speak in distorted fragments of their professional knowledge. See John Webster, *The Duchess of Malfi*, ed. Elizabeth M. Brennan (London: A & C Black, 1983), 4.2.

55. See David Farley-Hills, *The Comic in Renaissance Comedy* (Totowa: Barnes & Noble, 1981), 149; Rosemary Gaby, "Of Vagabonds and Commonwealths: *Beggar's Bush*, *A Jovial Crew*, and *The Sisters*," *Studies in English Literature* 34 (1994), 409–11; R. J. Kaufmann, *Richard Brome: Caroline Dramatist* (New York: Columbia University Press, 1961), 169–72; and Catherine M. Shaw, *Richard Brome* (Boston: Twayne, 1980), 132–33.

56. Gaby summarizes these constraints: "We hear of doxies screaming in labor, we hear a great deal about 'beggar niggling' and . . . we are made aware of the hardships and indignities of begging" ("Of Vagabonds," 410).

57. B. Taylor, *Vagrant Writing*, 9.

58. For example, Clack says in reference to the beggars that his "way of justice" is "to punish 'em first, and be compassionate afterwards" (5.1.120–21).

59. It is also worth noting that it is not clear how seriously we should take Clack's authority or his actions here. Clack is clearly a comic butt in the tradition of officious law enforcers like Justice Shallow, Elbow, or Dogberry, and his attempts to reinstall the "true identity" of the beggars could easily be played as bumbling officiousness.

60. Alan Everitt, "Farm Labourers," in *The Agrarian History of England and*

Wales, 7 vols., gen. ed. H. P. R. Finberg, vol. 4: *1500–1640*, ed. Joan Thirsk (Cambridge: Cambridge University Press, 1967), 464–65.

61. In the prologue Brome includes his play among "romances / Of lovers" who experience "travel and distress" while acting as "afflicted wanderers" (Prologue, 8–11). Here he turns travel into one of love's trials, which both speaks to the situation of the four lovers and fails to do justice to the complexity of his own representation of travel in the text.

62. Martin Butler reads the play as a "dramatic testament . . . set in a lovingly drawn English landscape as a measure of all that is worth preserving in the present crisis" (Butler, *Theatre and Crisis*, 277). I take Butler to understand that landscape to include not merely topographical features, but also the traditional social practices I discuss above.

CHAPTER 6: THE BELEAGUERED CITY

1. Michel Foucault, "Questions on Geography," in *Power/Knowledge: Selected Interviews and Other Writings, 1972–1977*, ed. Colin Gordon (New York: Pantheon, 1980), 70.

2. Edward Soja, *Postmodern Geographies* (London: Verso, 1989), 7. See Henri Lefebvre, *The Production of Space*, trans. Donald Nicholson-Smith (Oxford: Blackwell, 1991); Michel de Certeau, *The Practice of Everyday Life*, trans. Steven Rendall (Berkeley: University of California Press, 1988); and David Harvey, *The Condition of Postmodernity* (Oxford: Blackwell, 1990).

3. Harvey, *Condition of Postmodernity*, 204. As will become clear, in the early modern period it is not only "objective conceptions of time and space" that reproduce social life.

4. The "tradition" I discuss here is arguably a much-embattled one. Work by social historians such as Christopher Hill (*The World Turned Upside Down* [New York: Penguin, 1972]), Susan Amussen (*An Ordered Society: Gender and Class in Early Modern England* [Oxford: Blackwell, 1988]), David Underdown (*Revel, Riot, and Rebellion* [Oxford: Oxford University Press, 1985]), and Keith Wrightson (*English Society, 1580–1680* [New Brunswick: Rutgers University Press, 1982]) has done a great deal to unsettle the hegemony of a historiography both monarchical and political (in the narrow sense of the term) in its scope. However, the new historicism has largely maintained a monarchical focus. Seminal work by critics such as Stephen Greenblatt (*Renaissance Self-Fashioning* [Chicago: University of Chicago Press, 1980]), Louis Adrian Montrose ("'Eliza, Queene of Shepheardes,' and the Pastoral of Power," in *Renaissance Historicism*, ed. Arthur F. Kinney and Dan S. Collins [Amherst: University of Massachusetts Press, 1987], 34–63), Leonard Tennenhouse (*Power on*

Display [New York: Methuen, 1986]), Jonathan Goldberg (*James I and the Politics of Literature* [Stanford: Stanford University Press, 1989]), and Steven Mullaney (*The Place of the Stage* [Chicago: University of Chicago Press, 1988]) has largely focused on the semiotic relations between literature and the monarchy, and in doing so has ironically adhered to the emphases of an older, political historiography.

5. These are actually only two in a series of history plays produced in the 1590's that deal with an internal assault on London. The others are *The Life and Death of Jack Straw* (1591), *The Siege of London* (1594; a lost play seen by some as a possible source for Heywood), *Sir Thomas More* (1595), and *A Larum for London* (1599). Dates for some of these plays are controversial and are important here only as approximations. Dates are drawn from *The Cambridge Companion to English Renaissance Drama* (ed. A. R. Braunmuller and Michael Hattaway [Cambridge: Cambridge University Press, 1990]), except in the case of *Siege*, which the *Companion* does not mention. This is not necessarily an exhaustive list of "invasion plays"; it represents all of those that I have been able to identify. Moreover, *A Larum for London* only loosely belongs to this category—the story of the invasion of Antwerp, the play, as the title suggests, is nonetheless most concerned with the possibility that such an invasion be re-enacted in London. Thus, in certain ways the assault on Antwerp can be understood as an imagined invasion of London, and the citizens' response to the assault is crucial to the play's call for military preparedness in London. I have chosen the Heywood and Shakespeare plays because they offer the most extensive representation of the spaces and practices of the city and, as I say above, they both represent an invasion of the city from without.

6. I should point out at the outset that I do not take either of these two plays to be representative of *all* of the texts in each playwright's canon. For instance, in contrast to the sociospatial homogeneity of *2 Henry VI*'s London is the richness and particularity of the spaces in the *Henry IV* plays. Thus, the "Shakespeare" and "Heywood" I refer to throughout are only those of the plays I take up here.

7. Thomas Heywood, *The First Part of King Edward the Fourth*, in *The Dramatic Works of Thomas Heywood*, 6 vols. (London: John Pearson, 1874), 1:10. The text does not divide the play material into acts or scenes, so citations are of page numbers. All further quotations are drawn from volume 1, and will be cited in the text.

8. In Leadenhall market, items such as poultry, canvas, and woolens were sold, but Leadenhall is most famously associated with grain; Simon Eyre built a granary there in 1445. At the same time, the market was also used for the building and storing of properties used in pageants (S. Schoenbaum, *Shake-*

speare: The Globe and the World [Oxford: Oxford University Press for the Folger Shakespeare Library, 1979], 63–64).

That Falconbridge talks of selling pearls as if they were grain suggests a profound inversion of value; his control of the spaces of commerce will lead to a radical undermining of London's economy. The pearl is not only an exotic object suggestive of international trade and England's imperial conquest of far-off regions, it is usually understood as being priceless, as something that should not be sold or traded. Compare Othello in his death speech, who, "Like the base Judean, threw a pearl away / Richer than all his tribe" (*The Tragedy of Othello*, in William Shakespeare, *The Complete Works*, ed. Alfred Harbage [New York: Viking Penguin, 1969], 5.2.347–48).

9. Critics of the play have failed to notice the rebels' aim to control the commerce of the city. Instead, they have tended to read these scenes as enacting only "a carnivalesque fantasy of unlimited consumption" (Kathleen McLuskie, *Dekker and Heywood* [New York: St. Martin's, 1994], 56). See also Charles W. Crupi, "Ideological Contradiction in Part I of Heywood's *Edward IV*: 'Our Musicke Runs . . . Much upon Discords,'" *Medieval & Renaissance Drama in England* 7 (1995), 231.

10. For an argument that makes claims nearly opposite to my own, see Theodora A. Jankowski, "Historicizing and Legitimizing Capitalism: Thomas Heywood's *Edward IV* and *If You Know Not Me, You Know Nobody*," *Medieval & Renaissance Drama in England* 7 (1995), 305–37. Jankowski reads the play as asserting "the intrinsic power of the merchants/capitalists of London as well as the close connection between government and capital" (316). As will become clear below, it is my contention that the detail with which Heywood delineates the spaces of the city in terms of guild culture reveals that his sympathies are with that culture, one that can only problematically be aligned with capitalism. Moreover, the play articulates the tensions and not the close connections between the Crown and the city.

11. Mullaney, *The Place of the Stage*, 10.

12. Ibid., 13

13. Ibid.

14. Mullaney argues that the coherent symbolic order made possible by ceremonies and rituals begins to break down at the end of the sixteenth century, as those rituals can no longer speak to an urban population that includes foreign workers and nonguild industries. While I agree that this urban transformation takes place, I do not think that the ritualistic symbolic order ever fully defined or encompassed the socioeconomic life of the city. What Mullaney sees as defining I see as always in tension with other forms of material practice.

15. Lefebvre, *The Production of Space*, 38.

16. Ibid., 45. "Abstract space" is a complex concept in Lefebvre's work. What is most important to stress here is Lefebvre's insistence both that abstract space is socially produced and contributes to the reproduction of social relations, and that in a peculiar way the objective description of such space in a sense *becomes* that space.

17. Ibid., 39.

18. Here Lefebvre differs from de Certeau, who insists upon and privileges individual acts of resistance to a rationalized spatial order. See de Certeau, *The Practice of Everyday Life*.

19. In doing so I am obviously discussing landscapes of custom in a context different from that which I adduced in the Introduction, but it should not surprise us that custom is an important category off of as well as on the estate. The important point is that the landscape of custom that I examine here articulates the values not of tenants but of substantial property owners, the masters (and, as we shall see, the ambitious apprentices and journeymen) of the guilds.

20. For a recent discussion of the ideological nature of certain Lord Mayor's shows, see Sergei Lobanov-Rostovsky, "*The Triumphes of Golde*: Economic Authority in the Jacobean Lord Mayor's Show," *ELH* 60 (1993), 879–98. As the above definition of representations of space states, Lefebvre stresses that they are ideological, but it is important to point out that so are representational spaces—in particular, the ceremonial spaces defined by civic rituals such as the Lord Mayor's show.

21. Mullaney, *The Place of the Stage*, 19.

22. After the 1390's, we see the emergence of the "livery companies," which are "the incorporated societies which craft and trade gilds became by means of royal charters" (Steve Rappaport, *Worlds Within Worlds: Structures of Life in Sixteenth-Century London* [Cambridge: Cambridge University Press, 1989], 177). However, the two terms—"livery company" and "guild"—continue to be used interchangeably, and I do the same in this chapter.

23. Mullaney, *The Place of the Stage*, 20.

24. I do not mean to draw a simple distinction between symbolic and non-symbolic material practices—to argue that trade practices, for instance, are in no way symbolic ones. Instead, I want to suggest that an overemphasis on ritualistic practice on the part of Mullaney and others wrongly diminishes the significance of spatial practice, which, as Lefebvre is aware, is shot through with symbolic elements.

25. In a forthcoming essay, Jean E. Howard has convincingly argued that

the "us" inside the walls is not an all-inclusive category. Rather, she sees the play as privileging "the world view of what I would call the burgher class, the nonaristocratic householders of London, whose identity was bound up with their productive labor, their patriotism, and their companionate marriages." At the same time, Heywood's "burgher histories . . . show so clearly who is walled in and who is walled out when citizens rule the roost" ("Other Englands: The View from the Non-Shakespearean History Play," in *Other Voices, Other Views: Expanding the Canon in English Renaissance Studies*, ed. Helen Ostovich and Graham Roebuck [Newark: University of Delaware Press, forthcoming]). The citizens I refer to throughout are all representatives of or are invested in this burgher class.

26. A. L. Beier, *Masterless Men: The Vagrancy Problem in England, 1560– 1640* (London: Methuen, 1985), 5.

27. Thomas Dekker, *The Wonderfull Yeare, 1603* (London: The Bodley Head Quartos, 1924), 44.

28. *The Ancient Customes and Approved Usages of the Honourable City of London* (London: n.p., 1639), 13.

29. There are a number of possible reasons for this—the residence in the suburbs of many vagrants; the presence of controversial institutions such as brothels or playhouses; tensions arising from the jurisdictional ambiguities characterizing the city's relationship to both suburbs and liberties.

30. It is important to point out, however, that just as the suburbs are over-determined, so are rebellion and vagrancy. The latter, for instance, has been described by A. L. Beier as "a protean concept"; vagabondage laws "reflected a conviction in the ruling élites that vagabondage was a hydra-headed monster poised to destroy the state and social order" (Beier, *Masterless Men*, 4). Much the same can be said of social uprisings.

31. I am stressing the historical particularity of this rebellion, but of course the trope of the rebellious "many-headed multitude" is a common one. Conventionally, though, it is an aristocrat or patrician who either defends the assaulted space from the mob or convinces them to give up their attack (think not only of Cade in *2 Henry VI*, but also of the mob swayed by Antony in *Julius Caesar* or those who revolt against Basilius in Sidney's *The Countess of Pembroke's Arcadia*, who are first valiantly repulsed and then persuaded not to fight by Zelmane); what is striking about Heywood's version of this motif is that it is the citizens who repulse the mob.

32. John L. McMullan, *The Canting Crew: London's Criminal Underworld, 1550–1700* (New Brunswick: Rutgers University Press, 1984), 28.

33. For an account of royal expansion of the rights and powers of the

guilds, and of the failure of this expansion to control suburban industrial activity, see George Unwin, *The Gilds and Companies of London*, 3rd. ed (London: George Allen and Unwin, 1938), esp. 243–66.

34. Rappaport, *Worlds Within Worlds*, 23–24.

35. For an exhaustive discussion of the status of guild labor at this time, see Rappaport, *Worlds Within Worlds*. Rappaport downplays the actual threat posed to the guilds by changing patterns of labor while also acknowledging the cultural perception of that threat. This stance is in part a function of his emphasis on guild rather than non-guild labor. Others, such as McMullan, have focused on the development of a seasonal, unattached labor force in the suburbs (see McMullan, *The Canting Crew*, 20–23).

36. Robert Tittler, "The Emergence of Urban Policy, 1536–58," in *The Mid-Tudor Polity*, ed. Robert Tittler and Jennifer Loach (Totowa: Rowman and Littlefield, 1980), 82–83. Tittler goes on to address royal legislation from the 1530's designed to shore up the eroding authority of the livery companies. For more on this, see Unwin, *Gilds and Companies*.

37. For example, the long-established cloth trade, England's primary commercial industry, had London as its center, but depended both on its Antwerp market, which collapsed around 1550, and on the country-wide production of cloth. See S. T. Bindoff, *Tudor England* (London: Penguin, 1950), 17–24.

38. See Unwin, *Gilds and Companies*, 262.

39. The primary way of acquiring citizenship in the sixteenth century is through apprenticeship in a particular trade. In such instances, one's "freedom" is intertwined with the affairs of a particular livery company, but the custom of London allowed, among other things, "the son of the member of one company [who] was apprenticed to a member of another . . . [to] claim membership of his father's company, in which circumstances his own apprentices would eventually become free of that company" (Robert Ashton, *The City and the Court, 1603–1643* [Cambridge: Cambridge University Press, 1979], 50). Heywood may gesture toward this linkage of freedom and paternity, but this is not the primary way in which either city or guild reproduces itself.

40. I am arguing that Heywood's representation of the guilds is a nostalgic one that understands the life of the guilds as being inseparable from the life of the city. It is worth noting, however, that arguably Heywood longs not for a time gone by, but for one that never was. In other words, one might want to consider if the smoothly operating, all-inclusive guild structure that he represents ever existed. I would want to resist any narrative that fully assumed that the guilds had previously constituted a kind of organic community. One could also make the same point about the city as a whole: Leah Marcus has discussed

the way in which London was "scarcely monolithic, more a patchwork of local differences than a single, uniform political and geographical entity" (*Puzzling Shakespeare* [Berkeley: University of California Press, 1988], 165).

41. Anonymous, *A Breefe Discourse, Declaring and Approving the Necessarie and Inviolable Maintenance of the Laudable Customs of London* (London: Henrie Middleton for Rafe Newberie, 1584), 5–6.

42. Ibid., 6–7.

43. Ibid., 4. The author of this text alternately sees custom as in conflict with law and as another version of it.

44. *By the Mayor; An Act of Common Council Prohibiting Strangers to Use Any Trades Within This City* (London: J. Windett, 1606), 2.

45. Another definition of "custom" emerges in this period: "the practice of customarily resorting to a particular shop" or "business patronage or support." The OED's first example of this use of the term is drawn from *The Taming of the Shrew*, in which one character swears that another "shall hop without my custome sir" (OED 5). Here "custom" refers to the privileges not of the guild but of the consumer, who might not offer his or her custom to those defending and defined by the "antient customs" of their fathers. That is, the custom of the consumer (or customer) potentially disturbs those customs integral to the reproductive logic of the guilds and to certain visions of the city.

46. Thomas Heywood, *An Apology for Actors* (London: Nicholas Okes, 1612), F3v.

47. For arguments that suggest the play unproblematically conforms to Heywood's prescriptive definition of the history play, see Irving Ribner, *The English History Play in the Age of Shakespeare* (Princeton: Princeton University Press, 1957), 273–78; David Bevington, *Tudor Drama and Politics: A Critical Approach to Topical Meaning* (Cambridge, Mass.: Harvard University Press, 1968), 241–42.

48. This yoking of city and court is neither unusual nor particularly sinister in this period; countless early modern texts conflate city and court, perhaps because the city's growth as a center of conspicuous consumption is in part fueled by the court's expansion under the Tudors and Stuarts. However, Heywood understands the popular confusion of city and court as potentially threatening to the London of the citizens.

49. For an account of the homologous relationship between the chaste female body and the inviolable social space, see Peter Stallybrass, "Patriarchal Territories: The Body Enclosed," in *Rewriting the Renaissance*, ed. Margaret W. Ferguson, Maureen Quilligan, and Nancy J. Vickers (Chicago: University of Chicago Press, 1986), 123–42. Barbara Baines relates Jane's siege metaphor to a similar treatment in Shakespeare's "The Rape of Lucrece," and sees it

drawing "the parallel between personal and political rebellion" (*Thomas Heywood* [Boston: Twayne, 1984], 19).

50. Lena Cowen Orlin makes much the same argument, discussing, among other things, the "language that links the rebels' assault on London to the king's assault on Jane" (*Private Matters and Public Culture in Post-Reformation England* [Ithaca: Cornell University Press, 1994], 119).

51. The comparison of female love object to precious jewel is a familiar poetic one, and the emphasis is usually on the singularity and irreplaceability of the beloved. However, in this context the comparison is ironic and suggests the commodification of Jane.

52. Jean Howard discusses Jane's autonomy within and active contributions to the household as evidence of what early modern patriarchy would see as her problematic agency—problematic because "she is *more* than a passive object in such situations, [she] is also an agent, one who could choose whether or not to remain faithful to her husband." See "Other Englands: The View from the Non-Shakespearean History Play." I tend to see Jane Shore's affair with Edward less as choice than as the result of coercion.

53. Orlin, *Private Matters*, 123.

54. Mowbray Velte, *The Bourgeois Elements in the Dramas of Thomas Heywood* (New York: Haskell House, 1966), 25.

55. There are also sinister overtones to the way in which Edward passes in disguise through the London streets, "survay[ing]," as one character puts it, "the manner of our city" (p. 76). "When kings themselues so narrowly do pry / Into the world, men feare; and why not I?" (p. 78).

56. While below I refer to a specific historical phenomenon that motivates the play's representation of Edward, I should also point out that it is conventional to associate Edward with abuses of royal prerogative. The most obvious example is in his willful marriage to the widow Gray, which disrupted plans for alliance by marriage with France. Both Heywood and Shakespeare (in the *Henry VI* plays) take up this event. However, this fact does not invalidate the reading that is to follow. Rather, it suggests why the story of Edward is an appropriate vehicle for exploration of the contemporary issues that interested Heywood.

57. Unwin, *Gilds and Companies*, 158–59, 170. For my account of incorporation and royal patents I rely mostly on Unwin's magisterial work.

58. Ibid., 158. It is important to note that by the Elizabethan era some of the older established guilds held *de facto* if not *de jure* monopolies by virtue of their powerful institutional presence.

59. Ibid., 294. For a brief, clear description of the monopolies debate and

its relation to royal prerogative, see Alan G. R. Smith, *The Emergence of a Nation State* (London: Longman, 1984), 130.

60. Ashton, *The City and the Court*, 81–82.

61. Unwin, *Gilds and Companies*, 256.

62. See Ashton, *The City and the Court*, 53–54, for yeomen's complaints about the domination of livery companies by noncraftsmen.

63. Unwin, *Gilds and Companies*, 257–58.

64. Ashton, *The City and the Court*, 83.

65. In my Introduction I suggest that landscape of sovereignty "takes two related but distinct forms: it reflects and shapes the ambitions and imperatives of those who control or would control the kingdom; and, more broadly, it represents the conceptual annexation of distinct cultural spaces in the name of monarch or (a culturally homogenized) nation." Here I have the second definition in mind, although the first is hardly irrelevant.

66. George Unwin's description of monarchical fundraising makes clear the unwanted demands the Crown was wont to make of city guilds: "During the whole period of the Tudors and Stuarts . . . the city companies furnished one of the chief financial resources of the Government. . . . Elizabeth raised a compulsory loan of £20,000 in 1579 for the suppression of the Irish rebellion . . . Participation in State lotteries was twice forced upon the companies by Elizabeth, and once by James I." It is also worth noting that "The Government's demands for men were more frequent and probably scarcely less burdensome than their demands for money" (Unwin, *Gilds and Companies*, 240, 241).

67. Phyllis Rackin, *Stages of History* (Ithaca: Cornell University Press, 1990), 201. For a recent account of Holinshed that argues for the middle-class and multivocal nature of the *Chronicles*, see Annabel Patterson, *Reading Holinshed's Chronicles* (Chicago: University of Chicago Press, 1994).

68. Quoted in Thomas Cartelli, "Jack Cade in the Garden: Class Consciousness and Class Conflict in *2 Henry VI*," in *Enclosure Acts*, ed. Richard Burt and John Michael Archer (Ithaca: Cornell University Press, 1994), 57.

69. Brents Stirling, *The Populace in Shakespeare* (New York: Columbia University Press, 1949), 163.

70. Ibid., 165; *2 Henry VI*, 4.5.4–55. All quotations are from *The Riverside Shakespeare*, ed. G. Blakemore Evans et al. (Boston: Houghton Mifflin, 1974), and will be henceforth cited in the text.

71. Alexander Leggatt, *Shakespeare's Political Drama* (London: Routledge, 1988), 16. Shakespeare's central strategy for discrediting Cade's rebellion is to present his ideas as a hopeless muddle of monarchical ambitions and populist

utopian ideals. This muddle leads to mixed goals for the city: Cade wants to destroy the Tower, the clearest symbol of the Crown's authority, but also, as we shall see, to stage his own royal entry and appropriate the trappings of sovereignty. Cade reduces the distinctive spaces of London to which he elliptically refers to objects to be attained or destroyed, and we encounter no citizenry that infuses them with an alternative meaning.

72. "The Quene's Majestie's Passage Through the Citie of London to Westminster the Daye Before Her Coronacion," in *Elizabethan Backgrounds*, ed. Arthur F. Kinney (Hamden: Archon, 1975), 16. While the text was published anonymously, David Bergeron has convincingly attributed it to Mulcaster (*English Civic Pageantry, 1558–1642* [Columbia: University of South Carolina Press, 1971], 13).

73. "The Quene's Majestie's Passage," 26–27 (my emphasis).

74. See Unwin, *Gilds and Companies*, 240–41, for a description of the Crown's economic dependence on the city and city companies.

75. Wendy Wall quotes Sydney Anglo, who observes that "there is one feature of the pageants for Elizabeth which marks them off from their predecessors. This is the degree to which they . . . give advice on a right course of action" (*The Imprint of Gender* [Ithaca: Cornell University Press, 1993], 120). Of the city's gift of a Bible, Wall notes that "the mayor's reminder that the city had paid for the whole event created a coercive sense of obligation that had to be acknowledged by the queen publicly" (12).

76. Obviously what separates this spectacle from Heywood's play is the fact that the threat of shifting spatial practice is missing from it. Heywood's play, like the image of the guilds here, suggests the interpenetration of conceptions of the city and guild labor, but this procession does not address the threat to the guilds.

77. Ronald Knowles makes plain the connection between Cade's gesture of rule and the "real King Henry VI['s]" royal coronation ("The Farce of History: Miracle, Combat, and Rebellion in *2 Henry VI*," *Yearbook of English Studies* 21 [1991], 185).

78. To be more precise, I should suggest that Cade ignores the logic of the *Elizabethan* royal spectacle. As Jonathan Goldberg has shown, in some ways the Jacobean royal entry comes closer to Cade's imposition of his will onto the spaces of the city than it does to Elizabeth's scripted exchanges. See Goldberg, *James I*. It should also be pointed out that, as David Bergeron has shown, the formal differences between royal entries and coronation processions are negligible in the Elizabethan period (Bergeron, *English Civic Pageantry*, 11–64).

79. Cade also plans to "pull down the Savoy . . . [and] th' Inns of Court" (4.7.1–2); "all the records of the realm" are to be burned (4.7.14); Cheapside,

London's foremost commercial street, is to become a place where Cade's "palfrey [shall] go to grass" (4.2.69), but presumably not before the rebels "take up commodities upon [their] bills" (4.7.126–27). The irony of King Cade's projected reign is that, in gaining control of London, the rebels would destroy much of what is distinctive about it. Moreover, London in Shakespeare's play does not represent, as in Heywood's, a social landscape unified by the spatial practices of the guilds, but is instead a heterogenous collection of structures to be defended by the aristocratic caretakers of the city appointed by the fleeing citizens.

80. Broadly put, the difference is between dramatized versions of a political historiography that privileges time over space—that, to paraphrase Foucault, sees time as dialectical and space as dead and fixed—and of a social historiography that understands the spaces of the city themselves to be richly historical.

81. See, for example, 4.8.23–25.

82. See Rackin, *Stages of History*, 50–51. In the sources (Hall and Holinshed), Peter's claim is not validated, but, as Rackin notes, Shakespeare's validation is a seriously qualified one.

83. Richard Helgerson, *Forms of Nationhood: The Elizabethan Writing of England* (Chicago: University of Chicago Press, 1992), 214. While this makes sense for this play, I agree with Jean Howard ("Other Englands") that this formulation does not do justice to Shakespeare's second tetralogy. Helgerson argues that Heywood's play is an example of one in which citizens actively participate in the forging and maintenance of the political nation.

Index

In this index an "f" after a number indicates a separate reference on the next page and an "ff" indicates separate references on the next two pages. A continuous discussion over two or more pages is indicated by a span of page numbers, e.g., "57–59." *Passim* is used for a cluster of references in close but not consecutive sequence.